BOOKS IN THE BLOOD

BOOKS
IN THE BLOOD

memoirs of a
fourth generation bookseller

ANTHONY ROTA

PRIVATE LIBRARIES ASSOCIATION

OAK KNOLL PRESS

2002

Published by the Private Libraries Association
Ravelston, South View Road, Pinner,
Middlesex HA5 3YD, England

Published in North and South America by Oak Knoll Press
310 Delaware Street, New Castle, Delaware 19720, U.S.A.

1,700 copies (of which 950 for sale)
ISBN 0 900002 96 4 (UK)   1 58456 076 2 (USA)

A CIP catalogue record for this book is
available from The British Library
and in the United States on
application to The Library of Congress

Printed in Great Britain by St Edmundsbury Press

Composed in Abrams Augereau

Designed by
David Chambers

for Jean
who shared these years
with me

CONTENTS

ILLUSTRATIONS

ACKNOWLEDGMENTS

I am indebted to many people for help cheerfully and speedily given when in the course of writing these memoirs I needed to check facts, verify dates and so on. I have particularly to thank John Baskett, Clifford Bryant, Herbert Cahoon, Gay Elwell, Robert Fleck, Keith Fletcher, Richard Ford, and, as so often, Carol Rothkopf; John Critchley and the staff of the A.B.A. office; Shelley Cox (Southern Illinois University); Inge Dupont, Robert Parks and Rigbie Turner (Pierpont Morgan Library); George Fletcher (New York Public Library); Richard Landon (Fisher Library, University of Toronto), Vincent Giroud (Beinecke Library, Yale University); Cathy Henderson (Harry Ransom Humanities Research Center, University of Texas) and Katherine Reagan (Cornell University).

My thanks too to Mary Deval and Beryl Sims for lending photographs, and to Nicolas Barker and *The Book Collector*, together with the Executors of the late Simon Nowell-Smith for permission to reprint the last-named's obituary of my father. Excerpts from the Prologue to this book were published by the Ampersand Club in Minneapolis in 1989 as *Life in a London Bookshop*. Earlier versions of the reminiscence of Norman Holmes Pearson and the chapter entitled 'Beware of Little Old Ladies' were published in a memorial issue of the *Hawthorne Journal* and the newsletter of the Antiquarian Booksellers' Association respectively. I thank the Ampersand Club, Matthew J. Bruccoli (editor of the *Hawthorne Journal*) and the ABA for permitting me to print revised versions here.

My gratitude and belated sympathy go to Pauline Little who had to wrestle with successive drafts and virtually illegible manuscript revisions and produce a text clean enough to submit to my publisher. I am greatly obliged to John Byrne for his painstaking reading of that text, catching literal errors, non sequiturs and just plain mistakes with consummate skill. I thank Christopher Hurst for reading the manuscript and making various helpful suggestions. Once again I count myself fortunate to have had David Chambers of the Private Libraries Association as my publisher. He has acted as a most supportive editor and also as designer and production manager, bringing the highest standards of care and attention to each role.

My especial thanks go to my colleagues George Lawson and Peter Scott for not protesting overmuch when I shamelessly used them as sounding boards when I wanted to try out an anecdote before including it in or rejecting it from the text that follows. Lastly I thank my wife and my sons, Julian, who works with me, and Gavin, who doesn't, for reading my manuscript, offering invariably sound advice and nipping many incipient mistakes in the bud: those that remain are mine alone.

Anthony Rota

PROLOGUE

For as long as I can remember I have been fascinated by the details of other people's jobs, of how they do them and how they feel about them. Do airline pilots feel nervous just before setting many tons of expensive machinery down on a ribbon of tarmac which they hit at 110 miles per hour? When brain surgeons are scrubbing-up before an operation are they planning which instruments to call for and in what order, or are they contemplating what they would like to eat for dinner that night?

Having been asked so often what it is like to work in a bookshop I prepared an answer by selecting a week from an old office diary and giving a fairly full account of it. I called that account 'A Week in the Life of a London Bookshop'. All the stories in it are true and together they give a picture of the variety that is the spice of a life spent dealing in rare books and manuscripts. Here is that week.

First I want to dispel some commonly held illusions. I have lost count of the number of times that people have said to me 'It must be lovely to work in a bookshop and read books all day long!'

Yes, it *is* lovely to work in a bookshop, but there is precious little chance of spending much of the day reading – and bookselling is far from the ideal pursuit for those in search of a quiet life. Laws against sexual discrimination make it illegal to advertise in specific terms for a young *male* assistant, but I am often tempted to include in our 'situations vacant' notices some such words as 'bookshop wants assistant, male or female; must be able to bench-press at least 200 lbs', for a bookseller's job is a very physical one. Books, especially those with illustrations printed on art paper, can be very heavy.

And let me mention here that whenever I have bought a large collection of books in a private house they have always been

15

shelved as far from the front door, and thus from the nearest point that a vehicle can be parked, as a perverse Fortune could arrange.

Moreover, since bookshelves are not elastic, any attempt to preserve logical order in one's shop involves constant bending and twisting exercises as a run of books is taken from the top shelf of one bay, carried across the shop and placed on the bottom shelf of another. I sometimes think that the Antiquarian Booksellers' Association invented the whole concept of aerobic exercises. Rudyard Kipling said in one of his more frequently quoted poems that 'Half a gardener's work is done upon his knees'. I can confirm that the same is true of antiquarian booksellers.

Perhaps I should say something about the kind of shop in which I was working in 1988, the year from which my diary entries are drawn. It was a ground floor, open access bookshop in Covent Garden, a busy part of London, in the centre of the bookselling and publishing district, an area now thronged with tourists. Our ground floor retail area was supported by an equivalent space in the basement for reference materials and reserve stock and by the same amount of office space upstairs. In an adjacent building we had four more offices. If you think the ratio of offices seems disproportionately high I should point out that ours is to a large extent a mail-order business, although our London customers visit us regularly. When our country customers are in town they, too, come to see us, and many European and American visitors also arrive each week. Even so, more of our customers come through the letter-box than through the door. This means that of our total staff of just over a dozen in 1988 (it seemed more on Fridays, fewer on Mondays) about a third were concerned with secretarial and accounting duties. Much of my own time was spent in writing letters, taking 'phone calls and in general managerial tasks. I saw all the 'difficult' books which were brought in to the shop for us to buy – those which junior staff were not familiar with or which on grounds of rarity or association seemed likely to be costly. I read and sometimes edited catalogue descriptions prepared by my staff. On a good day I even got to write catalogue descriptions myself (which is where I began in 1952). I shuttled back and forth between the shop and our warehouse in a North London suburb 10 miles away. On more days than not some question or problem arose in our trade association – either nationally or internationally – and as an officer I had to pitch in to help resolve it.

Although we deal primarily in modern English literature we are potentially interested in buying and selling good books right across the field of the humanities, no matter what their age. We would always reckon to have on hand a few good examples of modern bookbinding, a selection of autograph letters from distinguished authors, a good range of fine printing and so on. We issue catalogues, but these are really only the tip of the iceberg: indeed we once calculated that of every ten books that came into the shop only one ended up in the catalogue, the other nine being sold before getting that far, mostly because of our fairly elaborate system of recording customers' wants. We also sell many collections intact.

Within the firm we all specialize. When I was not being 'Personnel Director', 'Welfare Officer', 'Financial Controller' or 'Catalogue Designer' my own particular areas were and remain the 1890s, novelists and poets of the 1930s and 1940s, but most particularly literary manuscripts and archives.

In choosing a typical week in my working life, the temptation was of course to gild the lily, and to string together seven particularly interesting days. I say seven days because, a bookseller's week is not a Monday to Friday nine to five affair, however hard one might try to make it so. I remember being called from the bath-tub one Sunday night by a customer in the Philippines who had just got our latest catalogue and wished to lose no time in placing her order. Then it is rare for me to be introduced to new acquaintances at a dinner party without being asked the value of their family Bible (probably late 19th century) or of their set of Walter Scott's novels (probably incomplete). While it was tempting, then, to select seven especially interesting days and pretend that they did in fact all happen in the same calendar week, eventually I decided not to cheat: well, only to cheat a little. I have used a very small amount of poetic licence in as much as I selected a week in which quite a lot happened, and then transplanted into it just one occurrence from seven days before.

In all this my intention is not so much to reflect on these particular happenings, *per se*, as to allow them to illumine some of the possibly unexpected considerations which colour a book-dealer's working life.

Let me delay no longer. Let me begin to quote from my diary for the week commencing Saturday May 21st, 1988. If you think it odd to pick a week that began on a Saturday, well, I did warn you about poetic licence.

Saturday May 21st & Sunday May 22nd.

A sad weekend. With my wife I drove up to the small Norfolk town of North Walsham to make an assessment of the books and remaining literary papers of my old friend, the poet, critic and biographer, Kenneth Hopkins, who had died less than four weeks before at the age of 74.

Kenneth had stayed true to his vocation as a writer all his life and in consequence all his life he had been poor. Like W. H. Davies, author of *The Autobiography of a Super-Tramp*, Kenneth had begun his literary career by having some of his poems printed at his own expense, and peddling them from door to door from a knapsack on his back. As you will gather he was an idealist. As I have told you, he remained poor.

He once published a rather good essay on being an impecunious book-collector. He called it *Book Collecting for the Financially Unstable* (1985). Certainly he was a book-collector *par excellence* although he built his library on a shoestring.

He had a good nose for a book. Perhaps in unconscious preparation for writing two of his three major literary studies, *The Poets Laureate* and *Portraits in Satire*, he began to accumulate minor nineteenth century verse. Indeed to describe it as 'minor' is if anything to exaggerate: much of it was by authors whose names are unknown today. After thirty or more years of collecting in this fashion

Kenneth had put together a remarkable assemblage of works of this genre, an assemblage which it would have been impossible to duplicate by the time of his death. The works of the great poets of the nineteenth century survived: their texts are to be found in major libraries everywhere. What Kenneth Hopkins had put together was something altogether different – a collection of editions which had all but disappeared. It was a great resource for the study of the minor writing of the century, and also of 19th century typography and book production. We sold that collection to the McFarlin Library at the University of Tulsa in 1980.

Its sale made life a little easier for Kenneth, though he continued to write under several different *noms de plume*: occasional books of detective fiction, compilations of literary quizzes, even a ghosted autobiography of Liberace, and excellent lyric poetry. (His love poems by the way are really quite splendid.)

Kenneth was my father's friend for many years and mine for more than thirty. It was therefore a melancholy task to go back to the bungalow which no longer echoed to the shafts of his dry wit.

Forming an assessment of the books was a problem indeed. I should explain that there were books in the dining room, there were books in the living room, there were books in the guest bedroom (a civilized arrangement to be sure): there were books in the master bedroom; there were books running in triple rows of shelving, just too high to reach without a stepladder, all round the long and narrow hallway; and the study, of course, was lined with books, some of them double-banked. On top of this, if you will forgive the pun, there were books in the attic.

Nursing a sick wife had left Kenneth no time for dusting the books and in consequence the spiders had had a field day. Spiders dead, spiders alive, and spiders at various stages in between were everywhere. As my wife will bear witness, soiled shirt-cuffs are an occupational hazard for antiquarian booksellers.

My difficulties in assessing Kenneth's books were manifold. First there was the vast array of subjects. There were books on local history and topography. There were books he had used in his occasional teaching work. (He taught a couple of semesters at Southern Illinois University and more recently at Her Majesty's Prison in Norwich; I never asked him which class was the more difficult.) There were books he had been sent for review.

Then again Kenneth was more interested in text than edition: he was as happy with a second impression as with a first. As for condition, he worried about it scarcely at all. Always short of money he bought only the cheapest copy he could find. Thus in Kenneth's library one might approach a promising looking run of, say, H. S. Merriman's novels only to find that the first three were reprints virtually without value, and the fourth a first edition lacking the fly-leaf, while the fifth, also a first edition, had what appeared to be the remains of a bacon sandwich wedged between chapters nine and ten. The sixth, however, might prove to be a very desirable presentation copy from the author to a lifelong friend. There were no quick solutions. Sorting the wheat from the chaff would be a time-consuming job.

All that was possible this weekend was to make a rough assessment and formulate a plan of action. We then had to come to terms with the rather eccentric heir to the estate, Kenneth's son, whom I had not met before. Once his confidence had been won, and the investment of our time seemed a reasonable wager if we put a fair and reasonable proposition to him, we were able to settle on a date for a return visit, when with one of my staff, I could go through the library volume by volume, taking due note of the many inscribed and presentation copies, setting the good things on one side, and arranging for many of the books which had come from jumble sales and charity shops to be sent back to a similar fate.

Monday May 23rd.

An elderly lady from the North of England came in by appointment. Quite unused to the world of rare books and manuscripts, she had telephoned earlier on the introduction of the Bodleian Library. She was a descendant of William Wilberforce, who led the campaign in England for the abolition of slavery. She had inherited his diary for the years from 1783 to 1786. The Bodleian Library wished to purchase it but required an independent valuation. As in the case of Hopkins's son, our first priority was to win the owner's confidence. We had to convince her of our *bona fides* and thus persuade her to leave the precious journal with us for a day or two. (Even after forty-five years or more in the business I do not feel happy about valuing unique material off the cuff: I would not care to take one glance at a Wilberforce diary and immediately put a finite value on it in monetary terms.)

I cannot overemphasise that mutual confidence and trust are all-important in relations between dealer and client. Much effort has to be put into the early establishment of such confidence. One thing the dealer can do at the start is demonstrate his familiarity with the material. For example he might find in a library he has been asked to make an offer for, a book which has an interesting bibliographical point. I think of the first edition of Norman Douglas's volume about travelling in Italy, *Alone*, 1929. The earliest copies have as a postscript on page 140 a warning against the 'Fine Champagne' sold by a certain hotel in Rome. 'It is a scandal that one of the best hotels in Europe should sell such poison – at ten francs a thimbleful.' At the insistence of the hotel management the offending leaf was cut from the copies remaining unsold and another inoffensive leaf was substituted. Telling the story and-showing the critical leaf can help to break the ice.

Most people who call on the services of a bookseller love stories about books, and the dealer should not hesitate to tell one or two, preferably stories linked to specific books in the collection or library under discussion. When such stories can only come from long experience, the owner is probably grateful for evidence that the bookseller concerned knows his or her field.

But let us go back to the Wilberforce Diary. Ron Taylor, our 'in-house history specialist' gave himself a refresher course in Wilberforce in preparation for the valuation exercise. Then when we saw the diary we first satisfied ourselves that it was genuine. In 99 cases out of 100 this can be done more or less instantaneously, almost by instinct or 'gut reaction': it is only the rare, difficult case that requires careful comparison of handwriting, analysis of paper and ink and that sort of thing.

But back to Wilberforce again. We next considered how the years covered by the diary related to Wilberforce's career: whether the material had been published and so on and so forth. Finally we came up with a suggested 'fair market value' (the price at which a hypothetical willing seller and willing buyer might agree). Happily in this instance our figure proved acceptable to both parties and that particular document is now safely preserved in the Bodleian.

On the same day I had an infuriating and frustrating experience. Science fiction *afficionados* will not need me to tell them that *Orphans of the Sky* by Robert Heinlein is an important and 'difficult' book: 'difficult' in the sense that it is hard to find in the first edition. The two stories comprising this 'novel' were originally published in the journal *Astounding Science Fiction* in the early 1940s, but were not published again until the British publisher, Victor Gollancz, brought them out in one pair of covers in 1963. The book is a science fiction classic. It tells of a civilisation evolving over generations in a huge spaceship lost between the stars, the inhabitants having no awareness of the existence of the rest of the universe, except as a myth.

We had a fine copy in the dust-jacket. Because of its rarity, particularly in such condition, we asked £225 for it, or, say, something approaching $350.00. In March we had reported a small batch of Heinlein first editions to a customer on the Eastern seaboard of the United States. He took all the others but turned this one down, saying the price was more than he wished to pay. A week or so after that an English science fiction collector was shown the book on one of his periodic visits to our shop. He too turned it down. On Monday May 23rd I received a telephone call from Connecticut. The American customer said, 'I'd like to have that last Heinlein after all.' 'Splendid,' I replied, 'It's yours.' I went straight downstairs from my office to the bookshop on the ground floor and said to our resident 'sci-fi' expert: 'I've just sold the *Orphans of the Sky*.' 'Oh dear,' he said, 'So have I!' The other collector, the Englishman, had come in not ten minutes before to say that he too had changed his mind. Some days the bookseller's lot is hard indeed.

Also on Monday, our box-maker came in with a particularly lavish box for a particularly important book. For once, in marked contrast to my usual request that the price be kept down, I had been able to say 'To hell with the expense!' The book which was to be so expensively housed was T. E. Lawrence's classic *Seven Pillars of Wisdom*, a book with a complicated bibliographical and textual history.

That curious and controversial figure, Lawrence of Arabia, had united rival Arab factions in successful revolt against the Turks, thus significantly aiding the progress of the British campaign in the Middle East in the First World War. His triumph was achieved at great personal cost. He undertook savagely testing journeys across the desert, travelling on camel-back and enduring great hardship. In *Seven Pillars* he not only recounts all this, but also writes poetically of the beauty of the desert – and of its mystery, and the mystery of man's spirit.

The first manuscript of the book was lost, allegedly on Reading railway station, and Lawrence had to begin the painful task of re-writing this long work. In 1922 he had the text printed (in double column) on the presses of *The Oxford Times*. There were just eight copies. Four years later, in 1926, he brought out another edition, slightly cut. This time there were some 218 copies, lavishly illustrated by the best of the war artists (Eric Kennington and Paul Nash for example). He sold some to subscribers to help defray the cost of printing and gave others to those who had served in the campaign or helped with the production of the book.

The copy we are now concerned with was the one which he inscribed to his friend, E. M. Forster. It was Forster who helped Lawrence make cuts in the 1922 text for this 1926 printing. Pencilled marks in Forster's copy indicated just where the cuts had been made. Loose sheets of Forster's distinctive typescript gave the text of the passages that had been cut.

In 1930 Forster, then aged 50, met and became very attached to a young policeman, Bob Buckingham. It was to him that Forster inscribed his copy of *Seven Pillars*, immediately below Lawrence's original inscription. Many years later we bought this spectacular copy of a great book from Buckingham's heirs.

It happened to be lying on my desk one day when an English collector, whom I had known for some little time, but not at all well, arrived to join me for lunch. His taste in books was reasonably eclectic, but I had no idea whatsoever that he was even remotely interested in Lawrence. He had never spent more than £200 with me at any one time. On being shown into my office he asked what interesting books had come in lately, 'Well, there's this,' I said, showing him the Lawrence. 'How much is it?' he asked. '£23,000.' I replied, 'May I think about it overnight?' he enquired. I thought that this was no more than a face-saving 'power-play' and that that would be the last I would hear of the matter, but to my astonishment, I received a telephone call within an hour of parting from him: 'I'll take it,' he said. We arranged to make a box to protect it. Lawrence used several binders to produce the 1926 edition of *Seven Pillars* and hardly two copies look alike. (I once had one bound in wooden boards made from the propeller of one of the planes which flew in the desert campaign.) Forster's copy was lavishly bound in full russet morocco, and we were able to match the shade almost exactly and produce a case worthy of the contents.

Tuesday May 24th. Nostalgia Day.

I had a visit from Capt. Peter Marr, almost exactly my contemporary and one of the first customers for whom I was given responsibility when I joined the firm. I had just finished my National Service: Peter Marr was still doing his. He was in the Army and had been seconded to serve with the Brunei Defence Force in Sarawak. He told me that he used to sit under a bivouac sheet in torrential tropical rainstorms reading our catalogues. I often wondered whether the letters which brought his orders, damp-stained and rain-smudged, travelled the first few miles in a cleft stick carried by a native runner.

Peter Marr's special interest was in the writings of Jack London. In the 1950s London's first editions were still cheap and relatively easy to find. Most of the Marr collection was formed in those early years, first from Sarawak and then from Lancashire when he returned to civilian life. Then he married.

Children came along and had to be educated: it was goodbye to book-collecting. We lost touch. It had been with delight that I heard his voice on the telephone the previous week. Then he said that the time had come to sell his beloved Jack London collection and I found myself experiencing very mixed emotions. I was glad to have the chance of buying the books, but sorry that the man with whom in my youth I had felt such empathy should be parted from them, gathered as they were under such adverse conditions.

Now, this Tuesday, we met again. As we started to unpack the cartons in which he had brought the books down from Lancashire in his car, my face fell. Condition was the problem. We have always advised collectors to buy the best copies they are likely to be able to find and at least the books Peter Marr had bought from us had started out in good shape. Alas that was not true of some of his other purchases. Moreover time had not used them well. They had not shared that bivouac in Sarawak with him, but one or two of them could not have been in worse shape had they actually done so.

Thirty years ago there was a market for inferior copies, provided the price was sufficiently keen. Now that market seems to have dried up completely. It was heartbreaking to have to explain this to Peter Marr, for of course our offer reflected this sad state of affairs. It was an unhappy experience to see him struggle to come to terms with this, and to see what a wrench it was for him to part, not just with his Jack London collection, but with an entire period of his life.

Later the same day the Head of Special Collections at Columbia University came in. We had recently negotiated on his behalf the purchase of the Benckendorff Archive, the surviving papers of the last Czarist Ambassador to the Court of St James. As Columbia already had the archive of the last Tzarist Ambassador to Washington, this new acquisition fitted like a glove.

The ink on the purchase agreement was scarcely dry. As Columbia's agents we had been in competition with the British Library and with a university in Japan. It had been a cliff-hanging finish. Until this moment the curator had not seen the papers for himself and had had to rely on the reports we had sent him. Because of the 'confidence factor', the importance of which I have already stressed, he had been willing to commit many thousands of dollars on our recommendation alone.

It might be asked if this kind of situation did not leave the door wide open for abuse. I can only say that the world of rare books is a very small one and that, whilst it might be possible to abuse a client's confidence once, it is unlikely that the market would offer a negligent, or worse still, a corrupt dealer, a second chance. Happily the librarian from Columbia was delighted with his purchase. The fact that neither he nor I spoke Russian did not affect the issue.

This deal, an important one for my company, came about through happenstance and combined many of the factors which are already forming a thread running through this diary. We all know that research libraries are, by and large, short of funds. It is also common knowledge that there are odd pockets of money out there – sometimes in the strangest places. Columbia had bought something from me a year or so before. To be sure it could have been classified as Russian, just about, but it was not obviously so. The librarian had told me then that he had a trust fund dedicated to Russian material and that it was not easy to find good things to spend the money on. Eighteen months later my right-hand man in our Manuscript and Archives department, John Byrne, happened to be dining with the former head of the manuscript department of one of the London auction houses, now a freelance cataloguer and appraiser. She mentioned casually that she was working on the Benckendorff papers. She had no idea that my company, with its emphasis on English literature, would have any professional inter-

est in the matter. In fact my colleague saw the possibilities in a flash
– and the rest, as they say, is history.

The all-important elements in a successful bookseller's armoury
were perfectly combined here:

1. An intelligence network that gives early warning of what is
coming up.

2. A thorough knowledge of the market, of who wants what; and
of where funds are available.

3. Complete confidence between client and dealer.

4. Sharply honed negotiating skills: more necessary than ever in
a closed auction situation such as this: knowing just when to raise
the stakes and when to make the final bid.

5. A network of experts on call, who can be brought in to give
specialized help and advice in whatever sphere is needed (in this
instance in Russian history and in early photography: there were
valuable glass negatives and prints included).

6. A great deal of luck.

There is a coda to this tale: it is a story against myself. On this
Tuesday the librarian from Columbia confessed to a great interest
in and appetite for papers relating to the work of the Freudian, Otto
Rank. I sensed another under-used fund. 'I'm glad to know that, I
think I know where I can put my hand on some things you would
like', I said.

Calling on the Old Boy network I wrote at once to my friend, the
biographer, Vincent Brome, whose papers we had sold some years
before. 'Dear Vincent.' I said, 'You wrote the biography of Sigmund
Freud. Can you put me in touch with any sources of original material relating to his disciple, Otto Rank?' Back came the reply: 'Dear
Anthony, How nice to hear from you. I think I can help you. You
will find they have some excellent things in Columbia University!'

Wednesday May 25th

There was an auction at Christie's. Among the books to be sold
was a copy of Evelyn Waugh's *P.R.B.* (an essay on the Pre-Raphaelite
Brotherhood), often, if slightly inaccurately, described as his first

book. In fact it was preceded by a juvenile work, published when the author was only twelve. Precocious publication is perhaps one of the principal dangers of having a publisher for a father. (Waugh's father was a partner in Chapman & Hall.) Waugh was still up at Oxford when in 1926 his father caused *P.R.B.* to be printed – in an edition limited to only fifty copies.

Earlier in the week a customer in California had asked my advice about this book with a view to having me bid for him at the sale. We had considered the auctioneer's pre-sale estimate, which was a range of £1,500 to £2,000. In my early days in the trade saleroom estimates were certainly available in London, but they had to be asked for specially. It is only in recent years that the London houses have followed New York practice and published estimates in their catalogues. The trouble with this system is that the estimates become self-fulfilling prophecies. My customer wanted *P.R.B.* badly. Fifty copies is a small limitation and though, considering its rarity, the book comes on to the market comparatively often (usually the same few copies changing hands again and again), we sensed it might be quite a time before another opportunity arose. We therefore decided to exceed Christie's top estimate by 75% and set ourselves an absolute limit of £3,500.

I went into the sale a confident man. I came out a sadder and wiser one, having seen my limit passed and the book knocked down to someone else for £3,600. I cheered myself up by recalling the occasion when, in the 1950s, I went with my tutor, my bookselling *guru*, Anthony Newnham, to Foyle's bookshop in Charing Cross Road and found on the shelf a copy of *P.R.B.* priced at a mere £5. Needless to say, we bought it – and went home by taxi to celebrate.

Thursday May 26th

Another auction sale, this time at Sotheby's. On this day the sale contained nothing that we wished to buy for our own stock, but a collector on the continent of Europe, who buys extensively at auction, using us as his agent, had sent a number of bids for the sale. His commissions are never simple or straightforward. For example he might say 'If you buy Lot 390 for less than £800, increase the bid on 459 to £650. If, by the time you reach Lot 472 you have spent less than £1,000 on my behalf, increase all my subsequent bids by 30%. If you buy Lot 473, double the bid on the next Lot. If the title-page of Lot 497 has the 'rue de Seine' address in the publisher's imprint bid £70, if not bid £50' – and so on and on. One almost needs a computer in order to cope with the complexity of his instructions. Remember, too, that a good auctioneer might sell at the rate of 120 to 180 Lots an hour, i.e. two or three Lots per minute. 200 an hour is not unheard of. At that speed one has precious little time for reflection.

On this day we bought precisely one Lot for our continental client – and that for a hammer price of £8. Since the accepted and general rate for such work is 10%, our gross remuneration in this instance was exactly 80 pence (or about $1.20) – less than the cost of a bus ticket to the auction room.

My next job for this day was by way of being a self-inflicted wound. As a member of the committee of our trade association I had agreed to hold a watching brief on the arrangements for a T. S. Eliot centenary exhibit at the Antiquarian Book Fair which the association was sponsoring at the end of June. I had not liked the original description of the exhibit in the Book Fair catalogue and in consequence now had the task of writing new copy and providing a fresh layout for the Eliot entry – all against a tight deadline of course. Blushing slightly at my effrontery in attempting to sum up Eliot's career in two paragraphs, I did what had to be done.

As I was finishing this task I received a telephone call from an old customer. His French parents in-law had just bought a house at Cap-Ferrat. In former days it had been an hotel where Jean Cocteau used to stay. My customer was going down to visit and wanted an appropriate present.

By a stroke of good fortune we had in stock a first edition of Cocteau's which bore a presentation inscription from the author. Moreover it incorporated a little sketch – not much more than a squiggle really, but still a sketch. The book was priced at £65. My customer was delighted and said what good booksellers we were. I accepted the compliment but thought of the part luck plays in the establishment of a reputation. We happened to have something suitable in stock, which made us 'good' booksellers. As a matter of fact we were pleased to sell the Cocteau so easily, for English book-sellers seldom have good fortune with French books. If one has a copy on *vergé d'Arches* the French collectors want it on *vélin*. If one has a copy in the original wrappers, the French want it in a lavish binding by Legrain, or vice versa. With French books and French collectors it seems one seldom wins.

Friday May 27th

A day to repeat the Cocteau conjuring trick – or to pull another bibliographical rabbit out of a hat. I had a call from the daughter of a bookseller, the late Harold Edwards of whom I shall have more to say later. Sally, like Edward Booth-Clibborn the day before, needed a book for a present – this time a wedding-present. She wanted an attractive example of something printed at the Golden Cockerel Press, but she had to have it within the hour. (A 'shotgun' wedding, I wondered?)

I promised to check the shelves and call her back. With the help of our private press book cataloguer, I examined ten or a dozen possibilities in Sally's price range. I called her back and she immedi-ately plumped for our own first choice: Thomas Carew's *A Rapture*, (1927) with engravings by J. E. Laboureur. Bound in batik boards, the edition was limited to 375 copies. This one had a bookplate stat-ing that it had once been the Press's own exhibition copy. It was priced at £110. Sally sent a despatch rider round to collect the book. A bookseller's daughter, she presumably learned about cash-flow problems at her father's knee and sent a cheque at the same time. Would that all our customers paid so promptly.

Next I took a call from that staunch bastion of civilisation, the London Library, a subscription to which remains one of life's great bargains. A reader had 'lost' their copy of *Alice in Wonderland*, not the 1865 first edition, happily (for only half a dozen copies of that are believed to have survived) but the '30th thousand.' Would I look out for one please? I said I would, but I fear that the hunt continues to this day.

A packet arrived from the daughter of the poet, Roy Campbell, one of the very few English writers to serve on Franco's side in the Spanish Civil War. The packet contained thirty autograph and typed letters written to her mother, between 1970 and 1979, by the liberal South African novelist, Alan Paton, author of *Cry the Beloved Country*. The letters were about a projected biography of Roy Campbell which Paton was to write. In them Paton condemned Campbell's anti-Semitism and also said he was not prepared to ignore Campbell's reaction to Mrs Campbell's affair with Vita Sackville-West. Teresa Campbell wanted us to buy the letters from her, but only on the understanding that, on reselling them, we would ensure that they would go into sympathetic hands. We were happy to make that pledge.

This was the day on which one of my co-directors had gone up to Liverpool to take a preliminary look at a private library formed by a man who had spent all his working life in adult education. He was secretary of the Liverpool Film Society and a founder of the Left-Wing Mercury Theatre. His library was reputed to contain 20,000 volumes. My colleague telephoned to give me his first impression.

There were closer to 10,000 than 20,000 volumes (sighs of relief), they appeared to be arranged in no sort of order (groans) and some of the 17th century books were imperfect (howls of anguish), but the collection still deserved attention. Much was fit only for the outside stall, what in former days was called the 'sixpenny box,' but there were real gems dotted here and there. I decided we would form a consortium with a general bookseller, who still had the equivalent of a 'sixpenny box,' with a view to making a joint offer.

Thus the week ended as it had begun, with the prospect of man-handling several tons of miscellaneous books, hard but satisfying labour, carrying with it the near certainty of exciting discoveries.

'Such,' my diary for the week concluded, 'is my life: aching back and dirty shirt cuffs – and I love it.'

31

Bertram and Anthony Rota, at Bodley House, *c.* 1964

CHAPTER ONE

HOW IT ALL BEGAN

ONE SPRING MORNING in 1952 I was sitting at my desk in the Headquarters of No.1 (Overseas) Ferry Unit at RAF Abingdon. An orderly brought the mail. Addressing me by the initial of the short form of my first name, by which I was known throughout my National Service days, he called 'There's a letter for you this morning, T'. I took the envelope and recognized my father's hand. My parents' marriage had gone sadly wrong twelve years before. I stayed with my mother but remained on good terms with my father.

His letter brought the news that his second marriage had also broken down irrevocably. The silver lining to that cloud was that Marjorie, his second wife and one-time secretary, had left the firm, and my father asked if I felt free to reconsider going into it myself. He told me to take as long as I liked before replying. I thought about it for almost four minutes before reaching for the phone, and saying an excited 'Yes, please', a decision I have never had cause to regret. Oh I am sure I could have made more money in other fields, but what other jobs could have brought me such unalloyed pleasure – pleasure in the materials I deal in and in the people I work with?

I often wonder how my life would have turned out had my great-grandfather's taken a different course. Bertram Dobell (1842-1914) of Huguenot descent, was the son of a tailor. His father's serious illness and early death brought the family to penury. In order to support them he was obliged to take a job as a grocer's delivery boy. In due course he was promoted to serving at the counter. In later years he was not forthcoming about this period of his life, seeming almost ashamed of it, though it was an honourable way of making a living: perhaps as a senior and respected figure in the book trade he thought he should have been able to boast of a more formal education. In any case he worked hard and saved hard, and in 1869 when he was twenty-seven, he opened his first bookshop in the Kentish Town district of London, (not in 'a town in Kent,' a howler which an editor at Bruccoli, Clark injected into an essay I wrote about my great-grandfather for *The Dictionary of Literary Biography*, (Vol. 184, 1998).

Bertram Dobell is chiefly remembered today for discovering and identifying Thomas Traherne's *Poetical Works*, 1903 and *Centuries of Meditation*, 1908. He is also remembered as the champion of the work of James Thomson ('B.V.'), especially *The City of Dreadful Night and other poems* (Chicago, 1899; London 1910). As a bookseller he published almost 250 catalogues, notable among them being one listing 623 items from the collections of Robert and Elizabeth Barrett Browning. One of the items listed was the set of corrected proofs of 'Red Cotton Nightcap'. In 1913 he offered for sale a collection of 1,400 privately printed books; assembling them was no mean achievement.

Around the turn of the century Westminster City Council were taking an officious stand against the booksellers' custom of putting a '6*d*. box' outside their shops, the council claiming that these were 'obstructions' under the Metropolitan Police Act of 1839. My great grandfather's business was chiefly concerned with the antiquarian books he sold inside his shop, but because the ban represented a serious threat to the income of some of his neighbours he decided to tackle the council head-on. He therefore caused to be erected outside his shop at number 54 Charing Cross Road a 6*d*. shelf that he certainly had no real need of, but it was enough to offend the Clerk to the Council and his street inspector. They duly charged Bertram with an offence and he appeared before the magistrates in January 1902. A master of the art of public relations, he saw to it that every national and London newspaper was represented in court and, further, conducted his defence through the correspondence columns of *The Times*, many notable authors of the day coming to his aid. The magistrates and the council knew when they were

Julian Rota, at Long Acre

beaten. He was undoubtedly guilty, but they fined him just one shilling and no further prosecutions were brought.

When Bertram Dobell died in December 1914 his sons Percy (a true scholar) and Arthur took over his business. Their sister, my grandmother Evelyn Jane Rota (née Dobell), had served as amanuensis to Bertram Dobell and it was to her that Percy and Arthur turned when they persuaded their nephew, Cyril Bertram Rota, my father, to enter the business. 'Give us your boy and we will teach him all we know,' they said. My father worked for his uncles for four years and then started in business on his own. That is why I do not think it is stretching things too far to claim that I am a fourth generation bookseller, and my son Julian who has worked alongside me these last years, is a fifth. Perhaps there really is some bookselling gene in our blood. Certainly as soon as I had passed through the stage when every little boy wants to be an engine driver, it seemed to be the most natural thing in the world to plan to join my father in his bookshop, with its wonderful musty aroma.

How did I learn the job? Partly by reading but mostly by experience, for in 1952 there were no ready-made training schemes for antiquarian booksellers of the kind that the ABA tried to set up with its diploma course over forty years later. There were occasional lectures it is true, but most of us had to learn on the 'sit by Nellie' principle, which literally involved sitting next to someone who was doing the job, watching them very closely and then trying to feed a leather binding, catalogue a first edition, make a simple collation or whatever the job might be, on one's own.

To learn about bibliography I read Carter's *ABC for Book Collectors*, Percy Muir's *Book Collecting: a Series of Letters to Everyman*, and McKerrow's *Introduction to Bibliography*. Alack and alas, Philip Gaskell's *A New Introduction to Bibliography* was not published until many years later. As the months and years went by I read much else that Carter wrote, lectures and essays by such wise men as Simon Nowell-Smith, Michael Sadleir and others. I little thought then that I would one day add to the literature myself.

Then, too, I read voraciously the 19th and 20th century English and American literature in which the firm specialized. I devoured such mainstream writers as Huxley, Lawrence and Hemingway but did not neglect the more esoteric writers such as F. W. Rolfe, Baron Corvo.

I remember that the first cataloguing task that I was set involved the listing of a virtually complete collection of the works of the three Powys brothers, John Cowper Powys, Llewelyn Powys and T. F. Powys. Having in front of me at one time almost the full range of each man's output from early to late, from rare to comparatively common, was an educative experience.

To train me in another part of the work my father handed me one morning what appeared to be a random selection from the incoming mail, although in fact I think he chose each piece rather carefully. 'Draft answers to these letters for me please', he said. 'Here are some examples of the sort of thing we usually say and the way in which we usually say it. Always write the kind of letter that you yourself would like to receive. When you have finished drafting it, read it through and look at it through the eyes of the recipient.' My father took as much care over every letter he wrote as other men might take over a sonnet or a short story.

Anthony Newnham, my father's co-director, was a hard task-master but learning practical things from him was still a delight. He taught me how to judge fine bindings and how to tell the work of one binder from another. I remember that he put this to the test one cold and wet morning by making me stand with him in Sackville Street and look into the window of Henry Sotheran & Co, where rows of fine bindings were arranged. In most cases I had to judge solely from the spines as I went along the row, saying for example, 'Sangorski, Sangorski, Bayntun, Bayntun, Bayntun, Sangorski, Bayntun, Sangorski.' If I got one wrong then, rain or no rain, I had to go back and start again. I thought of this many years later when Phil Bradfer-Lawrence invited me into the warmth and comfort of the library in his Norfolk home and showed me that part of his Lawrence of Arabia collection which comprised copies of the first published edition of *Seven Pillars of Wisdom*, 1935, each bound

Anthony Newnham

by a different designer-binder to his or her design. Phil had not attempted to dictate what he wanted: each binder was invited to express in leather exactly what the book meant to him or her. When I saw it I suppose the collection ran to about thirty examples. Among those contributing were Sally Lou Smith, Philip Mansfield, Bernard Middleton, Ivor Robinson and Arthur W. Johnson. To have a little fun on the evening I was there Phil had turned the labels face downwards and I was invited to identify each binder from the style employed. If I did not particularly cover myself in glory, nor did I make a complete fool of myself and I thanked Anthony Newnham's shade accordingly.

But I digress. During my first year or two in the firm my father used to take me with him when he was called to a house to make an offer for books. I watched him sort the volumes into piles according to his buying price. There would be a pile at half-a-crown and a pile at five shillings, a pile at ten shillings and a much smaller pile at a pound. This system made the eventual reckoning up much easier and yes, in 1952 and even in 1954, fine first editions in the dust-wrappers could still be had for this kind of money.

All this time Anthony Newnham was also teaching me something about printing on a hand-press. Ant, as he was familiarly known, lived at this time at No. 4 Great Ormond Street in Bloomsbury, just round the corner from an admirable public house called 'The Lamb and Flag' in Lamb's Conduit Street. He kept his printing press close by, in an unheated basement, reeking of damp, in Orde Hall Street. A great believer in territorial designations, he called it the Orde Hall Press. (He told me that if he were ever ennobled he would arrange to be called Lord Four Great Ormond Street.) Three pieces that Ant printed with immaculate taste, if marginally less skill, come immediately to mind. One was the first separate edition of *The Voice*, an essay by Bernard Shaw which Ant produced for his friend, soon to become mine, Harry Mushlin. The second was the conceit by the Elizabethan John Lyly, 'Cupid and Campaspe' ('Cupid and my Campaspe play'd | At cards for kisses; Cupid paid'). Ant printed this for the coming-of-age of Sarah Rothschild, presenting her with the complete edition of 21 copies. What else could one give a girl who had everything? ('At last he set her both his eyes; | She won, and Cupid blind did rise.') But what I remember best was the third, a pamphlet of poems by George Sims, taking as its title the Portuguese word 'Saudades.'

Before the days of computer typesetting it was comparatively common, as it had once been universal, to set type by hand with the aid of a composing-stick. One evening after work we braved the chill damp of the Orde Hall Street basement and Ant explained to me the 'lay of the case', the time-honoured arrangement of the 'sorts' of type or characters in their boxes. He then gave me a poem to set. I think I managed only the first couplet before it was time to clear up and catch the last train home, but I remember those two lines very well:

Today, again, frail and fitfully,
Like laughter over coppice walls,

Then, or on subsequent evenings, I learned much of the attractive language of the hand-press – quoins for locking up a forme; quads, thicks and thins, ems and ens for spacing; make-ready, bite and bonk, this last the impression that the hardness of the type made on soft paper, and not the other subject that always seemed to be uppermost in Ant's mind! After damping handmade paper so that it would better take the ink, adjusting the make-ready to get a better impression, playing with spacing and making microscopic adjustments, I came to understand just what went into producing a page of perfect print. In other words I learned what it took to print a fine book. I also learned enough about what accidents could occur along the way, causing bibliographical variants as a by-product. I have often said since that nobody should be allowed to attempt the writing of a descriptive bibliography until they have printed a text for themselves.

Let me now press the fast forward button and move from 1952 when I was a callow apprentice, to 1975 when my elder son, Julian, was in his second year at Highgate School. As one of his extra-curricular activities he had joined the Printing Society, which produced programmes and tickets for school concerts and plays, and things of that sort. I passed the school on my drive home after work, and on this day it had been arranged that I would collect him from the school gate and take him home. After the ritual exchange of greetings Julian began tentatively: 'Dad, I've got ink all over my white shirt. Do you think there'll be trouble?' Now before our marriage his mother worked first for Cassell's and then for Collins, and I was able to say 'Julian, as long as it is printing ink I think you will be all right.' And so it proved.

PAYING FOR LUNCH

In my early days in bookselling I was constantly hearing from the old-timers about the bargains that used to be found on the book-barrows in the Farringdon Road. It seemed to me even then that some of the tales were pretty tall ones, for such barrows as I saw around Seven Dials and in Soho seemed to contain only imperfect copies, odd volumes and the rejects from jumble sales. At this time – the mid 1950s – my father and I often used to lunch together in the saloon bar of a pub on the corner of Great Windmill Street and Brewer Street in Soho. The menu ran the whole gamut from A to B – or perhaps C on a good day. In the course of a week one might be offered roast lamb, roast beef, roast pork, steak and kidney pie and liver and bacon. Then it was back to roast lamb again.

Now it happened that just outside the pub was a barrow which usually contained the sorts of books that I have described. My father, bless him, was an incurable optimist and would often keep me waiting for my lunch while he ran his eye over the detritus laid out on the barrow. Then came a day when not one discovery but two made it all worthwhile and justified his efforts fifty times over. For five shillings he bought a mint set of the three volumes that make up the 1885 first edition of George Meredith's novel, Diana of the Crossways, *one of the more desirable Meredith titles to appear in the three-decker format.*

Nestling next to Diana *was a little volume in yellow paper wrappers, again in pristine condition. This proved to be* John Sherman and Dhoya *by 'Ganconagh', a nom de plume used by W. B. Yeats when writing this volume for Fisher Unwin's Pseudonym Library in 1891. This treasure cost my father a further half-crown. Afterwards we spoke jestingly of these two bargains paying for the day's lunch but, metaphorically speaking, they paid for lunches for the whole year. Of course it was impossible to hurry my father past the barrow after that but his best endeavours failed to turn up a desirable book on any subsequent visit.*

CHAPTER TWO

MY FATHER
LOSES HIS TEMPER

AND WE BUY A 'SPOTTED TIGER'

I worked closely with my father for fourteen happy years. From time to time I saw him mildly cross, usually with inanimate objects such as a car that would not start, a lock that would not turn or a window that would not shut, but sometimes with a person who had let him down.

Only twice did I see him lose his temper in any serious way, not with me I hasten to add, the first occasion occurring just a few months after I joined the firm. My father was negotiating the sale of H. G. Wells's manuscripts and correspondence files which are now in the University of Illinois. The papers had been stored in a bank vault in Hampstead where they were inaccessible to scholars and where time was doing them no favours. Wells's family wanted them sold abroad, if at all, because of the nature of some of the correspondence, both letters received and copies of letters sent. (It was felt there might be acrimony and possibly litigation if they were readily available to readers at an institution in say, Bloomsbury or Oxford.) To handle the sale of such an archive was a great feather in my father's cap and probably the most prestigious single deal he had undertaken since founding his own business thirty years before. I remember being taken to meet Wells's daughter-in-law, Mrs Marjorie Wells, and to see the archive while it was stored in her house. The depth and range of the material were overwhelming. One statistic that I remember clearly is that the pile of drafts, both manuscript and typewritten, for *Tono-Bungay* stood virtually three feet high.

Then one morning the telephone rang. It was Mrs Wells, sounding decidedly acerbic, and asking very brusquely to be put through to my father. He spoke to Mrs Wells and a few moments later came out of his office literally shaking with rage. He told Anthony Newnham and me what he had just heard. Mrs Wells said that 'a person calling himself Dr Schwartz' turned up on her doorstep out of the blue, saying he had heard she was selling her father-in-law's papers, a transaction which Mrs Wells had thought to be confidential. He had proceeded to tell her that my father was really out of his league in a deal of this kind and he, Dr Schwartz, could get her a better price. In an attempt to prove it he had pulled large bundles of £5 notes from his overcoat pocket. He refused to take 'no' for an answer and she had eventually had to shut the door in his face.

Although Schwartz had not succeeded in getting the handling of the affair himself, he had shaken Mrs Wells's confidence in my father's discretion and in the book trade as a whole. She was minded to withdraw from the sale. We had no written contract with her – we seldom do in cases of this sort – and although my father was able to give Mrs Wells a degree of reassurance there and then, some fence-mending would clearly have to be done.

At this point in my life I had only met Jake Schwartz two or three times, when he had called at the shop to sell us things. He was a colourful character whose reputation had preceded him. A swarthy man, with a leonine head, he had practised as a dentist in New York. He seemed to have made a success of that, for he came to live in England bringing with him enough capital to start a bookselling business. An eccentric character with a hide like that of a rhinoceros, he once issued a catalogue from his Ulysses Bookshop which in 1932 offered for sale at the contemptuous price of one halfpenny a book which was then as fashionable as was D. M. Thomas's *The White Hotel* in more recent times.

In the days when auctioneers at Sotheby's wore black jackets and sponge-bag trousers, and when jackets and ties were *de rigueur* for bidders, I saw Jake arrive for a sale in a sports shirt, aquamarine towelling shorts and open-toed sandals worn sockless. I was also to see him thrown out of Sotheby's when he gate-crashed a party there, not once, not twice but three times in the same evening. He could talk the proverbial hind-leg off a donkey and he certainly had a flair for books, turning up many rare and precious things, sometimes by the simple expedient of materialising on a doorstep and asking the author or the owner to sell.

On the day in question, the phone rang again, just after Mrs Wells had called. It was Jake asking to speak to my father. 'Bertram,' Jake began. 'I know what you must be thinking, but I was trying to help you.' This was too much for my father who told Jake that that was the sort of help he could manage without, thank you, and slammed the phone down.

Fifteen minutes later a cab drew up at the door and deposited Jake, who hurried in and asked for my father. 'I'm not sure he'll see you, Jake' said Newnham. 'You've really annoyed him and you might do better to wait until he's calmed down.'

This caused Jake to go into a song and dance routine about his acute distress at having upset his 'friend'; how he wouldn't sleep that night; and how awful it was to be misunderstood, this monologue being delivered at full volume and at a rate which ruled out any chance of interruption. My father came into the shop and expressed his displeasure. Jake swore he was only trying to negotiate a higher price so that 'everyone would benefit'. My father turned away and started back towards his office. Jake dropped to his knees and raised his hands in supplication. Still on his knees he followed my father across the room at a truly astonishing rate. By now he appeared to be weeping. 'Would my father ever forgive him?' he asked. Finally, probably in hope of a return to a quiet life, Bertram said he would try to put the matter behind him.

Jake, still on his knees, making quite a spectacle of himself in the shop, said that nothing would do but that we should all three agree to be his guests at dinner the next week in order to show that we did indeed forgive him. He finally wore us down and a date was set.

On the following Tuesday Bertram, Newnham and I turned up at the well-appointed apartment which Jake shared with the stage and screen actress Anita Bolster, his companion for many years. Glasses of sherry were pressed on us. Conversation from our side of the table might have been a little stilted, but Anita was not to blame in any way, and Jake never did know shame, and rattled on as though nothing had happened. Then he picked up a bottle and said 'Have some more sherry. It's the best. It's Tio Pepé. It's thirty shillings a bottle, but what do I care?' So saying he tipped the bottle and refilled my father's glass, and then moved to Newnham's and to mine, without altering the angle at which he held the bottle and thus spilling sherry on the carpet all the way.

After dinner Jake showed us a painting by D. H. Lawrence. A caption on the back called it 'The Tiger'. But it was a singular tiger indeed, for it had a leopard's spots where one would have expected stripes. We bought the picture just the same and, if memory serves me correctly, sold it later to Edward Nehls, editor of the groundbreaking three-volume composite biography of Lawrence.

Good Jake Schwartz stories are legion. For example in the course of a South Coast buying trip my wife and I found ourselves in Brighton, where Jake and Anita had taken a large and elegant apartment with a fine view over the sea. Jake had urged us to call on him and so we rang and said we were in town. 'Come round. Bring a bottle,' Jake said. We might very well have taken a bottle of wine with us in any case, but we thought it rather strange to be instructed so to do. When we duly presented ourselves at the appointed hour, which would have been seven or eight o'clock in the evening, the master of the house received us in his dressing-gown and then sat down at a marble-topped dressing table and proceeded to finish his supper, which consisted of sardines eaten straight from the can.

Jake seemed incapable of doing business in a frank and open way, with all his cards on the table. We had further proof of the truth of this in 1965, when he walked into Bodley House and said he had a rare Dylan Thomas item to show us. It was *In Memory of Ann Jones*, the fifth in the series of Caseg Broadsheets, of which just 500 copies were printed in Wales in 1942. In his bibliography of Dylan Thomas, published in 1956, John Rolph remarked that all the Caseg

Broadsheets were now scarce, 'on account of their physical frailty'. Certainly it was a little time since we had had a copy and we were therefore pleased to buy the one that Jake offered. On the next day he came again with another copy. We bought that also, remarking that we wished we had known about the second copy when he offered us the first. On the third day he appeared with three more copies. Rather than have the broadsheet turning up all over London, we bought those as well, asking if he had any more. Jake's reaction to an unusual question was always to release impenetrable clouds of verbiage which masked his answer, much in the way that RAF aircrews used to foil German radar by releasing showers of the reflective metal strips called 'window'. Sure enough Jake turned up again 48 hours later with ten more copies, which he swore really were the last that he had. He gave us a suitable discount on the original asking price and we bought them all, but how much simpler it would have been if he had said straightforwardly in the first place that he had found a cache of fifteen copies and named his price for the lot.

Sometimes months or even years would go by without our seeing Jake or hearing from him. I remember that he turned up in 1972, bringing us Wyndham Lewis material consisting of one or two minor manuscript pieces, some correspondence, books from Lewis's library and so on. He said he had bought it from the author's widow. 'Is this all there is Jake?' In reply came such a stream of words that it was impossible to find a straight answer anywhere in it. Later it became apparent that what he had sold me was about one third of the available material. As soon as he had my cheque he cashed it and went back to buy some more from Mrs Lewis. In the course of a week I bought three groups of Lewis material from him. I added about one third to the total price I had paid and began offering the complete collection to possible purchasers.

I was a little surprised when a few days later I had a visit from one of the trustees of the Wyndham Lewis estate, a man I knew quite well. 'Anthony,' he said. 'Don't you think you've been a little hard on Mrs Lewis. Could you not give her some more money?' I was very surprised at this turn of events and quickly pointed out that I had not dealt with Mrs Lewis at all: I had bought from Jake Schwartz what he in turn had purchased from her. It transpired that Jake had told the trustees, perhaps after they approached him as they had now approached me, that the sums he had paid to Mrs Lewis were paid on my behalf. Since I now learned that they amounted to only about thirty per cent of the price I had paid Jake I was less than pleased to be linked to them in this way. Happily I had documentation to support my version of events.

Speaking of documentation, on days when Jake was – exceptionally for him – reluctant to lower his first (usually rather high) asking price, he would say that he didn't mind in the least whether one bought the material or not because he had such and such an amount in the bank. He would then insist on showing his bank passbook to demonstrate that he did indeed have, shall we say, $80,000 in his current account. We were not the only people to be shown the evidence of his wealth. Warren Roberts, when he was Director of the Humanities Research Center at the University of Texas was also among those made privy to this information.

I have made Jake sound all bad but he had his better side and was probably more of a rascal than an out and out rogue.

THE BOOK QUOTIENT

Of the hundreds of homes I have been in to buy books, to sell books or just to look at books, whose contained the greatest number of volumes?

Since I never counted, I am not in a position to give the answer in absolute terms but I do think I can make a comparative judgement. Let us consider the size of the house or apartment and decide the winner by dividing the perceived number of books, rounded off to the nearest thousand, by the approximate number of square feet of floor space. I call the answer the book quotient.

I already know to whom I am going to award the prize. Who were the candidates? They included Bill Wreden, with the entire basement of his mansion in Palo Alto given over to book-shelves (but he was disqualified because he was a dealer); Fred J. Hoffman, in Milwaukee, compiler of that invaluable reference work The Little Magazine; *and Professor Gordon Ray of the Guggenheim Foundation, at his exclusive Sutton Place address in Manhattan. Each of these last two men had bookstacks in his city centre apartment. Then there was Oliver Stonor (who wrote not only under his own name but also as 'Morchard Bishop', a pseudonym he took from the name of a village which he saw on a signpost in Devonshire), who filled a large and rambling house in Morebath, near Bampton in North Devon, with source books for his writings, review copies and bargains picked up at a rate surely faster than any man could read; Kenneth Hopkins, poet, critic and author of* Book Collecting for the Financially Unstable, *whose house in Norfolk almost literally burst at the seams from storing too many books (see the diary which forms the prologue to these memoirs); and lastly W. H. Chesson in his small terraced house in Kew. I bought the Hopkins library in 1988 and the Stonor library two years later, but let me announce without further ado that the prize for having the highest 'book quotient' goes to W. H. Chesson, owner of the smallest house occupied by any of my candidates.*

Chesson can best be described as 'a man of letters'. Although he was only credited with the authorship of three books he translated and edited rather more and was a publisher's reader. His first wife was Norah

Chesson (née Hopper), a contributor to The Yellow Book. *After her death, Chesson, old and far from well, married again, presumably seeking companionship and someone to look after him. His chosen bride this time was the person who used to clean the house for him – at least that was what she was supposed to do but from what I saw of the place shortly after Chesson's death in 1953, she didn't make much of a job of it.*

I will admit that circumstances were against her. When Eric Barton of the Baldur Bookshop in Richmond called us in to look at the books with a view to making an offer for them, we found books everywhere. There were books piled high on both sides of every tread of the stairs. More books were stacked on the piano lid, reaching right up to the ceiling. Chesson's bedroom contained a solid stack of books about six feet high, with just a tiny passage left from the door to the hollowed-out space for his truckle bed. A thick layer of dust covered everything and it was not possible to read the titles of the books without knocking the dust off first. Anthony Newnham and I laboured at this for an hour or two, gaining an ever stronger impression that the library had already been picked over by people who knew what they were doing. By this time the second Mrs Chesson had joined us and had started to follow us from room to room, cursing us for what appeared to her to be a negative attitude, and her late husband for not having left her more money. In the end we selected just five volumes, the best of which was W. B. Yeats's Poems, 1895, *and beat a hasty retreat. To our delight and surprise, when we got all the dust off, the light brown cloth covers, with their overall design in gilt, looked remarkably clean and fresh, and the book was sold in less time than it took to find it.*

SLIMER

HARRY ADAM KNIGHT was the pseudonym of John Brosnan and Leroy Kettle.

JOHN BROSNAN (1947-2005) was born in Australia but lived most of his life in Britain. He published many books about movies and movie-making (including the particularly well-regarded *Movie Magic*, *Future Tense* and *James Bond in the Cinema*). Three of his horror books (*Carnosaur*, *Slimer* and *Bedlam*—the last two written with Leroy Kettle, all under the pseudonym Harry Adam Knight) were made into movies. Their most successful book was *The Fungus*. Two other horror books were published as by Simon Ian Childer, *Tendrils* (with Leroy) and *Worm*. And they published a collection of humorous pieces—well, they thought they were funny—called *The Dirty Movie Book*.

John also wrote several science fiction novels—the *Skylords* trilogy, *The Opoponax Invasion* and *Mothership*, as well as a range of SF thrillers such as *Torched* (with John Baxter) and *Skyship* and comic fantasy novels *Damned and Fancy* and *Have Demon, Will Travel*.

He wrote a much-liked column for the UK magazine *Starburst* and scripts for the comic *2000 AD*, as well as a range of TV novelisations.

LEROY KETTLE (born 1949) also published the science fiction conspiracy thriller *Future Perfect* in 2014 with Chris Evans and, before retirement, worked in the civil service as one of the principal architects of the UK's Disability Discrimination Act.

Both John and Roy first started writing in SF fandom and published humorous fanzines which were enjoyed by the few people who read them.

CHAPTER THREE

THE CUSTOMER
IS ALWAYS RIGHT

– WELL ALMOST ALWAYS

Certain wags in the book trade have suggested that Blades' *Enemies of Books* should include a chapter on the wives of collectors. Certainly there were some wives who resented the portion of the family's income that was spent on books, and others who were opposed to the growing incursion of bookshelves on the available space in their houses. One such was married to our customer Dr Eamon Norton, a genial Irishman who had a busy general practice in the Yorkshire town of Wakefield. He collected *inter alia* the first editions of Hilaire Belloc and G. K. Chesterton and regularly rang us from his surgery to order from our catalogues. He always finished by saying 'Now remember, don't send the books home, send them to the pet shop'. The shop in question was owned by a friend of his and was situated on the corner of the next street. Its proprietor kept late hours and whenever Dr Norton answered a night call, he would first see to the needs of his patient and would then park at the side door of the shop on his way home. His friend would ask him in for a chat and Dr Norton would slip a couple of volumes from a recently arrived parcel into his night bag and so smuggle them into the house. He would fit them on a shelf before going back to bed. He assured me his wife never suspected a thing.

Then there was Irving Steen, who was 'something in the city,' and lived somewhere in the Surrey stockbrokers' belt: we never did learn exactly where. Tall, well-groomed, with silver hair beneath his bowler hat, he gave the impression of being a man who had his own way in this world – except perhaps within the walls of his home.

He would come to see us two or three times a year, when his wife was away visiting her sister or was otherwise out of town. On these periodic visits he would select publications of the Limited Editions Club, or possibly some private press books, never taking more than could comfortably be carried in one parcel. He would write a cheque, usually for several hundred pounds, and would then depart by taxi. No, he didn't want catalogues, thank you. No, he wouldn't wait for a receipt and we were certainly not to send one, and no, he wouldn't leave his address so that we could tell him when we had particularly attractive things to offer him. He too swore that his wife didn't notice that there were more books to dust every time she came back from a trip.

Happily most wives are more supportive of their husbands' book collecting hobby: some of them being glad to indulge their husbands in such an innocent pastime and pleased to see an asset being built up rather than having money squandered on gambling or worse.

Of course some collectors' wives had legitimate grounds for complaint. One wife, mother of a young family, came to me in tears one day and begged me not to sell her husband any more books. As it happened her husband bought only the occasional first edition from us but he had a compulsion to buy any book that interested him and his purchases from general second-hand bookshops were so numerous that they wrecked the household budget, filled his suburban house to the exclusion of almost everything else and were wrecking the marriage. A few days later the husband came in and asked me to help him 'take the cure' by arranging to buy most of the books from him. He lived not far from my home so I agreed to call on the next Saturday morning.

Books had indeed taken over the house. They were piled on the beds, under the beds and so filled the wardrobes that the collector's clothes had to be stored in folded heaps on top of the books on the floor. It was not possible to get into two of the smaller rooms because the entire floor space was literally covered with books. I worked all that Saturday morning and the next, sorting the wheat from the chaff, sorting the first editions from the reprints and loading the former into my car. The books I took away represented perhaps no more than one in twenty but still filled a large car twice. For the rest I introduced a general bookseller, Ike Ong of Skoob ('Books' spelled backwards), who had to make several trips with a large van to clear his purchases. That was the end of the story for some ten years or so, but I wasn't really surprised when at the end of that time this sufferer from bibliomania came back to me and begged me to undertake another clearance, this time from his new house, which proved to be smaller but to contain an even higher ratio of volumes per square foot of floor space.

Pictures rather than books were the cause of overcrowding in the home of T. E. Hanley, of Bradford, Pennsylvania. He had so many paintings that he ran out of wall space and had to close the shutters across the windows to provide more room for hanging. If we ignore an unhappy early marriage of short duration, we can say that Dr Hanley was a bachelor most of his life, marrying again only after his mother died at an advanced age. He took as his bride one of two sisters who performed as exotic dancers and I understand that the three lived very happily together. Certainly Ned Hanley's wife and her sister did nothing to curb his book-buying. He built important collections of Bernard Shaw, Lawrence of Arabia, Beckett and the Powys brothers, to name only a few, and he had the intelligence and foresight to buy modern manuscripts by these writers before it was the fashion to do so. Neither my father nor I ever met him: we did business with him solely by correspondence. What made his custom different from that of most collectors was his insistence on paying for all his purchases, large or small, in three equal instalments, one month apart. Thus he might buy a book for $150 in December and pay for it in January, February and March with cheques of $50 each. While that was going on he was quite capable of buying a manuscript for $1,500 in, say, January, and paying for that $500 a month in February, March and April, thus demonstrating how easily he could have paid cash for the earlier transaction. I suspect he felt that booksellers owed him a little credit. One thing that could be said in his favour was that you could almost literally set your watch by the timely arrival of his payments. In the end all his significant collections were bought lock, stock and barrel by Dr Harry Ransom for the University of Texas.

REFLECTIONS ON BOOK FAIRS

I remember passing through New York one year at the time when the book fair was being held in The Armory on Park Avenue. Time was at a premium and I had not long enough to pay a proper visit to the fair and make a thorough inspection of the booths, so I decided not to go at all. Then fate intervened. I was to lunch with Howard Woolmer, a bookseller from Revere, Pennsylvania with whom we did much business. He suggested that we should meet just inside the entrance to the fair.

I duly surrendered my complimentary ticket, took a few steps in and paused to look around me. The English dealer Ian Hustwick had a booth only a few yards away. I had known him since the 1950s, when he managed the ground floor of Quaritch's old building in Grafton Street, and when he called out to me I went across to speak to him. After a brief exchange of pleasantries he said to me 'Isn't this your cup of tea?', holding up a particularly scarce and desirable modern first edition. It was Gertrude Stein's Portrait of Mabel Dodge at the Villa Curonia, *being one of the 300 copies printed in Florence and issued free of charge, in floral wrappers, in 1912. I bought it without hesitation, just as I would have done had Ian offered it to me in London.*

Turning on my heel, I saw the distinguished American collector Robert H. Taylor in the middle distance. The book in question was right up his street and when he visited me in London six weeks later I sold it to him without any difficulty. Such is the mad world of book fairs. Ian Hustwick need not have left home in order to sell me the book. Bob Taylor must have walked right past it. It is true that Ian and I both made a profit on the transaction (as did the Taylor Estate's heirs when his library was sold after his death) but on this occasion the real winners were the airlines which carried this rare Gertrude Stein piece across the Atlantic three times in as many months.

CHAPTER FOUR

JOCELYN BROOKE

BROOKENALIA, a.k.a. ROTAFESTE

Anthony Newnham, who was the junior director of Bertram Rota Ltd when I joined the firm in 1952, not only taught me elementary bibliography, not only how to set type and print from a hand-press, not just how to catalogue books and manuscripts accurately; he also broadened my horizons by introducing me to books I hadn't read. One of the writers he recommended was Jocelyn Brooke. This was long before the *Orchid* trilogy had been reprinted in paperback; at this point *The Military Orchid* was the only work of his to have reached a second impression while all the others had been remaindered. On a visit to England Mrs Alfred Knopf even went out of her way to meet Jocelyn in order to tell him how much money her husband's firm had lost by bringing out one of his books, *The Image of a Drawn Sword*, in America. This lack of commercial success was sad, for the quality of Jocelyn's introspective autobiographical novels was of a very high order, or so Anthony assured me.

I was later to come to the same view myself but I had not read more than two words of his when my wife asked me one day 'What shall I read next? Do you have any ideas?' and I suggested that she tackle Brooke, beginning with the *Orchid* trilogy. Before she was forty pages into the first volume she was hooked and proceeded to work her way steadily through the rest of the canon.

It was in 1958 that Jocelyn wrote to the bookshop from his cottage in the little village of Bishopsbourne, just outside Canterbury, a village famous in the literary world as home to Joseph Conrad. The fact that Richard Aldington's brother Tony, a retired solicitor, was landlord of the village pub was a further point of literary reference. Jocelyn's letter asked us if we would be interested in buying any or all of half-a-dozen books which he no longer needed. If so he would send them up for our offer. They included four books by Edith Sitwell, inscribed by their author to Denton Welch, whose journals Jocelyn had edited for publication in 1952. I seem to remember that there was also a Shakespeare & Co. edition of *Ulysses* among them. We made a selection and a price was soon agreed. A month or two later Jocelyn wrote again. He apologised for troubling us once more and offered a further selection. Once again there were things we were pleased to have and business resulted. Six or eight weeks after that a further letter arrived, again apologetic in tone: he was, he said, so sorry to trouble us with another tiresome offer; he did hope we wouldn't mind too much. In my reply I asked him when it was too much trouble for a bookseller to buy books. I was merely stating the obvious when I said that a bookseller was only too glad to be offered good books and that I hoped he would continue to favour us with such offers as he thinned down his shelves. The following months brought more such exchanges until finally I thought it time to try a different tack, even if it did involve telling a white lie. In response to a fresh offer of books I replied that the arrival of his letter was a happy coincidence, for my wife had just remarked to me how much she had enjoyed *The Dog at Clambercrown* (Jocelyn's book about life in the Elham valley where he lived). This was true. The 'Dog' was the pub in the hamlet of Clambercrown, not far from Bishopsbourne; it was no longer licensed and had reverted to its old status as a dwelling. Such was Jocelyn's modesty that when some months later we were driving through Clambercrown with him, he pointed to a cottage and said that it used to be a public house, which caused Jean to say, 'You mean *that* is *The Dog at Clambercrown*'. He asked 'How do you know?' 'We've read the book of course', Jean replied. 'Really?' said Jocelyn, who had obviously forgotten Jean's earlier praise of it.

In writing to Jocelyn about 'The Dog' I had untruthfully added 'As it happens my wife and I will have occasion to be in the Canterbury district in a week or two. If you wanted we could arrange to call in and collect the books that you have so kindly offered us. If you wished I could at the same time look over your shelves and point out other books that I would like to buy if you could spare them. I should also like to have a word with you about the manuscript of an essay you wrote on D. H. Lawrence.' Back came a letter from Jocelyn agreeing to our proposal and suggesting some dates.

Thus began a firm friendship which lasted until Jocelyn's far too early death in 1966. He did not drive and seldom came to London, though we used to travel down to Bishopsbourne two or three times a year. Before our first child was born it was our practice to collect Jocelyn from the cottage which he shared with Mrs Ford, the nanny who had looked after him as a child, and whom, presumably in an echo of childhood, he always called 'Ninnie'. We would drive down the Elham valley (yes, past Clambercrown) into Folkestone, the town where Jocelyn grew up and where his family had had a flourishing wine merchant's business. We lunched there often, in the dining room of the rather grand Metropole Hotel. We always tried to drink wine from Brooke's, the wine merchants which still bore Jocelyn's name. He would take advantage of being near a branch of Sainsbury's, and would slip in to buy their celebrated breakfast sausage and equally famous fruit cake. We would then go back to Bishopsbourne for tea.

Later, when our first-born still travelled in his carry-cot, we would take him with us on our visits; he would sleep under Jocelyn's apple trees while Jocelyn served a lunch which he himself had cooked for us. His speciality was chicken tarragon and very good it was too. Over coffee Jocelyn would perhaps play some modern French music on his antiquated gramophone. We used to speak of these occasions as days of *poulet et Poulenc*, also referring to them as *Brookenalia*. Jocelyn for his part called them *Rotafestes*. Whatever they were called, these days were happy ones and we came to feel very close to this shy, rather lonely man. Fortunately our visits caused an increase in the exchange of letters between us rather than any diminution. Jocelyn was an entertaining correspondent and we still have every letter and card he ever sent us – some 150 in all.

Jocelyn had accumulated a considerable number of books. (He was a critic – and a very perceptive one too – for both *The Times* and *The Listener*) and of course he bought many books apart from those that were sent to him for review, but he was never a book collector in any serious fashion. Thus the books that I was anxious to buy for stock were soon dealt with. I was able to place the manuscript of his perceptive essay on D. H. Lawrence in the Lazarus collection (now in the University of Nottingham). I then bought the manuscripts of some of his writings about Denton Welch and managed to find a home for those. Then it occurred to me to try to sell for him the original materials (manuscripts, typescripts and proofs) for all his published books, together with manuscripts and typescripts of juvenilia and other unpublished work. To this end I compiled a check list of his writings, supplemented it with a selection of the favourable reviews his books had received, and had John Ryder turn the resultant text into a layout for Bill Hummerstone to print at the Stellar Press. I used the resultant four-page leaflet as a promotional tool, partly publicising Jocelyn's writings generally and more particularly helping to market his archive. The first page of the text is reproduced overleaf. I sent one copy, with a catalogue of the papers, to Dr Harry Ransom at the University of Texas and he duly bought the archive for the Humanities Research Center. The first purchase Jocelyn made with the money was of a new record- player and some Poulenc discs to go with it.

Jocelyn, John Ryder, Bill Hummerstone and I collaborated again in the following year, 1964. I persuaded Jocelyn to set down on paper a splendid story that he told about Arthur Machen and the composer John Ireland. The latter, while working on his 'Legend for Piano and Orchestra', was eating a picnic lunch at a remote spot on the South Downs when he realized that he was surrounded by a group of children playing and dancing in total silence. They were all dressed in white and he soon realized they were 'no ordinary children'. He looked up again a few seconds later and they had vanished. He sent a full account of his visionary experience to Arthur Machen who replied very briefly, 'Oh, so *you* have seen them too?'.

Books and Pamphlets by Jocelyn Brooke

Six Poems. *Jocelyn Brooke, Oxford*, 1928
Limited to 50 numbered copies, signed by the author
Notes on the Occurrence of Orchis Simia Lamarck in Kent. *The Journal of Botany, November*, 1938
One of a small number of copies offprinted
A New British Species of Epipactis. By B. J. Brooke and Francis Rose. *The Journal of Botany, April*, 1940
One of a small number of copies offprinted
December Spring; poems. *John Lane, The Bodley Head*, 1946
The Military Orchid. *The Bodley Head*, 1948
The Scapegoat. *The Bodley Head*, 1948
American edition published by *Harper & Brothers, New York*, in 1949
A Mine of Serpents. *The Bodley Head*, 1949
The Wonderful Summer. *John Lehmann Limited*, 1949
The Image of a Drawn Sword. *The Bodley Head*, 1950
American edition published by *Alfred A. Knopf, New York*, in 1951
The Wild Orchids of Great Britain. *The Bodley Head*, 1950
Limited to 1,140 numbered copies, of which 40 were signed by the author and specially bound in white parchment. 12 sets of sheets were sold to the *Collectors' Book Club* for issue by them in special bindings
The Goose Cathedral. *The Bodley Head*, 1950
Ronald Firbank. *Arthur Barker Ltd.*, 1951
The Elements of Death and other poems. *The Hand and Flower Press, Aldington*, 1952
No. XII in the *Poems in Pamphlet* series
The Flower in Season. *The Bodley Head*, 1952
Elizabeth Bowen. *The British Council*, 1952
One of the series of supplements to *British Book News*, which was later called *Writers and Their Work*
The Passing of a Hero. *The Bodley Head*, 1953
Private View; four portraits. *James Barrie*, 1954
Aldous Huxley. *The British Council*, 1954
In the *Writers and Their Work* series. A revised edition was published in 1958
The Dog at Clambercrown. *The Bodley Head*, 1955
American edition published by *The Vanguard Press, New York*, in 1955
The Crisis in Bulgaria. *Chatto & Windus*, 1956
Conventional Weapons. *Faber and Faber*, 1961
American edition published by *The Vanguard Press, New York*, in 1961, as *The Name of Greene*
Ronald Firbank and John Betjeman. *The British Council*, 1962
In the *Writers and Their Work* series

Books Edited by Jocelyn Brooke

The Denton Welch Journals. Edited and with an introduction by Jocelyn Brooke. *Hamish Hamilton*, 1952
Denton Welch: Extracts from his Published Books. Edited and with an introduction by Jocelyn Brooke. *Chapman & Hall Ltd.*, 1963

Leaflet for the Jocelyn Brooke Archive

When Ireland's *Legend* was published it was dedicated to Arthur Machen. John Ryder turned Jocelyn's short text into a handsome if rather slim book which Bill Hummerstone had his Stellar Press print immaculately. The edition consists of just 65 numbered and signed copies. We arranged a lunch to launch the publication: the number dining was in proportion to the size of the edition – just Jocelyn, John and I. We ate at Stone's Chop-House and I remember that Jocelyn began with gull's eggs. He quipped that this was the only time any edition of his had seemed likely to sell out! Stone's Chop-House was an appropriate place for us to celebrate for it was there in the 1870s that those who would become founder members of the Sette of Odd Volumes used to gather informally before that bibliographical dining club was inaugurated.

We continued to visit Jocelyn and to exchange letters with him. I bought from him a manuscript notebook of Denton Welch's, decorated with pen-and-ink drawings. I also handled the sale of various items of Welch memorabilia. Jocelyn had custody of the carved angels which can been seen in the background of certain photographs of Welch. Jocelyn came by all of these things through his friendship with Eric Oliver, Welch's latter-day companion. Jocelyn's edition of the *Denton Welch Journals* remains a splendid example of how such a text should be edited.

Then in 1966 came an evening when Jocelyn had a pork pie for supper, walked down to Tony Aldington's pub for a drink and complained of feeling rather unwell. He returned home early, went to bed and died in his sleep. We lost a good friend, and the world lost a writer who had never quite achieved in his lifetime the reputation and the market that he richly deserved. Some of the things he said to me will remain with me for ever. For example he told me he had been commissioned to write an article about Ronald Firbank for the new edition of the *Encyclopaedia Britannica*, 'How do you convey the flavour of Firbank in 200 words?' he asked me, wryly. 'Ninnie', Mrs Ford, was dead by this time and so was his mother who used to come over to take tea with us in our early days as visitors to Bishopsbourne. Jocelyn's sister, Mrs Urmston, asked us to help clear up the Estate. So it was that we were in Ivy Cottage once again a few months after Jocelyn had died, helping one of the professional executors, an awfully pleasant young solicitor, to sort through the books and papers. It was agreed that I should sell the remaining library, Jocelyn's working library, intact, and this I did, to the University of California at San Diego. To sort correspondence, saving author's letters and throwing away electricity bills, the lawyer and I knelt on the rug in front of the fireplace. The cottage had been empty for some months and was thoroughly damp. I felt my right knee grow cold and wet in a way it had not done since I knelt to propose to my wife on the banks of the Thames in 1955. A river, the Nailbourne, flowed under the village, only breaking through the surface and showing itself every few years, always, it was said, when some disaster was imminent. That is why the Nailbourne was called the Woe Waters by some of the older villagers.

'Hmm! we don't want that', said the lawyer, tossing a bound typescript across the fireplace towards the open dustbin that we had brought in. I shot out a hand and caught the typescript in mid-air and found it to be an unpublished novel written when Jocelyn was still a very young man. It had very definite homosexual overtones which is why the lawyer had decided to cast it in the bin. I thought I knew Jocelyn better than he did, and that destroying several hundred pages of his prose would be a crime. Happily I was able to persuade the lawyer that it would be best if the manuscript was placed in the bosom of a research library where access to it would be subject to responsible safeguards. Now, if I meet Jocelyn again, as the clergymen assure me I will, I shall be able to look him in the eye.

LORD ALFRED DOUGLAS

I have written elsewhere about my changing attitude to book fairs, telling how my early enthusiasm turned to ambivalence and even to dislike of the wretched things. I wonder if the following episode played a subconscious part in this change.

One Sunday morning in the spring of 1973, business at the New York book fair was very quiet so I left my own stand and wandered round the exhibition rooms chatting to other exhibitors and admiring some fine books. I paused and looked into the glass case at Colin Franklin's stand and saw that he had a desirable copy of a particularly rare book in my own field. It was the first edition of Lord Alfred Douglas's Poems in the bilingual edition (parallel texts in French and English) published by the Mercure de France in Paris in 1896. The edition showed its French pedigree by existing in various degrees of limitation, each printed on more exotic paper than the last. The copy in front of me was one of only five on Japon vellum. The sheets had been folded to produce pages of markedly different sizes, but this was only one of this copy's unusual qualities.

This was the author's first book. He was to have dedicated it to Oscar Wilde, but Wilde declined the honour, saying that the tragedy and scandal associated with his name would have served to weigh the book down. To add to its attraction, this copy bore a presentation inscription from the author. It was not inscribed to Wilde and the inscription was not signed 'Bosie', but it was couched in affectionate terms and, to my surprise, it was addressed to a woman.

As I stood admiring the book and ruminating on its worth, that wise and shrewd bookseller, Bill Fletcher, doyen of the British book trade, and a man some thirty years my senior in both age and experience, came up to me.

'What are you looking at, my son?' he enquired. I told him.

'What's so special about that then?' he asked. I explained.

'Then why don't you buy it?' Bill said.

Thinking that Colin had the volume fully priced, I replied to the effect that were I to buy it with a view to selling it again, I would in effect be trading gold for gold.

'Shall I tell you something, my son?' Bill responded. 'The price of gold [pause] is going up!'

'Thank you Bill,' I said. And promptly called out to Colin to place my order. I admired the book tremendously. It seemed to me the very essence of nineties publishing. Spurred into action by Bill Fletcher's sage words I thought to myself that I really could not go wrong.

We published an elaborate description of the book in a special catalogue. The result was a string of compliments but not a single valid order. (One lady wrote and asked for the book, only to return it without comment when, six months later, we hinted that we would rather like to be paid.) The book then sat on the shelf in the bookshop until the spring of 1977, when we finally sold it for a trifle less than we had paid for it four years before.

CHAPTER FIVE

IN DUBLIN'S FAIR CITY

It must have been in the mid-1950s that I developed the habit of lunching with George Sims on his weekly visits to London. He was then and for a good many years my closest friend in the book trade. Over our food we would mimic our elders and betters (George did a brilliant impression of the rich Virginia accent of Dr John Gordan, Curator of the Berg Collection, a man we both enormously respected). We also discussed books that had come into our respective stocks, forthcoming auctions, and such issues as which was the rarest modern book. Ezra Pound's *A Lume Spento* and the first edition of F. W. Rolfe's *Don Renato* were two of the candidates, only six copies of the latter being known to have survived. Later I bought a seventh, but that is another story.

Over a nutty crumble or some such dish, in Vega, the vegetarian restaurant in Leicester Square (after a bout of food poisoning it was some years before George would again eat meat in London, though he had no such reservations in the country) our conversation turned one day to the topic of Irish books and the keen demand for Anglo-Irish literature of the late nineteenth century and after. I think it was George who suggested that a buying trip to Dublin might be very successful. Certainly it was he who drafted the advertisement in the *Irish Times* which trailed our visit. It described the sort of things that we wanted (proofs, signed copies, authors' letters and so on), promised that high prices would be paid and gave the address and telephone number of our hotel, The Four Courts. We chose this because of its associations with Jonathan Swift and because its windows looked out onto the River Liffey, James Joyce's Anna Livia.

In due course George and Beryl Sims and Jean and I arrived there from our short Aer Lingus flight one summer day in 1961. Jean and

George F. Sims

I were surprised to find that the bottom sheet on our bed wasn't quite large enough to cover the mattress and that we were not given a key to our room. Every time we went out or came in we had to get a chambermaid to lock or unlock the door. We were told that a previous guest had taken the room-key away three months ago and they had still not got round to replacing it. Our astonishment was complete when, around 6 o'clock in the evening, we ordered steak and chips only to find it was served with bread and butter, strawberry jam and a pot of tea.

A passion for the cinema was one of the things we shared with the Sims and learning that *On the Waterfront* was showing at the New Electric Cinema, we set off by taxi after supper. We gave the driver our destination and he ruminated on it quietly for a hundred yards or so. Then, without stopping the cab, he turned his head through 180 degrees and enquired 'Was it a particular film you were after seeing? Only it's not a neighbourhood I'd be taking the ladies to myself.'

At this time there were still several good bookshops in Dublin, notably Hodges, Figgis; Greene's; and Faulkner Greirson. We bought quite well in each of these and at the last of them helpful, erudite Michael Walsh asked whether we were planning to look at the Chester Beatty manuscripts while we were in Dublin. 'I didn't know they were for sale' quipped Sims.

Walking along Grafton Street we encountered George and Beryl's Berkshire neighbours, Harold and Olive Edwards. Harold was a friend and contemporary of my father's and when he was still a young man in a hurry to set right the wrongs of the world he used to speak on a soapbox in Finsbury Park, advocating either the communist or the anarchist cause – or perhaps both. In those days he had a bookshop in Theobalds Road but now, like George, he worked from his home in the country. He was both amusing and scholarly and went on to become the wittiest president of the Antiquarian Booksellers' Association that I can remember. Jean and Beryl got on well with Olive, who was younger than Harold and always immaculately turned out. We used, rather unkindly, to mimic her accent:

in saying her husband's first name she seemed to transpose the vowels, calling him 'Horald.'

Be that as it may, they greeted us warmly now. They too were on a buying trip, though their interests did not clash with ours. Harold dealt in English books printed abroad before 1800. They asked where we were staying and, on hearing our reply, Harold sniffed contemptuously. 'I might have known it' he said, 'I don't suppose you are eating properly either. We are at the Royal Hibernian. You must come and have dinner with us tonight.' We duly presented ourselves at their splendid hotel at the appointed hour. Harold asked what we would like to drink and then chose our meal for us from the menu. We thought this a little patronising but made no protest, since we imagined ourselves to be his guests, but when the bill was brought to him at the end of the evening, he looked at it and quickly said 'George, Anthony, you owe me £x each!'

Before passing on to the rest of our Dublin experiences I have two more things to say about Harold. In the lavatory of his bungalow outside Newbury he had a shelf crammed with books whose titles became *doubles entendres* by virtue of their location. One called *By Rushing Waters* was a good example. My other Harold story is less frivolous, but still shows something of the Edwards sense of style.

The Clique was the weekly publication in which booksellers listed books which they were seeking, either on their own behalf or for customers. In addition to long lists of titles it carried tablet advertisements for those interested in specialized subjects which might be anything from campanology to yodelling. I ran a series of such advertisements for books by fashionable authors and one week our advertisement read 'F. W. Rolfe, first editions by'. The usual response to such advertisements came in the form of postcards with the printed text 'We can offer' and then handwritten or typed descriptions of the books, which were usually fairly common ones, priced at just a few shillings each. One morning the postman brought a card from H. W. Edwards in reply to our Rolfe advertisement. It said, simply, 'We can offer Rolfe, F. W., *Don Renato*, 1909, Nice copy, £250'. This was the unrecorded seventh copy I mentioned above. A lesser man would have made much more of a song and dance about the book than Harold did, probably writing a letter at some length stressing the book's great rarity and expressing pride at having unearthed another copy, but that was not Harold's way.

In Dublin we began to follow up the replies to our newspaper advertisement. First we arranged to call on Seymour Leslie, brother of Sir Shane Leslie, at his house in Dun Laoghaire, the attractive district on the coast just south of Dublin proper. I got a very strong impression that he had a chip on his shoulder in that his brother had enjoyed the literary success which had been denied to him. We bought a few things from him including a fine copy of his brother's edition of Rolfe's *In His Own Image*. Seymour Leslie showed us his own book, *Of Glaslough In the Kingdom of Oriel*. He said, with every evidence of sincerity, that the only reason the book had not become a best-seller was that the illustrations were thought to be wrong for it by most of the critics.

The elegance of Seymour Leslie's drawing room, in a Georgian house with a glorious view, was in marked contrast, one has to say, to the squalor of our next port of call.

Back in the city we were visiting a writer whom the reference books would doubtless classify as 'minor'. He would have been around 70 years of age when we saw him and he had fallen on hard times. He was far from well and seemed to be living in one room, which was illumined by a solitary, fly-spotted, bare electric light bulb. His bed was unmade and to my memory's eye the sheets were grey with dirt. Dirty clothes lay in heaps on the floor and were draped over the furniture. The only chair in the room was occupied by a bowl containing our host's false teeth. He invited us to sit down and for the reasons given above this was something of an embarrassment.

Although we had called by invitation and at the appointed hour, and although he presumably wanted to do business with us, he found it necessary to launch into a diatribe against England and the

English. We waited patiently and when this came to an end were rewarded when this 'minor' writer produced a clutch of printed material dating from 1916 and the Easter Rising.

Such pamphlets and leaflets (by P. H. Pearse and others) were already scarce and have now become as rare as hen's teeth. We were pleased to see them but pointed out gently that some of them were not in the best condition. Cecil Salkeld (for it was he) pointed with glee to a blood stain and a boot-print on the front wrapper of one Padraig Pearse pamphlet and with heavy irony first apologised for the boot print and then added 'but I can assure you it is that of a Black and Tan!'.

Perhaps the most interesting visit we made was to the home of the widow of James Starkey who wrote, and who edited the *Dublin Magazine*, under the pseudonym 'Seamus O'Sullivan'. When the visit began it was rather like the jokes about the Australian pub with no beer, or one of the 'good news, bad news' stories. Mrs Starkey would see us (good) but she didn't think she had much for us (bad). There were still many books in the house (good), but Percy Muir, an able bookseller if ever there was one, had spent several days in the house some years ago picking what he wanted and had then had his purchases shipped home by goods wagon (seriously bad news). Being in Dublin anyway, and thinking that even this book trade Homer might have nodded, we decided to go through the contents of this tall, rambling house book by book. In the upstairs rooms Percy had done a very thorough job as we had expected. Whether the sheer quantity finally overwhelmed him or whether changing tastes and evolving reputations enabled us to pick things that Percy had left behind, I do not know, but we were in the end able to gather together quite a feast from the crumbs at the rich man's table. We asked if there were more books downstairs in the basement. 'Yes' we were told, 'there are some in the turf cellar'. I opened a cupboard there and found an enormously long run of the *Dublin University Review* filed in three or four stacks each six feet high. They did not seem to be in any kind of order. 'How thorough had Percy been?' I asked myself. I decided to find out. Near the bottom of the third pile I discovered it: the issue of the magazine that contained the first printing of W. B. Yeats's poem 'Mosada', one of the scarcest and most important pieces in the whole Yeats canon. I wonder that Percy did not hear my shout of jubilation in Takeley, five hundred miles away. This find alone made the whole trip worthwhile.

George and I looked round the turf cellar again. In the middle of the room was an old meat safe, a fairly primitive device, which was really a cube with 18 inch sides, standing on wooden legs. The door, which was jammed, and the sides were made of perforated zinc to allow the passage of air. How long had the door been jammed? we wondered. Was it so when Percy was in the house, if indeed he had penetrated to the cellars at all? We managed to prise the door open and instead of the earthenware butter and milk coolers one might have expected to find, we found crude wooden panels and shelves dividing the space into 24 pigeonholes. With one pigeonhole for J and I together, and another for XYZ, this provided the basis for a filing system. Tucked away in that humble meat safe were two years' correspondence from authors and actors: we had stumbled on the archive covering the genesis of the Irish National Theatre movement.

I liked Mrs Starkey very much. Born Esther Solomons, she developed quite a reputation as an artist. By the time that I met her Nature had played a cruel trick on her. Never of very great stature, she was bent almost double by arthritis and her wrists and knuckles were swollen to an extent that must have made the exertion of any kind of pressure quite painful. On our first visit George Sims and I quickly realized that there was more to look at than could be seen in the time we had allowed. Mrs Starkey arranged for us to come back the following afternoon. She promised that she would cook a salmon for the occasion and when we arrived we found that she had poached a whole one and had made wonderful fresh salmon sandwiches for us. I say 'us' but her poor hands were in such a state that the slices of bread were nearly an inch thick and were more than George Sims was prepared to tackle. I therefore found myself eating for two while he perused the shelves.

It is a cliché to say that the world is a small place, but on my return to London I found that Mrs Starkey was the aunt of Bethel Solomons Jnr., a consultant dermatologist who had been of great assistance first to me, and then to each of my sons, as occasion demanded. Since Bethel was also a customer of Bertram Rota Ltd, I was especially glad that our business with Mrs Starkey had left both sides well satisfied.

My next visit to her house was a sad one, undertaken some ten or fifteen years later, when Mrs Starkey had departed this life. The house had been empty for two or three months and I went back to it in mid-winter with my genial Bertram Rota colleague George Lawson. On what seemed the coldest day of a cold winter, we went into a house where our breath virtually froze in front of us. Mrs Starkey's friend and neighbour, a delightful lady called Robin Goodfellow, had done what she could to warm the house for us, but the most that could be achieved was to have one 500 watt bar of a reflector fire switched on. If one moved to switch on a second bar and put the rating up to a whole kilowatt, the fuse blew and there was no heat at all! Wearing a warm shirt, two sweaters, an overcoat and gloves, I did my part in making an assessment of the remaining books. Finally, numb from head to foot, I retired to the comfort of the Shelbourne Hotel and, remembering James Mason in a famous scene from *Lolita*, ordered a whiskey from room service and drank it while immersed to the chin in a hot bath. As my brain thawed out I began to ponder, and later to discuss with George Lawson, how the remaining books in the house should be treated.

Just as the gap between Percy Muir's purchases and my own first visit led me to take a view of the books that was different from Percy's, so the gap between my visit with George Sims and my visit with George Lawson made me see the books through different eyes. It is true that most of the high spots had gone, but a number of books that had seemed quite common ten or fifteen years ago had become scarce in the interim. Moreover some fledgling reputations had burgeoned into fully feathered figures.

Even so it was undeniable that most of the books remaining

were by minor writers, Irish writers it was true, but minor writers still. George and I came to the conclusion that if the books were kept together they would make a not insignificant assemblage of nineteenth and twentieth century Irish writing, not of the first rank admittedly, but of the second and third. The major writers were well represented in every library: few had really good, deep holdings of the minor figures. By their very number the minor Starkey books had an enhanced value, the whole being greater than the sum of the parts. It would be splendid if we could sell the books in Ireland, which was what Mrs Starkey's heirs wished in any case. On that note I returned to London, leaving George to hold discussions with the major research libraries in Dublin. Happily one of them shared our view of the significance of Seamus O'Sullivan's 'collection' of minor Irish poets and it remains in Dublin to this day.

SLEEPERS

'Sleeper' is a word that does not appear in Carter's ABC for Book Collectors. It signifies a book whose intrinsic worth and, more important-ly, market value has not been recognised by the bookseller who has it in his stock. When two or three booksellers were gathered together, chatting about old times, it would not be long before one boasted of a sleeper he had bought at ......'s, a firm which should have known better.

In my mind the term is inexorably linked with Dick Wormser, already when I met him the doyen of the American book trade. With his grey hair and his military bearing, he cut an impressive figure. One of the relatively few Americans to have held the Presidency of the International League of Antiquarian Booksellers, he wanted to know whether I would be up to leading the British trade association in 1971, the year in which we were to host an ILAB Congress in London. Dudley Massey, head of Pickering and Chatto, consultant to Christie's, and himself a former President of the ILAB, together with Ted Dring, joint managing director of Bernard Quaritch, invited me to lunch with Dick so that he could satisfy his curiosity. It appears that I passed muster, although all I remember is passing out, that a great deal of wine was consumed and that I was far from well afterwards, a conclusion I blamed on one rather dubious bivalve in a plate of moules marinières.

Be that as it may, when I saw Dick in a branch of Wheeler's that day, I remembered how he had played on me some years before the trick he tried whenever he came across a newcomer to the trade. Entering a bookshop he would make a beeline for the new employee, introduce himself and then, with a perfectly straight face, 'Tell me' he would say, asking, not for the poetry section or the architecture section, 'where are your sleepers?'

CHAPTER SIX

FORREST REID

– IN ANOTHER PART OF THE ISLAND

I first read books by Forrest Reid in my early twenties, soon after I had come into bookselling. With all the certainty and assurance of youth I declared then that I thought Reid one of the best prose stylists of the twentieth century. I must say that the following years have given me no cause to change that opinion. I was therefore delighted when I received a letter from a Mrs Wright in Newtonards in Northern Ireland asking if I would be interested in a long run of Forrest Reid first editions inscribed by the author to her late husband. My answer was very definitely in the affirmative but I found it impossible to make a sensible offer for the books without seeing the inscriptions and knowing the condition of the books. I therefore arranged to go to Newtonards to inspect them, offer for them and, I hoped, bring them home. Besides, experience had taught me that where there were books as desirable as these sounded, there were likely to be other good things as well.

A date was set for my visit and I duly reported at Heathrow at the crack of dawn on an autumn morning. This was in the early 1970s when 'the Troubles' were at the forefront of everyone's mind and when British troops had been on the streets in Northern Ireland for two years or so. This state of affairs was brought home to me when I was not allowed to take my briefcase with me into the cabin of the aeroplane: instead I had to carry my sheaf of papers on board in my hand.

In an hour or so the plane came in low over Belfast Lough and landed at what appeared to be an airport under siege. Reunited with my briefcase I went to the Hertz counter, signed the requisite forms and was handed the keys to a Ford Escort. 'Where is it?' I asked.

The Hertz representative took me to the door and pointed into what seemed to be the middle distance. 'There' he said, 'Just behind the line of oil drums'. The oil drums were filled with concrete and formed a barrier, keeping vehicles at least 200 yards from the terminal buildings.

Driving a strange car along unfamiliar roads is never the easiest thing to do and my confidence was not helped when I was stopped at an army checkpoint. While one soldier came to the driver's window to ask for my papers, another kept me covered with an automatic weapon on the nearside of the car. On the other side of the road was a pillbox and through a slit I could see another soldier looking at me down the barrel of a machine gun. I remembered from my National Service days just how easily automatic weapons could go off, even when not intended to. The soldiers soon waved me on with a cheery grin, but I was not surprised to find myself lost shortly after, having taken a wrong turning just past the pillbox.

I was mightily glad when I eventually reached Mrs Wright's house on the outskirts of Newtonards and looking over Strangford Lough. She was rather like everyone's idea of a favourite grandmother and her cordial welcome quickly helped me to relax.

When she brought out the books most of the scarce titles were there. *The Garden God* in its limp parchment binding, *The Bracknels* of course, *Following Darkness*, *The Gentle Lover* and *Pender Among the Residents*. There were perhaps a score of volumes in all, each in decent condition and most with a curiously formal inscription – just 'R. J. Wright from Forrest Reid', although in the case of *The Bracknels* (1911) Reid unbent sufficiently to put 'Bob Wright from Forrest Reid'. The dedication copy of *Pirates of the Spring* was there, but still with a brief and formal inscription. *Minor Fiction in the 'Eighties* was one of an edition of only six copies off-printed from the Royal Society of Literature symposium *The Eighteen 'Eighties*. There was also a typescript of Reid's unpublished play for dancers, *Lovers of Shulan*. Mrs Wright and I soon reached an agreement about the price, for I badly wanted the books and would have hated to leave Northern Ireland without them. We packed my briefcase and two carrier bags, and then over a light lunch, which Mrs Wright kindly provided, I asked her what else she might have for me. The other books in the house were not of interest and I wondered if she had sold some of her husband's books before, just holding back the Forrest Reid for sentimental reasons. What she did have, she said, was a series of letters from Reid to her husband. She told me that she did not think they were very interesting since the two men normally met once a week and talked for a couple of hours or so. She said I could have them one day but adamantly refused to let me have them or even see them there and then. I took my leave and drove back to the airport where I had to carry the three bags of books for what seemed an interminable distance from the car park to the terminal. My arms felt two inches longer by the time I got to the check-in desk. At the security gate I was made to take out every book so that the staff could fan each one open to be sure it was not a hollowed-out container for a gun or a bomb.

Back in London I savoured my purchases for a while before selling them *en bloc* to the Berg Collection at New York Public Library. I told Lola Szladits, who had by that time succeeded John Gordan as the head of the Berg, that the letters existed and she was as eager to secure them as I was. Over the years since then I wrote several times to Mrs Wright begging for an opportunity to offer for them but absolutely to no avail. I even suggested she should leave a note with her will to tell her executors of my interest but no word ever came.

Despite the formality of the inscription in the books, Wright and Reid were obviously close and Wright's help in 'drawing on a large stock of memories extending over many years' is acknowledged by Russell Burlingham in his *Forrest Reid, a Portrait and a Study*, 1953. I cannot therefore believe that the letters were of no interest, and I wonder whether the correspondence revealed either an association between the two men, or a shared orientation, that Mrs Wright found embarrassing?

I came across a similar situation once before when I was negotiating the purchase of some Hugh Walpole letters on behalf of the

University of Texas. The letters had been offered to the Ransom Center by the widow of a former secretary of Walpole's and consisted chiefly of letters of instruction and reports of progress sent home by Walpole on his travels around the world. As I surveyed the batch that had been sent to me for appraisal, gaps in the chronology suggested that some letters were missing. I wrote to the owner, pointing this out very gently and asking if some pieces might perhaps have been 'overlooked'. Back came another half dozen letters. There was nothing in them that can be regarded as really incriminatory although some did begin or end with salutations that might be regarded as excessively friendly, even for a successful middle-aged novelist writing to a young man in his employ, even if the young man in question had perhaps taken up his duties as much out of hero-worship as for salary. Reviewing the whole correspondence I suspected that I still did not have everything so I wrote again in what I hoped were tactful terms. I could not be too explicit in saying what I suspected but I wanted to say that the world's understanding and tolerance in these matters had grown out of all recognition during the fifty years since the letters were written. I emphasised the library's excellent reputation as a responsible steward of material in its care and stressed the importance of presenting posterity with the whole picture and not a partial one. In reply the widow sent me one last letter, the missing piece of the jigsaw. After this lapse of time I can say that it gave the date of Walpole's expected arrival in Liverpool, instructed the young man to meet the boat and to have booked for the two of them a room at the Adelphi, with a double bed.

Early one morning in May, 1974, I received a telephone call from that most urbane and civilized of booksellers, Colin Franklin. He said he was ringing on behalf of a customer of his who had a virtually complete collection of the publications of James Guthrie's Pear Tree Press. The only significant piece that it lacked was Blake's Songs of Innocence. *In his bibliography curiously entitled* British Modern Press Books (*Modern British Press Books would have been so much more euphonious*) *William Ridler called* Songs of Innocence *'The most considerable achievement of the press'. Although 100 copies were announced (at least that is the figure given in Will Ransom's* Private Presses & Their Books, *though Ridler says 300*) *Guthrie said in a letter to Ridler in October 1943 that publication was suspended when the war began and that no more than 17 copies were actually completed. This makes this intaglio plate book truly rare.*

Whether Colin Franklin thought that a little flattery would go a long way with me I do not know, but he went on to say that he had told his client that 'The one person who could find a copy of Songs of Innocence *for him was Anthony Rota'. I gave a nervous laugh by way of response and said I would get back to him.*

I then sought out John Byrne who was in charge of the firm's Press Books and told him what had transpired. We put our heads together and soon reached one conclusion : trying to find a copy on the open market, or searching high and low in case there was an eighteenth copy out there somewhere would be fruitless. The best course of action was to go after a copy that we did *know about. Happily a private collector with whom we had done a good deal of business over the years was fortunate enough to have the Pear Tree Press* Songs of Innocence *in his collection. John knew the man quite well and telephoned him to say that we had urgent need of a copy and were in a position to pay a price that was really exceptionally good. I believe John went on to give examples of other treasures that could be purchased with the large sum we were putting forward. As we thought, our man, who had bought the* Songs of Innocence *many years before, had no idea of the extent to which it had*

79

appreciated in value. Once we had told him he was only too happy to sell and so it was, that only an hour after he had asked me for this 'impossible' book, I was able to offer a copy to Colin. We sold the book for £1,000, an appreciable sum in 1974; Colin's customer was delighted to complete his collection; and Colin is still amazed that we were able to produce a copy so quickly. If only it were always so easy.

CHAPTER SEVEN

WHEN GREEK MEETS GREEK

BORIS HARDING-EDGAR

Despite my occasionally acerbic comments, Boris Harding-Edgar's appearances in these pages are as welcome to me as were his appearances in my life. He was, and happily remains, a big man, tall and quite heavily built. When I first knew him his hair was blonde and he wore a neatly trimmed beard. He was always something of a man of mystery. He traded under the name of Charles Rare Books and carried a briefcase bearing the gilt initials J-BC. Anthony Newnham used mischievously to suggest that Boris's name was really *Jean-Baptiste Charles* and that that was where his business name came from. A more prosaic school of thought had it that Boris used to have a shop in Charles Street, Mayfair, and that his firm's name derived from that. Word had it that he had come to London from Edinburgh and that he had received training as an architect. When at a later date he moved to No. 1 Heath Drive in Hampstead, which had once been T. J. Wise's home, some unkind people said how appropriate it was.

Because our specializations were almost identical (Boris did less with private press books and manuscripts than we did), we tended to move in the same bookselling circles, and though Boris was some ten years my senior, we got along together very well. This must have had much to do with Boris's natural charm, for our bookselling philosophies were very different. Boris used to say 'Book collecting is a disease and I am the doctor. It is a very expensive cure'. Whether he really meant that or if he was just teasing me I never knew. Certainly he liked a big mark-up. (I speak in the past tense because since he retired to Spain many years ago our paths have crossed only occasionally.)

I describe elsewhere how Boris and I were comrades in arms for a time, fighting as 'Young Turks', a.k.a. 'the Ginger Group', for our trade association to take a more pro-active role against auction rings and in favour of book fairs. At this time Boris had his business premises in the Hertfordshire village of Buntingford. His book-room therefore made a convenient stop when I was on my way to Cambridge, or to see Laurie Deval at Elkin Mathews in the village of Takeley outside Bishops Stortford. Quite often Boris would come with me on the second half of one of those trips. Therefore when petrol rationing was imposed it was natural that he and I should pool petrol coupons and share a car on buying trips round the country. Boris conducted the reckoning at the end of the trip: 'Petrol is 4/11d. a gallon, call it 5/-. I get thirty-three miles to the gallon, call it thirty. We went ninety-seven miles, call it a hundred. You owe me 19/6d. call it £1!' I put up with this rather one-sided arithmetic because I enjoyed Boris's company so. I remember when we once stopped at the County Hotel in Bedford for dinner and were told at what was barely 8 o'clock in the evening that dinner was finished. 'Finished!' Boris expostulated, 'What ever time did it *start*, then?'

He rang me one day and asked whether Frank Hammond, the Birmingham bookseller, who was an apologist for the auction ring, had telephoned me about the library of John Hampson Simpson, who, as John Hampson, had written the astonishingly popular book of the 1930s, *Saturday Night at the Greyhound*. 'Well I know he plans to ring you,' said Boris, 'and I thought we might go along together'. Then with what might have been arrogance or might just have been a jest, he said that if I went with him, since he had introduced me to the library, he would expect me to buy the run of the mill books, while he had the rarities..

A few days later I collected him from Buntingford in my father's Rover 14 Sportsman's Saloon, probably the only saloon car in which the driver could knock out the ashes from his pipe against the ground while remaining seated behind the wheel. After an hour or two's drive we parked in Birmingham, something that could still be done fairly easily in those days, and went into the shop. Frank Hammond's face when he saw me was an absolute study. Boris said to him, 'You know Anthony Rota, Mr Hammond. You said you wanted the best price for John Hampson's library and I guessed that you'd be asking Anthony to come up later so that you could compare our offers. I thought that if we were both here at once we could save you a lot of trouble.'

Muttering under his breath Frank Hammond took us up to the mezzanine floor where the Hampson library, strong in first editions and inscribed copies of books of the first three decades of the 20th century, was laid out on its foredges in the form of a letter 'U'. Boris said to me, 'You start at this end and I'll start at the other'. We'll meet in the middle and compare prices. I worked through my half of the books, conscientiously looking at every one, and when we met in the middle, Boris not having troubled to stoop down to examine too many volumes I noticed, I gave him my figure. Let us say it was £950. I left him to add his figure to it and to negotiate with Mr Hammond. I was astonished to hear him say, 'Well Mr Hammond, we've both looked at these books and we've added our figures together and we come to a grand total of – £950'. Hammond turned several shades paler and said '£950? That's not enough. I paid almost that. I've got to have more money.'

'If you've got to have more money, we've got to have more books,' retorted Boris, and started to help himself from the shelves, taking first a set of Richard Jefferies in half morocco, including the rare polemic *Suez-cide*, attacking Disraeli for his purchase of shares in the Suez Canal Company.

Eventually a deal was struck. We wrote Mr Hammond a cheque and his staff helped us load the books into the groaning Rover. We then drove back to Buntingford for a division of the spoils. We laid the books out on Boris's dining-room carpet, divided them into lots and held a private auction. The first books to come up for consideration were seven volumes of Algernon Blackwood's fiction. Boris said, 'You'll want those. What will you bid for them?' 'Five pounds,' I said. 'Ten,' he replied. 'Fifteen,' I said. 'Twenty-five,' he said. 'You keep them,' I said. We went on in this way for a little while, with my keeping the duller books only if they were really cheap, and trying to secure the better books even if they cost rather more.

Then we came to virtually a set of first editions of E. M. Forster's books, each bearing an affectionate inscription to John Hampson Simpson in some such terms as 'John with love from Morgan.' I was prepared to bid on these quite strongly but they fell to me very easily and pretty cheaply. Boris and I did our arithmetic at the end of affair and settled up. We then retired upstairs for a well-earned night's rest. After breakfast next morning Boris helped me load the car and said, rather plaintively I thought, 'Who exactly is Morgan?' I did not like to ask him in reply what he thought the M stood for in E. M. Forster.

Tony Doncaster, then proprietor of the Castle Bookshop at Colchester, once told me a story against himself, a story which showed what might be thought one of the unexpected hazards of the trade.

He was called to a large house in Essex to make an offer for the library. The owner said he was about to move and could not take the books with him. The owner was not present when Tony arrived but another member of the family let him in and showed him where the books were to be found.

Tony found them disappointing. They looked like a collection that had been picked over several times already, and as he worked his way along the shelves his face grew longer and longer. Then he discovered one rare book, one very rare book, rare enough to make the purchase of the whole collection worthwhile. Allowing a fair price for that single volume and virtually nothing for everything else, he reached what he hoped the owner would find an acceptable total for the whole shooting match. He duly submitted his figure in writing as he had been asked to do, saying in his offer that the books were disappointing and that there was nothing there that he really wanted. As he was shortly to discover, he had just dug himself a bear trap.

The owner accepted his offer by telephone and when Tony went along to collect the books he found – surprise, surprise – that the only really valuable book was no longer there. Since he had told the seller that there were no good books at all, he was in no position to complain, and had to pay up and look cheerful. He never did tell me what the great book was but a rascal had really used it to salt the mine.

CHAPTER EIGHT

SAVILE ROW

IN AMONG THE TAILORS

When I joined my father's firm in 1952 I brought the strength up from five people to six. There was room for us all in Bodley House in Vigo Street which was actually G1 Albany, a set of 'gentleman's chambers' from which John Lane had carried on his publishing business for many years. The kitchen and bathroom facilities were primitive and the pressure on the latter could be quite considerable at peak hours such as lunch time and the end of the day, but we were all very fond of the place and as our kind of bookshop it functioned very well.

During the late 1950s and early 1960s the so-called 'learning explosion' and the subsequent demand from new and growing university libraries in North America allowed us to expand the business. Fortunately we were able to rent the three rooms (one to each storey) over Napoleon's, the little newsagent's shop just a few yards down the road from us at No 8 Vigo Street. My father took the first floor for his office: in the upper stories we housed books in various subject fields, but which were not first editions of modern English literature. These rooms were first the province of Brian Harker, whom we recruited from Bernard Quaritch, principally as an office manager, and latterly of Ronald Taylor, who came to us from the Collectors' Corner division of the Folio Society, after spending many years as the principal outside buyer for Blackwell's antiquarian department. Ron and I had grown up as neighbours. Four years my senior, he used to see me safely across the road on the way to the kindergarten and primary school that we attended together. The school's frequent use of general knowledge lessons helped him develop the encyclopaedic knowledge he displayed in adult life, which was a constant source of astonishment and envy to his colleagues.

The business continued to grow, both in terms of staff and stock, for many good books seemed to be coming onto the market and the appetite for them among university libraries seemed insatiable. Soon there were fifteen of us (seven of us buying, selling or cataloguing rare books and manuscripts, and the rest providing backup services or handling our not inconsiderable business in new books). We reached a point where we could push out the walls in Vigo Street no further and, besides, having two buildings was inconvenient, even though they were so close together. In addition to these factors our Vigo Street rent was due to be increased quite dramatically. What is more new laws required us to turn serious attention to the plumbing in Bodley House, always an expensive undertaking in a listed building. We therefore decided that the time had come to seek fresh fields and pastures new.

We found the answer to our accommodation problem just twenty-eight yards from our own front door, in Savile Row, the street that is synonymous with the best bespoke tailoring in the world. Like Bodley House itself, which had been repaired, Savile Row suffered during the German blitz on London. Three fine houses, numbers 4, 5 and 6, had been demolished, and after the war they were replaced by a monolithic modern building with a covered forecourt and an underground garage. Walking up Savile Row to Sotheby's one day one of us spotted a TO LET sign against the ground-floor of this building – all 4,250 square feet of it, a huge space compared to what we were then occupying. The notion of having all our books not only under one roof but on one level, so that we did not spend all day running up and down stairs, appealed to us enormously but we knew that both rents and rates were high in Savile Row and did not dream that we would be able to afford what the building with the cumbersome title of Numbers 4, 5 and 6 would almost certainly command.

In the spirit of 'nothing venture nothing gain' we rang the agent and discovered an interesting and curious situation. A property magnate who was also a chartered accountant and tax specialist, who had built up a certain reputation among West End estate agents, had taken over the lease from the outgoing tenants when it still had quite a time to run at a high rent. He had done this not out of the goodness of his heart but in exchange for the latterday equivalent of 30 pieces of silver. In effect he then offered to subsidise the rent of the ingoing tenant from the capital sum he had received. There was clearly an enormous tax advantage for him in appearing to sublet at a loss. I never really understood how it worked but it was sufficient for us that these modern and commodious premises were thus affordable. Even so the increase in rent and rates would be quite formidable and in the uncertain world of antiquarian bookselling, we would be taking not so much a big step up, as a leap in the dark. With what later appeared to be uncanny prescience, my father, who was then 62, remarked that he would not be around for ever and that he would leave the final decision to me. With his support and that of other colleagues I took the plunge. My father enjoyed the luxurious new quarters for little more than a year before his sudden and far too early death at the age of 63.

The advantages of the Savile Row premises were considerable. Even on the wettest day one could park a car or lorry on the forecourt, but under the overhang of the building, and unload books without any fear of their getting even a single spot of rain on them. Then, joy of joys, the back door, in Heddon Street, was right next to the Post Office. The front half of the building was partitioned and decorated to the highest standard in the Wedgwood style. The back half lent itself to an arrangement of bays of shelving, work-stations and packing benches which allowed us to set up a virtual production line for assembling, invoicing, packing and shipping the large quantities of new books which we were at that time despatching to various North American universities under Dealer Selection Plans and Blanket Orders, as well as the books to fill standing orders from private collectors who asked us to supply all new books by given authors as they were published.

For the first time we were able to put all the books in our reference library in one place. This library, assembled over more than forty years by the time we moved into Savile Row, was supplemented by reference books from the businesses of Frank Hollings and G. F. Sims when we took them over. There was plenty of 'back-office' space where, for example, Arthur Uphill, now rejoicing in the title of Chief Manuscript Cataloguer, could work quietly at the job he was so good at: sorting authors' archives and preparing clear and comprehensive descriptions of them. He was able to spread himself – and his papers – without every visitor to the shop being able to see what he was working on.

The public area, well-lit and spacious, allowed us to display books in showcases as well as on shelves; moreover it made a magnificent setting for exhibitions and for parties.

The previous occupants had been Gossards, the makers of lingerie and foundation garments. We took down one piece of decoration they left behind them: it was a statue, or more precisely, if the pun might be excused, a bust. We used to quip that the keynote of the building had been changed from physical to spiritual uplift.

THE BITER BIT : II
but this time with a happy ending

Back in 1963, we nearly fell victim to a piece of trickery that was wholesale in its nature, rather than retail like that suffered by Tony Doncaster. One morning a burly American in his sixties, well dressed in bowler hat, velvet-collared overcoat, striped suit with a double-breasted waistcoat, and expensive-looking shoes, called to see me. The Freudian censor has obliterated his name from my memory banks, but I shall call him Mr Kintbury, that village between Newbury and Hungerford being where he lived at the time. After introducing himself with slightly old-fashioned courtesy, he produced two books and asked if we would be interested in buying them. They were both publications of George Macy's Limited Editions Club, not just any two picked at random but probably the most valuable and most readily saleable of all the Limited Editions Club titles. They were James Joyce's Ulysses, *with illustrations by Matisse, and Aristophanes'* Lysistrata *with illustrations by Picasso. In 1963 these were worth about $150.00 each. (The* Ulysses *would have been much more had it been one of the few copies signed by Joyce as well as Matisse : his poor eyesight kept him from signing the entire edition.)*

'These' said Mr Kintbury, 'are my calling cards. I have a house full of books down in the country. I will shortly be taking my family back to America and I don't want to take the books with me. If you would give me a fair price for them all I should be happy to sell them to you.'

I told him what I would pay for the two books he had shown me. He seemed pleased and left with me a copy of a pretty basic catalogue of the books that he had described. He said he would like me to write to him giving 'a ball-park figure' as some indication of what he might expect to receive. He said with half a wink and a roguish grin that something he could show his bank manager would be useful.

I had learned with my mother's milk always to be extremely cautious when putting prices on books I had not seen, and when there was talk of showing letters to bank managers it was my habit to be even more circumspect. Anyway I cobbled together a letter saying that if the books on the list were as described, and if their condition were satisfactory, then I thought it probable that Mr Kintbury might expect to receive between xx and yy thousand pounds for the collection.

Two or three days later I received a telephone call from the manager of the National Westminster Bank in Jermyn Street with whom we were dealing in connection with our purchase of successive tranches of the archive of Princess Marthe Bibesco. He came straight to the point : 'Mr Rota when are you going to pay Mr Kintbury the money you owe him?' 'Owe him' I expostulated, 'I don't owe him anything'. 'Yes' said the manager, 'You are buying his library for not less than xx thousand pounds'. Our burly but courteous American had almost succeeded in pulling the wool over the bank manager's eyes by first sending my letter and then telephoning to say that I had been to the house, inspected the books and confirmed the buying price. I hastened to assure the manager that things were not like that at all. I rang off, both distressed and angry that Mr Kintbury had come so close to blackening my credit rating in a quarter where it particularly mattered. When the rascal came into the shop again, presumably before the bank manager had had time to speak to him, he said he found my figures satisfactory and wanted to arrange a date for me to go down to examine the books. I decided to play along with this and made an appointment. When he had gone my colleagues and I went into a huddle and formed a plan of action. We would be pleased to buy the first editions and private press books for stock and would use most of the rest to help fill what was virtually an open order for good scholarly books for a new university library. Brian Harker, who was in charge of this last operation, would accompany me.

On the day in question we drove down the A4 and as we neared Kintbury Brian said to me 'When you introduce me I don't see that it is necessary for you to say that I am part of the firm'. So it was that I merely said that 'This is my colleague, Mr Harker, whom I have brought along to deal with the general books as opposed to those for my first editions stock'.

An hour and a half later we had examined all the books in this large country house standing in spacious grounds outside the village. If Mr Kintbury had owned the house he would indeed have been a man of substance. It transpired that he rented it and was moreover behind with *the rent. Be that as it may, he wasn't too happy with the figure for the general books. Brian said 'And I'm not too happy with the books either, Mr Kintbury. I have come up here today because Mr Rota asked me to. I left the South Coast at 6 o'clock this morning' (all perfectly true). 'Some of the books are not in the best of condition and that is all I can pay.' Kintbury eventually agreed and asked if he might have a cheque. As I was going through the motions of writing one out he asked when we would like to come to collect the books. At this a little man with the mien of a ferret, to whom we had not been introduced, but who had been going round the building writing in a notebook, looked a little startled. Brian and I eyed one another. 'Oh we'll take the books now, Mr Kintbury, then you can have your cheque right away', said Brian. 'Take them now?' queried Kintbury. 'But you'll never get them all into the car.' 'That's all right' said Brian. 'We have a large van waiting against just such a contingency.' So saying, he stepped out into the garden and gave a prearranged signal to the driver from our usual haulage firm, who had his vehicle parked in a gateway a hundred yards up the lane. Kintbury's face was a study as we loaded the books into the van. The ferret-like man didn't look very happy either and I drew him aside and asked his role. He said he was there on behalf of the bailiffs and had been expecting to clear all the furniture and the books the very next day. If we had been naïve enough to hand over the cheque and go back for the books at the end of the week we would have found empty shelves. Where Tony Doncaster's man had removed the one good book, Mr Kintbury had planned to remove the entire library.*

CHAPTER NINE

A GRIEVOUS BLOW

In November 1966 my father had been due to go to America to visit various of our customers. Instead he had his second heart attack. It was not a very severe one and his doctor, a heart specialist called Walter Somerville, who was a book collector, soon had him on the road to recovery. From his bed in the London Clinic B. planned a regimen that Dr Somerville approved of, and set a target date for a gentle, gradual return to work.

I went to see him on the eve of his discharge from the clinic and, guided by heaven only knows what intuition, passed an hour by reminding him of happy incidents from my childhood. I told him what a wonderful father he had been. I was to be eternally grateful that the conversation took that turn for I was never to see him alive again.

Una, whom he had married some years before, took him home to Ivor Court and there on 3 December he suffered a massive stroke and died. Una called me at 6 o'clock on this dark Saturday evening and said that things were bad and that I should come at once. Driving across Hampstead Heath I had a puncture and pulled to the side of the road to change the wheel. Because of the awkwardness of the camber at the point where I had stopped I could not jack the car up high enough to get the spare wheel into place. I struggled desperately to lift the car the extra inch that was needed. Literally hundreds of cars must have passed by before one stopped and its Pakistani driver got out to see if he could help me. He braced his back and heaved while I pushed the wheel and in a trice we got it into place.

When I finally got to Ivor Court my father's G.P. was still there. He assured me that everything possible had been done to save him. He added that the stroke was such that had B. survived it, he would

Anthony and Bertram Rota, at Bodley House, *c.* 1957

have been very severely handicapped. Knowing him as we did we could not have wished for that outcome. I went through to the bedroom to take my leave of him. He looked wonderfully at peace.

While I was with Una two of B.'s old friends rang to check on the progress of his recovery from the heart attack. I had the melancholy task of giving them the news. George Lazarus, who has a chapter to himself in this book, said 'I am so terribly sorry. I have lost my oldest friend' and put down the telephone.

For my own part I felt as though I had been kicked by a mule. In one blow I had lost my much loved father, my best friend and the ideal head of my firm. I had also lost the Court of Last Appeal. It is said that no man is finally grown up until his father dies. At 34, with a wife and two small sons, responsibility for my mother, who had never ceased to love my father, the need to look after Una and to ensure the safety of the jobs of the firm's dedicated staff. I certainly understood the truth of the saying that I have quoted.

As the news of my father's passing reached people in the world of books, Una and I were almost overwhelmed by the flood of letters of condolence that we received, evidence of how highly my father was regarded both by his customers and his colleagues. His obituary appeared in *The Times* over the signature of Edward Lucie-Smith. As I recall, he was one of the first antiquarian booksellers to be so honoured. Simon Nowell-Smith wrote a splendid memorial of him, for publication in *The Book Collector* and with the kind permission of that journal's editor Nicolas Barker, I reprint it as an appendix to the present volume.

In various unexpected ways many friends showed great acts of kindness at this time. One of them was George Lazarus, who had known me since I was in short trousers and was thus one of the few people outside the family allowed to call me by the short form of my first name. I should explain that it was George's invariable custom at this stage in his life to come to see us around four o'clock on Tuesday afternoons between the closing of the Stock Exchange and his visits to his 90-year-old mother at her home in Green Street. He would stride through the shop and without waiting to be announced would fling open the door of my office. Calling out a greeting without breaking stride, he would march on through the communicating door to my father's room. For all George knew, I might have been taking a nap or changing my trousers: it was not his way to be troubled by such considerations.

In my father's room George would sink into one of the two guest chairs and the two men would discuss new acquisitions and other developments relating to George's D. H. Lawrence collection, lubricating their thoughts with a glass of whisky. More often than not I was called in to join them. At that point George would usually retail the best of the new jokes going round the Stock Exchange.

On Tuesday, 6 December, at 4 o'clock precisely the door to my office was flung open and in came George. With a curt 'Good afternoon' to my secretary, that tower of strength, Anne Prior, George turned to me and said 'Come on, Tony, let's go next door' and, suiting action to words, he led the way to the *sanctum sanctorum*. Once there he took his usual chair and I went to sit in the other guest chair facing him. He was up in one bound and taking me metaphorically by the scruff of the neck, forced me round to the other side of the big desk and plonked me down in my father's chair, an act which seemed to me at the time to be verging on the sacrilegious. 'When are you going to America?' he asked peremptorily. 'But George, my father's not cold yet,' I said. 'Look,' he replied, 'it is vital that you show the world that the firm is going to carry on and that it will continue to be worthy of your customers' support. I'm not leaving here until you give me a date.' Eventually I agreed to arrange to make in March the trip on which my father should at that very moment have been engaged. 'Right. Now where's the whisky?' George enquired.

Countless others helped enormously in those difficult days. I had the wonderful support of my wife, and could count on the loyalty and dedication of the team at Bertram Rota Ltd. It seems almost invidious to single out particular names there but I owe a special debt to George Lawson, whom I was shortly to make my co-director. Without his help and the support of Anne Prior already mentioned, I am not sure I could have got through. Simon Nowell-Smith proved a staunch friend. Warren Roberts, Director of the Humanities Research Center at the University of Texas, showed his confidence in me in a way which led eventually to my purchase and resale to Texas of the Bradley Archive, as I shall tell.

The reactions of our bankers made an interesting comparison. I telephoned the manager of the clearing bank with which we had had an account since 1923. When I told him the news he said, the worry showing in his voice, 'Oh my God! I mean I am so sorry'. My next call went to a director of Charterhouse, our merchant bank, who had much the same cause to feel nervous. His response was 'My dear chap, I am so sorry. You are going to need help. Won't you come to lunch next week so that we can see what we can do?'. Harry Cahn, the Churchill collector, who made half his living from advising clients on their relations with bankers, became our banking consultant at this time and refused to take a penny piece for his services.

As I wrestled with the various problems that my father's sudden death brought us, I never felt that he was far away. In fact that feeling remains to this day. When faced with a business problem, perhaps a matter of taxation or finance, perhaps something to do with the staff, or with how to conduct a particularly difficult negotiation, I will be sitting with colleagues becoming more and more deeply embroiled in the ramifications of the matter and the possible consequences, when suddenly my mind will go back to an informal board meeting in my father's day. I will remember how at a similar impasse a slow smile would creep across his face and he would make a remark or crack a joke that eased the tension, showed us the funny side of our predicament, and in the relaxed mood that followed, allowed us to find a solution.

It is not only at fraught moments that I feel him near: I often think of him as sitting on a cloud, not playing a harp, but, with a glass of burgundy in hand, chatting about books with such old friends as David Magee, Anthony Newnham, Simon Nowell-Smith and Franklin Gilliam.

In the 1950s runners were still an important part of the mechanism of the rare book market : far more so than they are today. The term ought to be in John Carter's ABC for Book Collectors, but it isn't. A runner (in America the word 'scout' is more commonly used) is a self-employed bookseller without a shop, who does not issue catalogues and whose stock tends to consist solely of his mistakes, i.e. of books he bought for instant resale but for which he failed to find a buyer. A runner is just as good, or successful, as his memory for bibliographical issue points and prices. He makes his living by buying good books whose potential has not been fully recognised by the dealer who has them in stock, and selling them to a bookseller who rates them more highly. He usually works on a small margin, sometimes making no more than the courtesy discount he receives from the seller. Occasionally he will 'run' a book on behalf of the seller, which is to say he will offer it to one or more trade buyers on behalf of the owner, who may be moving old stock at a considerable discount, but not want the fact known. Often he will be asked if he knows of a copy of a particular book being currently on the market. There his good memory comes to his aid again and he may well recall seeing a copy three weeks before, in a bookshop the other side of the country. A really good runner will also remember the book's condition and price. If he is lucky he will buy the book and resell it at once to the dealer who has need of it. Being a runner is not the easiest way of making a living.

The runner I knew best was A. W. Howlett, who used to call on us in Vigo Street more days than not. He must have had a first name, but I never heard him addressed as other than 'Mr Howlett' nor referred to save as 'Howlett'. A quiet and shy man, he spent most of the Second World War in a German prison camp and this experience had certainly had an effect on him. When war broke out in 1939 he was running his own little shop somewhere on the southern fringes of London, selling new books, second-hand books and stamps. He once told us that he could make more money selling stamps than selling books. 'Pity I don't like stamps,' he added. At this time too, he was just making a breakthrough as a writer, getting stories and poems published in little magazines. By 1945 his years of imprisonment had left him unable to face the challenge of reopening his own bookshop and unwilling to spend each working day shut up in the confines of somebody else's, so, though he had plenty of offers of employment, he preferred the freedom of a runner's life, travelling the country on foot and by bus and train in all weathers, carrying with him a heavy load of books. These he always had in a cardboard carton which he carried by a string (which cut into his fingers cruelly). In later life he walked with a limp, as though perpetually carrying that heavy load at his side.

Although he kept himself clean, he cared nothing for clothes. He always wore a collar and tie but they were very loosely connected. Winter and summer alike he wore a raincoat, and like his greasy, sweat-stained hat, he wore it until it literally fell from him in tatters. In short he had the appearance of a tramp. Quite often he was stopped in the street by the police, who would demand to know what he was carrying in that heavy box. When they were not satisfied with his answer Howlett would ask them to take him to the nearest bookshop where, of course, the proprietor would gladly vouch for him.

One day he brought us a copy of the rare first edition of George Orwell's Keep the Aspidistra Flying, 1936, in wonderful condition and still protected by its tell-tale, bright yellow, Victor Gollancz dust-jacket. While my senior colleague Anthony Newnham was looking at it, Howlett named his price, which was as usual perfectly reasonable. (On occasions when Howlett thought his asking price was high he inadvertently signalled the fact by breaking into a quiet but perfectly audible hum.) On this occasion he merely said 'It's a mint copy. Pity someone has written his name on the title-page.' Newnham showed me the book as he replied 'We'll buy it anyway'. He paid Howlett from the till and then said affectionately: 'You daft thing. The name written on the title-page is 'Eric Blair'! Don't you know that 'George Orwell' is only a pseudonym for Blair? You've just sold us a copy signed by the author. Just a minute.' Newnham turned and took the book into my father's office. He came out again a moment later and said 'Bertram says "Thanks" and you are to have the same amount again,' reaching for the till once more, a gesture never forgotten by Howlett and a lesson in fair dealing learned by me.

CHAPTER TEN

I DISCOVER AMERICA

In the late 1950s and early 1960s it was by no means commonplace for rare book dealers, even those who took their business seriously, to make annual trips to the United States. My father used to go, sometimes lecturing and sometimes not, visiting our major institutional and private customers and, as a by-product, buying from American booksellers English books that they had on their shelves almost by chance, as well as American books that were needed by some of our customers in England. Every time he returned to London from one of these trips my father would say to me 'You must go next time', but he was clearly enjoying himself so much that I felt it would be a pity to take his place: my turn would come. In point of fact I intended not to go to America until I was able to take my wife with me but events intervened.

James Meriwether, a professor of English at the University of South Carolina, an authority on William Faulkner and possessor of a razor-sharp bibliographical expertise, rang me one day and said that after many years on starvation rations his university library had had a windfall. He said, and I do not know with what degree of truth, that a sum of money had been set aside for air-conditioning the freshman dormitories but that he had managed to get it switched to the book account. He would like me to fly out to discuss how it should be spent and if I did not find it convenient to come within the next couple of weeks he was sure that one of my competitors would.

This was the sort of language I understood and a week later I was on the plane to Columbia, South Carolina. As Ford Madox Ford said, *New York is not America*, and I have always been very glad that my introduction to the United States came about in South Carolina in the fall rather than in New York at some other time of year. Jim was a Southerner through and through and was determined that I should enjoy the southern experience. He showed me the dogwood trees, he fed me on sourdough muffins and he gave me Jack Daniels to drink out of a silver tumbler. He took me to the State Archive building where I saw rebel flags that women had made by cutting and dyeing their undergarments. He showed me what a disaster Reconstruction was for the South. I loved the people. I loved their slow pattern of speech and the shop girls' valediction of 'Y'all hurry on back now'.

There were in essence three libraries on the University of South Carolina campus, the undergraduate library, the graduate library and the South Caroliniana library. Jim told me that he wanted me to write a report on these libraries. I managed the first and last with no difficulty at all, but I had trouble in reaching Dr Rawlinson, the Director of Libraries, to get permission to visit the graduate library. What Jim had not told me was that I had landed in the middle of a shooting war between the English faculty (chiefly as represented by Jim) and the library establishment as represented by Dr Rawlinson, a man who all through the depression had turned back at the end of each fiscal year an unused portion of what was in any case a pitifully small acquisitions budget. The university was now having to pay the price of his short-sighted attempt to curry favour with the authorities: its shelves were full of gaps that would now cost five, ten or even twenty times as much to fill. At this point I was summoned, with Jim's boss, the chairman of the English department, Professor Jack Guilds, to the presence of Dr Thomas Jones, the president of the university, whom I had met socially at a party the night before. What did I think of Dr Rawlinson, he asked? I explained that I had been unable to see him and suspected that he was planning to be unavailable until my plane had carried me back to London. Dr Jones then said that Jim had had no right to invite me and to commission the report on the state of the libraries. To make matters right he, the president, would commission me to make the report to him instead. I was moreover to be back in his office at 2.30 that afternoon when he would personally introduce me to Alfred

Rawlinson. When the clock got around to half past two Dr Jones banged Rawlinson's head and mine together and sent us off to make a tour of the graduate library. I was struck by the fact that Dr Rawlinson did not introduce me to a single member of his staff. We then sat down in his office, a room which had a suspiciously clear desk. He reached for a directory of booksellers and asked me again what my name and speciality were. He proceeded to read through the list of first edition dealers in America which included the names of such great firms as Seven Gables Bookshop, House of Books Ltd, Gotham Book Mart, Brick Row and so on. 'There you are' he said. 'Don't know a single one of you'.

'If you know none of them Dr Rawlinson then I am proud that you didn't know my name either', I replied. After this outburst things could only get better and we were at least exchanging routine civilities by the end of the afternoon. I duly wrote my report. Jim got his money and came to London to spend it, buying from a number of the major dealers and doing a great deal to strengthen the library's English literature holdings.

My next trip to America took place in very different circumstances. As I have said, after my father's death George Lazarus would not leave the premises until I had fixed a timetable to make the trip to see our major American customers that my father would have undertaken had his second heart attack not got in the way. I eventually went in March 1967 for the better part of two weeks, visiting some five or six institutional libraries as well as a number of private customers and dealers. Then, as every year for the next twenty-one, I included in my journey calls on two customers in particular, the Berg Collection at the New York Public Library and the Humanities Research Center of the University of Texas at Austin. John Gordan, curator of the Berg Collection and proud scion of an old Virginia family, kindly gave me the use of a tenth floor apartment in a co-operative building virtually in the back yard of his brownstone on East 78th Street. I was to dine with him and his wife Phyllis (née Goodhart, whose father had been a distinguished collector of books and manuscripts). John rang me 48 hours before I was due to leave London to say that on the evening of my arrival he had tickets for a Schubert *lieder* recital by Hermann Prey at the Pierpont Morgan Library. It was to be a black tie affair but I need not bother to bring my evening things: he would lend me some of his. Well though this was meant, I pictured myself standing up in a suit borrowed from John, who was probably six inches taller than I, and decided that I would pack my own after all.

Came the day, and Phyllis hosted a small dinner party at the Cosmopolitan Club. I was seated next to Mary Hyde who, with her late husband Donald, had built such an impressive Samuel Johnson collection and assembled a fabulous library at Four Oaks Farm. Many years later she married Viscount Eccles, who was also a customer of ours. The marriage had the happy by-product of bringing Mary to London more often than was previously the case, but on this Manhattan evening in 1967 we found ourselves neighbours still in the auditorium at the Morgan Library as Hermann Prey got up to sing at 9 p.m. local time. This was two in the morning by my body clock and I confessed to Mary that I was beginning to have serious doubts about my ability to stay awake. 'Don't worry, Anthony', she said. 'I will lend you a couple of matchsticks for your eyelids'. She did not actually do that but she did nudge me gently at one or two crucial moments and I managed to avoid absolute disgrace during the recital.

Afterwards there was a reception in the East Room of the Morgan, where the director, Fred Adams moved about, meeting his guests and dispensing charm and bonhomie. When he came over to the Gordan party John said to him, 'You remember Anthony, don't you Fred?' Fred did and greeted me warmly, asking what had brought me to New York and the Morgan on this particular night. There in a room which housed a Gutenberg bible, and manuscripts by Thomas Hardy, Mozart and Wagner, John Gordan cut in with 'I told him you served the best ice-cream 'shapes' in New York, Fred.'

John and I did a little business the next day, and then I went down to Texas. A year or two earlier the proportion of our turnover that was done with the Humanities Research Center had risen to

F. Warren Roberts, *c.* 1962

one third and thinking that uncomfortably high, my father had set me the task of increasing our sales of entire collections and of archival material to other purchasers. Now I went to see Warren Roberts, the first of five directors of the Center that I was to work with over the years, and told him that although my father was gone, his spirit lived on in the firm and that the people who had worked with him remained there. I asked if he would at least give us one opportunity to show that we could still perform the kind of service for the University which he used to commission.

'How could you think otherwise, Anthony?' Warren replied.

Eventually a slot opened up in the busy schedule of Dr Harry Ransom, President of the University of Texas at Austin and founder of the Humanities Research Center, which at that stage did not carry his name, but simply shared his initials. (During the tenure of Dr Decherd Turner as director, the center changed its name to the Harry Ransom Humanities Research Center, but some of us thought that was mere tautology.) Dr Ransom greeted me kindly, spoke warmly of my father and asked what collections I had brought to offer the university. He said he would talk to Warren Roberts about them in due course but meanwhile wanted me to know that of all the catalogue descriptions that accompanied incoming shipments of manuscripts and letters from dealers on both sides of the Atlantic, those of Bertram Rota Ltd were the best in terms of accuracy and organization. Dr Ransom repeated this flattering remark in future years and I took great pride in it, remembering gratefully how my father and Anthony Newnham had trained me and how I in my turn had trained our chief manuscript cataloguer Arthur Uphill and my associate director John Byrne.

In a later year Dr Ransom performed a very impressive trick. His secretary telephoned Warren Roberts to say that a meeting Harry Ransom was having with some Mexican politicians seemed likely to break up soon and that if we were in the outer office in five minutes time Dr Ransom would be able to see us before his next scheduled appointment. Warren and I put on our jackets, smoothed our hair, straightened our ties and flew across campus to the president's

Harry Ransom, *c.* 1960

office. We had barely sat down when the Mexican gentlemen came out and Harry Ransom turned from them to us and came forward beaming, both arms extended, one to shake my hand the other to clasp my shoulder. After polite preliminaries about my health and the aeroplane journey he said to me 'Now Anthony, as I was saying to you last year' and proceeded to pick up in mid-paragraph exactly where he had left off twelve months before. I doubt he had taken minutes of our previous meeting and if he had there would have been no time to read them. I was very impressed.

On this visit in 1967 I set the pattern which was to hold for many years. In a two or three-week trip I would visit between seven and ten university libraries, sometimes speaking to gatherings of professional staff and sometimes talking to students who were English majors. As I have said I went to New York and to Austin each year. I always arranged for my time in Texas to fall so that it covered a weekend, for I soon had many friends in town and I liked the outdoor lifestyle that they followed. Each year I visited some old customers and each year I called on one or two new ones. I went pretty regularly to the University of Wisconsin at Madison and to the University of North Carolina at Chapel Hill, both of which were customers with whom I particularly enjoyed working. I also went to various branches of the University of California, to the University of Chicago, to Harvard, Princeton, Rice, the University of Houston, the Lockwood Memorial Library at Buffalo, to Stanford, to Delaware and to the Library of Congress. In addition I visited two or three dealers on each trip, always buying well in New York, sometimes having the good fortune to follow an English literature collection into the premises of Larry McMurtry's Booked Up in Washington DC.

The other Washington in my life at this time was Washington University in St Louis where my friend William Matheson was head of Special Collections. He was probably the most demanding librarian customer I ever had, which is perhaps why I found working with him so stimulating. Bill's wife, Nina, was, like him, a book collector as well as a librarian (she put together an astonishingly comprehensive collection of Nabokov's works, which is now to be found at the University of Texas) and moreover she was and remains one of the best cooks at whose table I have been fortunate enough to dine. When you throw in the fact that the Mathesons also kept a fine cellar it is small wonder that first St Louis and then when Bill moved back to the Library of Congress and Nina to John Hopkins, Washington DC and Baltimore featured prominently in my travel plans for many years.

Chapel Hill was a regular port of call for not dissimilar reasons. My principal contact there was Professor Mark Reed, the English faculty's representative on the library committee and a shrewd judge of a good book and a valuable archive. Wordsworth's chronologist as well as Wordsworth's bibliographer Mark also kept a truly impressive cellar and knows more about French wine than seems proper for anyone not born in that country. His wife, Martha is also a cook of quite extraordinary powers, and I often think that the most successful negotiation I ever brought off was an arrangement under which the Rotas and the Reeds could each claim 'hotel rights' in the others' home.

When he was Prime Minister, and trying to boost British trade overseas the late Harold Macmillan said in a famous soundbite 'Exporting is fun'. At the time it was fashionable to jeer at this, for exporting was very hard work indeed, but I have to admit it had its consolations.

After lunch one day in 1952 I went with Anthony Newnham to visit Sangorski and Sutcliffe, then the firm that we most often used when we needed bookbinding work done. Their premises were on the top floor of a workshop building in Poland Street in the heart of Soho, and one had to climb three flights of stone steps to reach them. Breathing hard from the ascent, we would be greeted by the proprietor, Stanley Bray. We would show him what we wanted done and ask if we could, with his advice, select the materials to be used. I grew to enjoy this part of the proceedings because it involved visits to two or three locations in the bindery and one thus got a virtual Cook's tour. I found that if I slowed down as I passed a workbench Stanley Bray would come back and explain to me exactly what was going on there. In the course of two or at most three visits one would be given a complete demonstration of all the various processes that went into producing a fine binding.

On this occasion Anthony and I chose the exact shade of Levant morocco that we wanted, Stanley uncomplainingly opening and rolling out one goatskin after another until we found just what we were looking for. Then we chose a marbled paper for the sides. Anthony had an antipathy, which I came to share, to the well-nigh ubiquitous Cockerell designs of the day and Stanley allowed us to pick from his diminishing stock of old Florentine papers that were altogether more unusual. These were kept in a chest near the bench of Sangorski's foreman, the redoubtable Mr Middleton, father of the Designer-Bookbinder and trade historian Bernard Middleton.

If I may digress for a moment, I remember an occasion around this time when I took to Sangorski's a copy of the Large Paper issue of James McNeill Whistler's The Gentle Art of Making Enemies, *1892. Though the contents were clean and fresh, the binding was soiled and worn and I told Stanley Bray that I would like to have the book rebound in full white vellum. I asked whether he could work in gilt in a corner of the upper cover a representation of Whistler's famous butterfly device. 'We've got a brass [i.e. a tool with the requisite image cut into the metal at the business end] for it somewhere'* he said, *striding off into the workshop. 'Here, Middleton'* he shouted, *'Where's Mr Whistler's butterfly?' for all the world as though the tool had been commissioned only a month or two before and was in use every day, although Whistler had already been dead for more than fifty years. In Stanley Bray's day Sangorski's was a truly remarkable firm.*

To revert to my afternoon visit with Newnham, Stanley stopped as we were passing the bench where he himself wrapped up every finished job. 'This is something up your street' he said, showing us a fine copy of W. H. Hudson's 'Romance of the Tropical Forest', Green Mansions, 1904. One of us remarked that it was indeed a lovely copy.

'You wouldn't have thought so when John Hanson brought it in', said Stanley. 'The first edition was in a right mess but he'd found a fine reprint and got us to swap the covers over. Turned out well, didn't it?' We had to agree that it was a remarkably fine job. What we didn't do was preach a sermon to Stanley on the iniquity of Hanson's instruction. To fake a book so that it had the appearance of being something that it was not, to 'sophisticate' it, was a serious crime in our eyes. My father used to say that in book-collecting, booksellers made the rules and if they didn't abide by them, the whole thing became an utter nonsense. Though Stanley probably thought he was merely improving the appearance of a rare book which happened to have worn and soiled covers, Hanson must have known that 'sophisticated' copies were bad news, especially if they were not described as such.

Anthony and I went back to the shop, but imagine our joy when, four days later, who should come across the threshold but John Hanson. He was ruddy-cheeked, stood about 5 foot 10 inches, was in his fifties I should think, and had thinning reddish gold hair. As usual he wore a double-breasted blue overcoat and a brown homburg hat. His nicotine stained fingers held a cigarette as always. He greeted us in his strong Canadian accent: it hadn't diminished for all the long years that he had lived in London.

We talked about the weather and we talked about the state of the trade until Newnham finally asked him 'Have you got something for us, Hanson?'

'Yes, something I think you will like,' he replied, and to our carefully

concealed delight he produced the sophisticated copy of Green Mansions. 'How about that?', he said.

'My, but that's a smart copy', Newnham replied. 'May I look at it?' He examined it carefully and passed it to me. I also admired it and passed it back. Then just a flicker of a frown crossed Anthony's countenance. It was so quick that Hanson was hardly aware of it. 'I'd like to show this to Bertram', Anthony said. And he asked me to go and fetch him. I quickly tipped my father the wink and he came out of his office, saying 'What have you got for us today, Mr Hanson? Oh, that's a pretty copy indeed. May I?'

He picked the book up and turned it around in his hand, studying it from every angle. Normally when endpapers are renewed as a book is being re-cased either in its old binding or a new one, a thin sliver of the new endpaper can be seen protruding above the text block towards the upper and lower edges of the boards. The difference between Sangorski's and a binder of lesser ability is that in the case of the Sangorski book this obtrusive piece of paper was so thin that it could scarcely be seen at all.

'Do you know,' my father said, 'I could almost swear that this copy had been re-cased.' At this even Hanson's naturally red cheeks could scarcely hide the blush that was beginning to form, but he blustered on. 'What ever makes you say that?' he asked. While making a great show of pointing out the tell-tale trace to Anthony and to me, my father gave Hanson a patient lesson in bookbinding technique. But Hanson wasn't finished yet : 'I should like to know who could re-case a book as well as that' he declared.

'Sangorski's?' asked my father. Collapse of stout party.

CHAPTER ELEVEN

NOT FOURTH AVENUE

It was 1967 when I made my first visit to New York and by then the legendary hunting grounds where generations of book scouts had apparently gleaned golden grains of books at bargain prices from the general chaff on display as a matter of course, were, to mix metaphors, just about fished out. Fourth Avenue was to New York what Farringdon Road with its barrows was to London and by the mid 1960s both had had their day. Even if that had not been so, even if the Avenue had still been at its fabled best, I really doubt if I would have spent much time there. My book-buying philosophy has always been this: when in a distant town for a limited period of time it makes better sense to go where you know you are going to see quantities of really good books even if they are priced to the hilt, rather than to spend an hour or more looking through piles of dross in the hope of finding one unsuspected treasure for a fraction of its true worth. On another page I tell of my father's good fortune at one particular London book-barrow but even in London I myself found it more profitable to spend my time where I *knew* good books were to be seen. One of the best buys I ever made, for example, was from the front room at Quaritch, when they were still in their elegant building on Grafton Street. It was an album of letters and other documents in the hand of Aircraftman Ross, the name used by Lawrence of Arabia when he sought refuge from a world that was too much with him and tried to make an existence incognito in the ranks of the Royal Air Force. The subject of the album in question was the development work he was engaged on with the Air Force's high-speed launches used as seaplane tenders.

Although I have no tales to tell of Fourth Avenue I did begin in 1967 to develop a round of New York bookshops that I enjoyed visiting and that between them could show me an enviable array of good material. Margie Cohn of House of Books used to say that she always made Bertram Rota Ltd her second stop on her trips to London. 'I go first to Elizabeth Arden and then to you' she would tell me. Omitting the beauty parlour I reciprocated when in New York. Margie's premises, upstairs off the street like so many New York bookshops, comprised two rooms, one public and the other where reserve stock was kept and the packing was done. In the public room one could always see a wide range of first editions of modern English and American literature in the best possible condition. Her prices were always fair and in her later years eminently reasonable. Margie prided herself on the handsome appearance of her letterpress catalogues and rightly thought it unfair that collectors who compared catalogues but not prices assumed that books cost less at, say, the Phoenix Book Shop down in the Village, just because Phoenix's cyclostyled lists were cheaper to produce.

After sitting and chatting for a little while, taking reputations apart and exchanging bibliographical gossip, I would tour the shelves, selecting for the most part American editions of English authors for which I had customers waiting in London.

Margie was always very kind to me but she must have seemed like a fairy godmother to the college boys who found their way to her when they were beginning their collections. If such book buying was stretching their student budgets beyond endurance she would both give them extended credit and buy them a square meal.

My next stop in New York was almost always at Seven Gables Book Shop, on West 46th Street, just off Fifth Avenue. The ground floor was occupied by a shop that sold everything that an angler could require. I remember always seeing a fine array of knives, many with cork handles, in an impressive display. Dedicated book hunters would ignore the knives, the rods and the reels and ring for the ancient goods lift which would, painfully slowly, take them up past the floor where Seven Gables, agents for Waller Barrett, kept a large portion of his library. Occasionally the lift would stop at that floor by mistake and the door would be thrown open to reveal for a moment what was for bibliophiles an Aladdin's cave. Seven Gables' public area on the floor above was hardly less of a treasure house. There one encountered the genial erudition of Mike Papantonio and his partner John Kohn. In addition one was generally warmly greeted by Marie the bookkeeper and Tony the packer.

Although the partners, later joined by John Brett-Smith, were very serious about their work, in particular Mike about American bindings and John about nineteenth and twentieth century English literature (of course their expertise spread far wider), doing business with Seven Gables was always great fun. My father, who knew no small amount about gastronomy, said that Mike and John kept the best lunch table in town. For my part I liked Mike's system for dealing with unanswered mail. 'Take a medium-sized suitcase,' (I paraphrase) 'fill it fairly full, so that the letters cannot slip about, lock it and place it in a left luggage locker. Take a bus or cab to the middle of Brooklyn Bridge and hurl both keys into the river. The letters will give you no further trouble'.

It seemed to me that those parts of the shop that were presided over by John Kohn were tidy and orderly while Mike's kingdom in the front room had a misleading air of chaos. Good books, in my case chiefly of the 19th century, were to be found in both sections. Something I was especially pleased to buy there was a book outside Seven Gables' specialised area. It was a copy of the sumptuous Festschrift printed on the house press of the Bauer type foundry to honour the great German book and type designer, E. R. Weiss. 273 folio leaves printed on the rectos only, in black and red, reproduce type specimens, ornamental initials, bookplates, binding designs and so on. G. K. Schauer in his *Deutsche Buchkunst*, 1963, goes so far as to call it 'one of the most important documents on design in the first quarter of the twentieth century.'

Buying books in a specialist dealer's shop that are outside his or her normal field is often a good idea, but you must remember that you don't have the dealer's specialised knowledge to guide you and protect you. The bookseller who is not familiar with the field may think a particular goose is a swan and price it at more than the specialist would. Nevertheless buying 'off-subject' books is a pastime that has always appealed to me. Thanks to my friend Robert Elwell (*q.v.*) I bought just such a book from Walter Schatzki's rather grand shop in Midtown. When he knew I was shortly to be in New York, Bob would clip for me coupons and advertisements for bargains at Sam Goody and the Record-Hunter. On one trip he introduced me to a bargain of a different nature. He told me that Walter Schatzki had a copy of the German language edition of the Cranach Press *Hamlet*, with the celebrated engravings by Gordon Craig. Moreover it was an inscribed presentation copy from the translator, Gerhart Hauptmann. The German edition contains six engravings fewer than the English language edition, but it was published a year earlier, so I bought the Schatzki copy and resold it quickly and profitably.

While I was with him Mr Schatzki showed me a trick I would have been reluctant to try on my own. We had been discussing vellum bindings and their unfortunate propensity to warp and curl on being taken from the chill and damp of many a British home of the 1960s and introduced to a warm, dry centrally heated American apartment. Mr Schatzki had the perfect solution. 'Wrap the offending volume tightly in newspaper,' he said 'and leave it in the icebox overnight. It will be fine in the morning.' I grinned cynically, thinking I was being teased, so Mr Schatzki marched me through to the kitchen behind the shop, opened the door of the icebox, pulled out a rather damp parcel wrapped in the previous Sunday's *New York Times* and invited me to unwrap it. Inside was a pristine Kelmscott Press book in the original limp vellum binding. 'Yesterday you wouldn't have given that copy shelf-room,' Mr Schatzki said.

I have said, or at least implied, that runners were more numerous in the 1950s than they are today, but one who has left no uncertain mark in recent times is the man known simply as Driffield: he appears to have neither first name nor initial, although he is frequently referred to and addressed simply as 'Driff'. Not solely a runner, Driffield will be remembered in book-trade history as the editor of Driff's Guide, *an egocentric listing of bookshops which achieved a certain notoriety because of the undoubtedly funny comments made by the editor, no matter whether or not they were true.*

The Guide made good use of acronyms, e.g. NEB (not enough books), WWA (well worth avoiding), WTA (worse than average), and FARTS (follows around recommending the stock).

Eric Barton, of the Baldur Bookshop in Richmond, now dead alas, was certainly an eccentric in the great British tradition. A difficult man at the best of times, he could be absolutely impossible on a rainy day, but he really did not deserve Driffield's description of him. Eric told me that he would have sued Driffield for libel had the latter been worth more than the clothes he stood up in. Others have said the same to me and indeed I felt the same way myself on one occasion. I thought it quite funny when he said that I was 'too proud to take money'. But I found it less than amusing when the instructions he gave for reaching 31 Long Acre from Covent Garden tube station led people in the diametrically opposite direction. Driff's Guide *certainly did fill some sort of a need because, by car, train and bicycle he visited a huge number and a wide range of bookshops all over the country. He was able to give a pretty up-to-date picture of which places were still open, which had recently opened and which had closed. He gave an indication of the stock, he gave suggestions about how to reach remote places and he gave pen pictures of some of the more notable proprietors. Alas he chose to exclude completely booksellers who did not have ground-floor, open access bookshops: no book-rooms, no offices, no places that required a bell to be rung before admittance was gained, none of these found their way into his book.*

In his comments and in a mimeographed journal that was little more than a scandal sheet, he did his best to pull down various members of the book trade Establishment, large and small, and undoubtedly damaged some dealers' business. In his writings he was certainly not a modest man.

I have spoken of him in the past tense although he is, I believe, still very much with us : it is just his publications that have died the death.

CHAPTER TWELVE

THE BRADLEY ARCHIVE

AN AMERICAN IN PARIS

Like many an American of his generation William Aspenwall Bradley had his introduction to France in the First World War. He so liked what he saw of Paris that he did not want to return to America. Furthermore he had met a clever and beautiful Belgian girl of good family, one Jenny Serruys, and wanted to marry her. He needed to find some sort of job which would pay him a decent salary and which would be acceptable in the eyes of Jenny's parents. Discovering that a number of his American friends were staying in Paris to write, and realizing that they would benefit from having a specialist agent to represent them, Bradley began his literary agency. He married Jenny Serruys and they were partners in the enterprise until his death. Apart from representing the American expatriate writers of the twenties and thirties, the Bradleys also looked after the interests inside France of various English and American writers who still lived and worked in the countries of their birth but who sought a continental market.

In *The Autobiography of Alice B. Toklas* William Bradley had been characterised as 'the friend and comforter of Paris authors.' He worked with the emigré Russian writers such as Aldanov and Bunin, as well as with Sinclair Lewis, Gertrude Stein and in the early days, Henry Miller. He was also instrumental in placing European writers with such American publishers as Alfred and Blanche Knopf, a firm which the Bradley agency represented in Paris. After Bradley's death in January 1939, Mrs Bradley continued the business through the troubled period of the German occupation of France. When the war was over she set about expanding the agency and handled European rights for Thomas Mann, as well as

Margaret Mitchell, *Gone With the Wind* having become a cult book in France. She also dealt with the French rights of successful thriller writers such as Leslie Charteris, James Hadley-Chase and Patricia Highsmith. The Bradleys carried on their business from a rather grand house on the Ile St Louis which was said to have been the home of Cardinal Richelieu at one time. By 1974 its attics were stuffed full of the agency's files. The archive contained approximately a quarter of a million pieces. Word reached me that Mrs Bradley was minded to sell. Through Mrs Bradley's London correspondent I got an appointment to see her and to examine the material.

The agency's files included 168 letters from Gertrude Stein and seventy from Alice B. Toklas. Other names of note among the 1,680 authors represented included Ford Madox Ford, Blaise Cendrars, Isadora Duncan, Ezra Pound, Jean Rhys, Vladimir Nabokov, D. H. Lawrence, Igor Stravinsky, Evelyn Waugh and Nijinsky.

The Scott Fitzgerald and Hemingway letters alone were worth a small fortune. I made an offer for the entire archive which was eventually accepted. We brought the papers back to London, where my colleague Arthur Uphill made a descriptive catalogue of them, on the basis of which we sold the archive to Texas. Warren Roberts later said that of all the many collections we had sold the University he thought this far and away the most important.

There is a postscript to this story. After Jenny Bradley's death I went back to the Ile St Louis to meet her nephew, Max Serruys, heir to her books and remaining papers. He and his wife were living in the Bradley house on the quai de Béthune. I was invited to Paris to inspect and appraise the material that M. Serruys had for sale. At the appointed hour I rang the bell and when the door was opened I began to greet the man I correctly took to be Max Serruys. '*Enchanté de faire votre connaissance, cher monsieur*,' I said, extending my right hand to shake his. Then I saw that his hand was in fact an artificial one. Quickly recovering myself (my father-in-law had lost his right hand as a subaltern at Gallipoli when a Mills bomb had exploded prematurely, so I was well used to 'the left hand shake' as practised by the Scout movement), I withdrew my right hand and put the other one forward. M. Serruys offered his left hand and as I took it in mine and began to squeeze it and pump it up and down I realized that that hand too was made of wood. The poor fellow, an industrial chemist, had suffered the loss of both hands when an experiment went sadly wrong and caused an explosion in his laboratory.

The Glaswegian artist and writer, Alexander Trocchi started to come into Bodley House around the time that his novel Young Adam *was published in England (which was in 1961, six years after its original appearance in Paris). Seven years my senior, he was tall and lean – almost cadaverous. I always found him pleasant, friendly and gentle. When* Cain's Book *was published in England in 1963 I read it and liked it enormously and, when I told him so, he proved very ready to talk about his work. Thus it was that I learned that, under the pseudonym of 'Frances Lengel', he had written pornographic novels for Maurice Girodias at the Olympia Press. The titles included* White Thighs, *and* Helen and Desire. *I remember one hilarious passage in which Helen was sold to a sheikh who liked his paramours plump and fattened Helen up on a diet of semolina. As 'Carmencita de las Lunas' he wrote* Thongs, *and as 'Oscar Mole' he translated* The Debauched Hospidar.*

But not all Alex's time in Paris was spent in producing the pornography which a farmer might regard as 'a cash crop'. In the years between 1952 and 1955 he was one of the founding editors of the avant-garde periodical* Merlin *which printed contributions by Samuel Beckett, Patrick Bowles, Christopher Logue and other interesting writers. In the 'sixties I was pleased to buy sets of* Merlin *from Alex, as well as copies of that curious book* Hedyphagetica *by Austryn Wainhouse, one of the co-editors of* Merlin. *Alex also sold me other good things by writers in the* Merlin *circle, but by far the best thing he brought me was the corrected typescript of Beckett's* Watt, *which had been one of the two books which launched the* Collection Merlin *series. I am also grateful to Alex for introducing me to Gregory Corso, perhaps best known for his* Gasoline, *who sold me letters and other original material by fellow members of the City Lights set. I still have as a souvenir of those days a copy of his work of fiction* American Express *(Paris, 1961) inscribed 'For friend Rota from Gregory'.*

I never saw Alex the worse for drugs and when I asked him about the heroin habit he was said to have, he made light of it. He told how he had shocked a BBC reporter who had asked him, over a live microphone, 'And where do you inject it, Mr Trocchi?' expecting, Alex thought, the answer 'In the arm', or 'In the thigh'. Instead he said to the listening millions: 'In the gents at Piccadilly Circus.' He tried to ease my concern for him by telling me not to believe everything I heard about addiction: 'Contrary to what they tell you, it is very easy to give up heroin. I gave it up three times last year.'

CHAPTER THIRTEEN

MORE HANDS TO THE PUMP

In the summer of 1963 something happened in the firm which was as significant in its way as the recruitment of Anthony Newnham some fifteen years before. Needing another member of staff, we advertised in the trade press and were struck by the application of a young Scot called George Lawson. From school in Edinburgh he had trained first at John Grant's bookshop in that city and then at Bredon's in Brighton, where he worked under Raymond Smith, who later had his own business in Eastbourne. When our advertisement appeared George had made the move to London and was working for an academic bookseller at a job which he did not find very satisfying. At his interview the breadth and depth of his knowledge of literature impressed my father greatly, causing him to remark that George was better read than anyone else of his tender years that my father had ever met. With the advantage of hindsight I can now see that George also displayed signs of the lateral thinking with which he approached any problem. We engaged him and, like Newnham before him, he had a lasting impression on the shape, style and direction of the firm. Also like Newnham, he was not cut out to be a nine till five man or a great one for following office routine. He did however bring a sense of fun back into bookshop life.

George's ability to see two moves ahead stood us in good stead on many an occasion, not least when a young collector of Firbank paid us one of his periodic lunchtime visits in February 1967, not long after my father's death. After chatting and gossiping for half an hour or so, the young collector, whose name was John Byrne, said to George, 'Well I mustn't stand here talking. I'm tired of my insurance job in the City and I'm off to Sotheby's to see if they can find a place for me.' Before you could say 'knife' George came back with

George Lawson

'Don't go up to Sotheby's. Let me just see if Anthony is back from lunch.' I was, and George explained the situation to me. At that time we had no vacancy but we were both so impressed by John's qualities that we engaged him on the spot and George set out that very afternoon to buy a desk and chair for him to sit at. *

John used that desk and chair, or a set-up remarkably like it, for the next 28 years, leaving us in 1995 to turn freelance. In the time he was with us he grew tired of hearing me boast to others that he had a mind like a steel trap, but it was true. He became first our specialist in private press books, both the classic presses (Kelmscott, Ashendene, Doves, Golden Cockerel and so on) and the new ventures (such as those of Michael Mitchell at his Libanus Press, Simon Lawrence at his Fleece Press, and Ken Campbell). Second, and I think more to his liking, he became quite brilliant at cataloguing and appraising modern literary archives. He quickly learned the soubriquets, addresses and potted histories of seemingly every significant twentieth century writer in English. He knew who signed himself 'Bunny' (David Garnett), who lived at Brackenburn (Hugh Walpole), and, for example, which poet (Robert Graves) had to appeal through Eddie Marsh, editor of *Georgian Poetry*, to Winston Churchill, then Home Secretary, to avoid his mistress being charged with attempted suicide after she threw herself out of a window.

Working with him on an appraisal was a delight: indeed it still is a delight, for we frequently call him in his freelance capacity when we need another pair of hands, or, for that matter, a 'steel-trap mind.'

One day I had a call from the University of Texas. Dr Ransom, then the Chancellor, had bought from a private observatory in the South West of France a library of important books on astronomy. I was asked if we would go over to France and see to the shipping and export formalities. 'Oh, yes,' my caller added, 'And Dr Ransom also

---

* John says this account is apocryphal. His recollection is that George said 'Weren't you thinking of going into the book trade?' To which John replied 'No.' Whichever account is correct, John was a welcome recruit.

bought the Observatory's telescope!' I said we would be happy to take care of all this, that George would see to it and we would charge the University for his time plus his expenses. George set off the following weekend and after a few days came back and reported that everything had gone very smoothly. He handed me his expense account. When I recovered my breath I said to George that I could not possibly send such a high figure through to Texas without a report explaining how the total had grown to this alarming extent. Twenty-four hours later he put a document in my hand which I can only précis and paraphrase here. It went something like this:

'Being too late to book a direct flight to Bordeaux [George has probably missed more planes than he has caught in the course of his lifetime], I had to fly to Paris, stay overnight and rent a self-drive car for the journey to the observatory. Unfortunately, at this short notice, Hertz could only offer me a rather large Mercedes, the petrol consumption of which does admittedly make the hire-charge rather high. . . . When I checked into a hotel near the observatory, I found that a major French public holiday was fast approaching. If we did not get the books and the telescope packed and loaded on board before that holiday began, we would miss a sailing date and there would be a long delay. Luckily I was able to find a manufacturer of packing cases who was of a sporting disposition and I persuaded him to accept a wager that he and his men could not build the necessary set of custom-made wooden crates in forty-eight hours. Settling this wager cost a further FF1,000.

Once at the observatory I soon realized that there was only one way to get its large telescope out of the building and that was through the open cupola. Lifting a precision instrument of this heavy weight and manoeuvring it through the opening in the cupola was clearly beyond the firm of packers I had engaged. But then I happened to discover that a detachment of the United States Air Force was stationed nearby. I drove over. I went into the N.C.O's Club and said I should like to meet any Top Sergeant who came from Texas. Happily one was found and I explained the predicament to him. As soon as he knew I was working for the state of his birth, he promised to take care of the problem, and promptly introduced me to a friend of his who was in the engineering section. More money changed hands (see attached voucher) and that evening a mobile crane and supporting crew arrived at the observatory and successfully extracted the telescope.

Dealing promptly with bureaucratic minutiae has never been a forte of the French and I was worried whether the shipment would obtain customs clearance before the holiday. I went to the docks, met a moderately senior *douanier* and made him a wager similar to that accepted by the packing-case makers. I bet him FF2,000 that his men could not stamp the necessary documents and have the packing cases on board before the shipping company's deadline. Naturally I lost the bet (see attached voucher) and the vessel sailed on time with books and telescope safely aboard.'

I duly sent on to Warren Roberts, the director of the Humanities Research Center at the university a modest bill for George's time, the rather more extravagant claim for expenses and George's account of how they had arisen. Warren was equal to the occasion. He wrote back: ' I'll pay your bill, Anthony, and I'll pay George's expenses, but only if you throw in the copyright in his account of the affair.'

NORMAN HOLMES PEARSON

One Spring morning in 1968 I was sitting in the far corner of a virtually empty dining room in the Forty Acres Club in Austin, Texas. Wags said that the club's name came from the acreage of carpet in the lobby but in truth the name was a reference to the size of the original campus of the University of Texas.

It was the breakfast hour and I sat contemplating with a jaundiced eye a glass of orange juice, a cup of black coffee and a small pile of aspirins. The night before I had dined not wisely but too well and now, to borrow a phrase from my friend Robert Elwell, the black bird of remorse had settled heavily on my shoulder.

Suddenly I became aware that a stranger had made his way right across the deserted acres of dining room and had settled himself at a table next to mine. I felt mildly piqued for I had deliberately sought out my corner in order to suffer in decent privacy. The stranger began to speak. 'Good morning' he said. I grunted. 'It looks as though it's going to be a really pleasant day.' I grunted again and raised my newspaper hoping that it would act as a barrier: light conversation was the last thing I felt able to cope with.

The stranger spoke again. 'Are you visiting the university?' 'Yes' was my monosyllabic reply. 'Are you lecturing?' 'No'. 'What are you doing then?' 'Consultancy.' 'Consultancy? That's interesting. What are they consulting you about?' 'Rare books' I replied, treating my interlocutor to a two-word answer for the first time. 'Rare books?' he said. 'Where are you from?' Thoroughly on the defensive now I reverted to a one-word answer: 'London'. 'London?' The stranger's face lit up. 'Who are you with?' 'Bertram Rota' I told him, expecting the information to sink like a lead balloon. Instead my interrogator's face lit up. 'Then you must be Anthony Rota' he said. 'I'm Norman Holmes Pearson.' The smile I was to come to know well divided his face from ear to ear. He extended a hand and invited me to join him at his table. My headache rolled away and I suddenly felt on top of the world.

Norman Holmes Pearson had been a customer of mine and of my father's before me for many years. We had corresponded regularly and he was one of the American scholars whom I most respected. We had countless friends and almost as many interests in common. I cannot say that I would have swum the Atlantic to meet him, but I would certainly have gone very far out of my way for the chance to shake his hand. Here we were now, running into one another quite by chance, fifteen hundred miles from his house and four thousand miles from mine. And I had spent fifteen minutes determinedly and resolutely discouraging every friendly overture he had made.

Norman seemed to find the episode as funny as I did and as we began to talk – inevitably about books and bookmen – time went by until breakfast stretched almost to lunch. We spoke about Norman's collection of 'dusty diamonds' – first editions by such authors as G. A. Henty and R. M. Ballantyne. He spoke too of his collection of 'art for the wrong reason' – drawings and paintings by men who were primarily distinguished as writers rather then artists. Victor Hugo, Hilaire Belloc and Denton Welch were among the 'artists' represented. We talked of the pattern of rare book buying in American universities in the nineteen sixties and of the implications for the private collector. We discussed the health of the book trade in England and America – and very much else besides. We parted vowing to meet more regularly, both in London and New Haven, a vow which I am pleased to say we faithfully observed.

Norman seemed to know innumerable celebrated American authors and his office at Yale was filled with mementos of them. He had a story or a quip – always a kindly one – about virtually any author one could name. He was an excellent raconteur and the art of conversation is the poorer for his having gone to his maker. He was a generous man, not merely in terms of public philanthropy but also in doing good by stealth. He was generous too in the amount of time from a busy and crowded life that he devoted to giving help, advice and encouragement whenever and wherever it seemed to be needed. He watched zealously over the literary reputations of the poet, H. D. (Hilda Doolittle) and the novelist, Bryher, taking especial pride in the achievement of these old friends.

He was a most considerate host. I saw him last when I visited Yale to conclude a piece of business that he and I were engaged in together. The business was not to Norman's benefit at all but that of Aurelia Hodgson, widow of the poet Ralph Hodgson. Norman was advising Mrs Hodgson on the disposal of her husband's books and papers and wanted some things for Yale. These I was to value for him so that he could be sure of paying a fair price. He recommended to Mrs Hodgson that she should sell everything else to me and this I am pleased to say she did.

On my arrival in Norman's office to discuss all this I was greeted with a choice of no fewer than four blends of tea. Later I was his guest at a lunch party to which he had invited not only my existing friends at Yale but also those people he thought I ought to meet. The menu had been arranged and wines selected with meticulous care. At the end of the meal Norman had to go off to give a lecture, but he would not leave the table until he had made sure that I would be properly looked after and duly escorted back to my train – yet one more example of the standard of behaviour and courtesy which was entirely natural and from which I never saw him deviate.

CHAPTER FOURTEEN

THE INTERNATIONAL LEAGUE

It happened that in 1971 I was the president of the Antiquarian Booksellers Association when it was Great Britain's turn to act as host to the biennial congress of the International League of Antiquarian Booksellers, the umbrella organisation for national associations of antiquarian booksellers across the world. It was becoming the custom that the congress be followed by an international antiquarian book fair attracting perhaps as many as 200 exhibitors. The congress itself was the responsibility of the League's committee but the physical arrangements, the social programme and the running of the fair were all down to the host association.

Planning started in 1970, when I was vice-president to bluff, genial George Porter, of the Cambridge firm of Galloway and Porter. We set up two committees, one under Tom Crowe (whose Norwich bookshop was a treasure-house), to raise funds and organise the social programme, and the other under Martin Hamlyn, of Peter Murray-Hill Ltd., to be responsible for the fair. I took the chair of a third committee, on which Tom and Martin sat, and we three were responsible for liaison between the other committees.

Dates having been agreed with the League, we set to work in earnest, Tom proving adept at twisting people's arms and getting large donations for our hospitality fund. We then persuaded the Government to give a reception for our foreign guests at Lancaster House. There was to be an opening reception at a West End hotel and a farewell banquet at the Savoy. In today's politically correct climate it is customary for congresses to have an outing for 'spouses' but in 1971 we unashamedly organised a fashion show for wives.

For our principal cultural event we were indebted to Diana

Parikian, dealer in emblem books among other things, and to her husband Manoug, the distinguished violinist, who was a collector of Armenian literature. The Parikians persuaded their friends, Sir Ralph and Lady Verney, with the permission of the National Trust, to allow us to use Claydon, their lovely house in Buckinghamshire, once the home of Florence Nightingale, to stage a concert. Mary Verney herself would play the harpsichord, and no less a diva than Elizabeth Schwarzkopf would sing for us. When Madame Schwarzkopf's agent submitted the programme, it seemed to me to lean too heavily on Hugo Wolf for the simple tastes of our audience and I asked, very diffidently, if the programme could be lightened a little and also whether, as a particular kindness to me, 'Plaisirs d'Amour' could be included (my friends Bob and Gay Elwell had had the Schwarzkopf recording of this song played at their wedding). Back came a feisty reply from La Schwarzkopf: if that was the sort of audience we were she would cheerfully sing Danny Boy!

When the time came the evening was a huge success. As we drew up at Claydon champagne was served on the terrace. One of the coaches lost the way, which meant that several more cases of champagne were served than had been budgeted for, but who was counting? After a delicious candle-lit supper Mary Verney played for us and Schwarzkopf gave us an hour of sheer magic.

The other high point of the week was to be a trip to Chatsworth by private train. In negotiating the hire of this train we asked a manager from British Rail if we could have a bar provided. 'Yes' he said, 'provided you guarantee to spend a minimum of £100 on drink'. 'Good gracious', I replied, 'my committee alone will spend that!'

A bad experience I had in a British Rail buffet car around this time caused me to write to the private hire department stressing what bad publicity it would be for British Rail if our 200 visitors from a dozen nations suffered a similar misadventure. Our contact, the manager, telephoned to say 'I don't know what you said in your letter but I have been told to come with you on the train in case there are any problems. You will have the footplate staff and the dining car staff from the Royal Train, with an inspector riding in the cab so that he can order the signalman to overrule red signals and give us priority. You will also have a separate carriage for your committee and one compartment of it will be filled with replacement light bulbs, clean towels and spare rolls of lavatory paper.'

In the event all went very well indeed. Coffee and drinks were served on the journey north from St Pancras. At Chesterfield we left the train and went by coach through the Peak District to the Duke of Devonshire's estate. There we had lunch before spending the afternoon in Chatsworth's magnificently landscaped grounds. When the house closed to the general public we went in to see a special display in the library. After that we had a picnic tea on the lawns before making our way back to Chesterfield and the waiting train. To the surprise of our French visitors, British Rail served us a splendid meal on the way south and to the astonishment of the Germans, we reached St Pancras exactly on time.

Before these events took place, but when we had finished drawing up the detailed plans, I sent a copy of the programme, together with a layout of how it would look in print, to the president of the League, Fernand de Nobele in Paris. 'How is this?' I asked. Back came the programme with not a word of enthusiasm or praise, merely a note asking me to make the League's logo larger.

SUPERLATIVES

Over the past forty or more years I have been interviewed many times by journalists writing stories for newspapers or articles for periodicals. They all wanted to deal in superlatives. What was the oldest book I had ever handled? What was the rarest? And above all what was the most expensive?

They might as well have asked me which was the heaviest, for I had no meaningful answers to any of these questions. For good or ill my memories are not filed in a way that allows for easy retrieval of this sort of information. There is, however, one question I was never asked but to which I could have given a clear, definitive and absolute answer: what book did I own for the shortest time? The answer is a copy of what was then thought to be the first and only edition of Winston Churchill's Mr Brodrick's Army, *1903.*

I owned it for about six minutes on a Thursday afternoon in 1955. I bought it in Louis Simmonds's bookshop at the junction of Fleet Street and the Strand. Louis sold new books and review copies downstairs and had a few second-hand books tucked away on the first floor. I had called in, as a number of us made a habit of doing, on my way to a one o'clock sale at Hodgson's auction rooms in Chancery Lane. Louis let me go upstairs (the first floor was not open to the public at large) and there I saw peeping out at me from a glass-fronted bookcase the dark red card covers of Mr Brodrick, *a book which I had never seen before and was not to see again for many a year. I paid Louis for that and a few other volumes, the Churchill costing me £10 as I remember, and then hurried across the road to get a seat at Hodgson's comfortably before the sale was due to start. In Hodgson's lobby I fell in with a friend, Harry Mushlin, the Bernard Shaw specialist who was a runner when I first knew him but who later traded from an office/showroom on a top floor in Bond Street. Looking at my parcel he said 'What have you got there?' Elated by my purchase I told him I had just bought that* rara avis, Mr Brodrick's Army. *'I'll give you three times what you paid for it,' Harry replied.*

'But you don't know how much that was,' I quibbled.

'Three times whatever it was,' Harry rejoined. Blinded by the percentage profit I passed the book over and took three crisp, new ten pound notes
in exchange. In the duller moments of the auction sale that followed the
extent of my folly slowly sank in. I tried to console myself by saying 'But
people say it /a collection of speeches attacking William St. John Brodrick,
a reforming Secretary of State for War/ isn't a very good book anyway.'

Five years, passed, and ten, and I eventually saw another copy or two.
Then I had a telephone call from my best Churchill customer, Harry
Cahn, of whom I have written more elsewhere in this book. He asked me
to value for him a 'most unusual' copy of Mr Brodrick which he had
been offered privately. When I saw it, it was 'unusual' indeed. Instead of
making 104 pages in the dark red boards that I have described the text was
crammed into a 44-page pamphlet which bore the price of 'Twopence'
where the edition we were used to seeing was priced at 'One Shilling'. My
first reaction was that the pamphlet must be a cheap reprint that had,
astonishingly, escaped notice till now, but the longer I looked at it the
more convinced I became that what Mr Cahn was offered was an earlier
version which the publisher, Arthur Humphreys, had produced in a small
quantity as a trial, perhaps to win the author's approval. This, I surmised,
he had failed to do. Churchill probably told him in no uncertain terms to
reprint the book in larger type with wider margins and a decent binding.
Fred Woods, compiler of what was then the best of the Churchill bibliographies, took the same view. Mr Cahn bought his copy of what is now
regarded as the true first edition and was well pleased. My reward came
a little while later when another copy of the trial edition turned up from
the same source and I was able to buy it. I sold it again for a good profit
but not for three times what I originally paid! This time I had it in my
hands for as many weeks as I had had my first Mr Brodrick for minutes.

CHAPTER FIFTEEN

AMOR LIBRORUM

The motto of the International League of Antiquarian Booksellers is *amor librorum nos unit* and it is certainly the case that a mutual love of books has brought me wonderfully rewarding friendships.

In writing about the Congress of the ILAB that was held in London in 1971, I told of the hard work that went into planning and fund-raising, and I said that the president of the League, Fernand de Nobele responded to the draft programme merely to say that the League's logo should be made bigger.

On the first day of the Congress my wife and I were present throughout the registration formalities; around noon the de Nobeles arrived, he short, fierce-looking and perhaps sixty years of age, his wife, elegant and gracious and younger. I heard him ask 'Où sont Monsieur et Madame Rota?'. Jean and I went forward and introduced ourselves. He was affable enough, I must admit. She, Laure, was charm itself. It was still with a certain feeling of apprehension that we went to their hotel that evening to take them to the opening reception. Laure appeared to speak no English herself and to understand our language very little if at all. Fernand understood us well enough but resolutely refused to speak anything but French. None the less we found ourselves warming to them and indeed I was so taken by Laure that I went home and settled down after midnight to brush up one or two irregular French verbs the better to communicate with her next day. As the week wore on we came to admire Fernand as well, despite his uncompromising toughness in the League's business meetings. Perhaps this was born out of his experiences as a 'maquisard' in the war. After the Congress was over but before they returned to France, he and Laure took Jean and me to lunch at the Connaught, always a special treat, and there, after inviting us to call him by his soubriquet of Nono, he

put to use knowledge he had gained during the week of my predi-
lection for white Burgundy and red Bordeaux. When we parted he
made us promise to give him warning of our next visit to Paris, so
that he and Laure could entertain us there.

In the following year we were indeed heading in the direction
of that most sybaritic of cities and wrote to Nono accordingly. A
postal strike meant that he was unable to get a reply to us. I rang him
when we checked into our hotel and thought what he said to me
translated into English as 'Can you come for lunch or dinner on
Tuesday or Thursday?' I replied that dinner on Thursday would
suit us very well. 'No, no, no,' he expostulated, 'I said lunch *and*
dinner on one of those days'. I explained that we would have our
sons with us, then aged 10 and 8. 'Bring them to the shop at noon' he
ordered, still speaking only French. At the appointed hour we duly
reported to the shop in the Rue Napoleon, where he carried on his
business in books on the fine and applied arts. Nono worked from a
little office, scarcely more than a desk and two chairs, curtained off
from the public area at the front of the shop. It seemed a very small
space for the man who was president of the League, and regarded
by many as the doyen of the antiquarian book trade worldwide. 'It
is important that your boys should know about café society' Nono
stated. 'So we will go across the road to the Café Flore and there
Laure will join us'.

It was obvious that Nono was well known in that establishment,
for we had no sooner sat down than a bottle of Pouilly Fumé and a
plate of hard-boiled eggs was set before us. Nono told us that he
stopped at the Flore every night before going home and always ordered a bottle of Pouilly Fumé. 'Sometimes Laure will join me and
sometimes I will finish it alone' he said. It was to this habit that he
later attributed his long life. Over our aperitif he told us that he was
taking us to lunch at the Eiffel Tower Restaurant: 'The food is
comme-ci, comme-ça but the view is *magnifique!*'

Suiting action to words, he went outside and hailed two taxis,
packing Jean, Laure and the boys into one, and taking the second
for himself and for me. Once inside this taxi and alone together,

with the glass screen cutting us off from the driver, he astonished me by speaking freely and easily in colloquial English. His refusal to do so in public was merely his way of ensuring that the importance of the French language in the workings of the League was not diminished.

At the Eiffel Tower he once again indulged my preference for white Burgundy and red Bordeaux but seemed put out when I declined a glass of *marc* at the end of the meal. I told him I had to work that afternoon. He said he thought that a very poor excuse, but that he and Laure would expect us at their apartment no later than 7.30. We took our leave and made our way to the Ile St Louis, where I paid a courtesy call on Jenny Bradley. She received us graciously and we had not been sitting in her drawing room for long when the clock struck four. 'Ah!' she said, 'c'est l'heure du thé. Monsieur Rota savait.' Sure enough there followed a tap at the door and in came the maid bearing the 'tea-time' tray of Lanson Black Label champagne and five glasses. Our sons' education was proceeding apace.

In due course we fed the boys an early supper, and left them safely tucked up in the hotel. At 7.35 we made our way through the market of Saint Sulpice and presented ourselves at the door of the de Nobele apartment. Nono opened to our ring. 'Anthony, que vous êtes en retard', he remonstrated, as there came a loud pop of a champagne cork from the depths of the apartment. We saw off the bottle of champagne and then repaired to Le Recamier, which Nono dismissed as only *'une maison du quartier'* but which was actually an extremely good restaurant. Without consulting us he ordered the house aperitif, which turned out to be a pink champagne cocktail, and then again there was white wine and red wine to suit my taste. At the end of the meal the *maître d'hotel* came over and put a bottle of *marc* on the table and said, 'Avec les compliments de la maison, monsieur'. 'Now', Nono said to me, 'You cannot refuse, Anthony'. Never in my life had I consumed so much alcohol in one day and it says something for the quality of the wines that were set before us that we felt no ill effects whatsoever, either that night or the following morning. This was the first of many happy evenings we were to spend with the de Nobeles in Paris and in London. We were even able to do a little business together. For example when Jenny Bradley died a few years later and I was invited to offer for the library that she and her husband had built up, I asked Nono to bid for the French art books, saving just the literature for myself.

Then came an event which proved embarrassing in the extreme. Nono turned up unexpectedly at the London Book Fair one year. We had on display a book of views of St Petersburg, a city with which he had particular connections, and after making a cursory study of it and being quite tough about the price, Nono bought it, paying me in brand-new notes produced from his back pocket. The price was, as I remember it, something in the order of £1,200. At the same Fair in the following year he arrived at our stand again and said he had something disturbing to tell me: the book which I had sold him last year was imperfect, lacking what was arguably the best plate. Horrified, I said as a reflex action that I would at once take the book back and refund his money. 'After a year?' he questioned. I said I would insist on it and proceeded to write him out a cheque. We arranged that I would collect the book from his hotel that evening. In the meantime I turned to my colleague, Ron Taylor, who was responsible for books in that area and said how angry I was that he should have allowed me to sell a defective book at all, let alone to a man who had until recently been president of our international trade body. Ron countered: 'Anthony, I collated that book when we bought it and it was perfect'. We agreed to inspect it together in the morning and when we did so, I must say that I found the absence of the plate impossible to miss. A trade association subcommittee was meeting on our premises that day and I took the opportunity of getting half-a-dozen further expert opinions. No one of us could see how even the most hurried collation could have failed to spot the rather crudely trimmed stub, so I telephoned Nicolas Barker, who was then Head of Conservation at the British Library and asked for his help. He agreed to have the book examined under an electron microscope in the Library's laboratory. It came back with an opinion which confirmed Ron Taylor's defence. Nicolas said that the stub appeared to have been made with a razor blade, almost certainly left-handedly. That the dreadful deed had been done very recently was borne out by two facts: seen in end-section the stub resembled a cream-cheese sandwich made with wholemeal bread (in other words the central core of the paper had only been exposed to the atmosphere for a very short time), furthermore tiny flecks of paper, scarcely visible to the naked eye, were still falling from the cut edge every time the book was moved.

Now Nono had told me that when the book had arrived in Paris in the previous year he had not left it in the shop but had taken it home and put it in the bookcase in the hall of the very apartment that I had visited. He said that it was only when he went to show it to a caller a few weeks ago that he had discovered that a plate was missing. I told him of the British Library laboratory report and he flared up at once, asking what I was implying. In reply I invited him to have the book examined by experts at the Bibliothèque Nationale, or by any other laboratory he would care to nominate, but he would have none of it. What was I to do? Here was a past-president of the French trade association and of the International League, a member of the Légion d'Honneur and a bookseller of the highest reputation – and yet the British Library report showed that there had been dirty work at the crossroads. I decided to swallow both my pride and the financial loss. I later discovered that Nono had once been systematically robbed by a manager whom he had treated as virtually one of the family: I do not think he could bear the thought that a second person close to him had also betrayed him. Somehow we managed never to speak of the matter again.

The years went by and we continued to meet for Lucullan feasts and for talk about the ILAB, on whose committee I was now serving. It was at a Congress in Paris, in 1988, that I was elected to the presidency that Nono had once held. Nono was by now alas too ill to take part in the proceedings but he was still able to go to his shop for an hour or so on most days and we were able to see him there for a few minutes before going to the formal opening of a special exhibition at the Bibliothèque Nationale. Nono had always encouraged me to take up work for the League and now gave me his blessing as I began a term of office dedicated to promoting its name and burnishing its reputation. We parted, each of us knowing that we should never meet again in this life, and each choking back the tears.

NOW, ABOUT THAT SILVER SPOON

Ten or a dozen years ago Jake Chernofsky, editor of AB Bookman's Weekly, was touring England with one of his associate editors, conducting interviews for an issue on the British book trade. While they were talking to me one or two matters relating to current trade practice and ethics arose and Jake asked me to write an article on the subject, which I duly did. In it I said inter alia that I thought that the 'cult of the dust-wrapper' had gone too far and that the premiums sometimes asked for the presence of a dust-jacket were becoming absurd. I had in mind a couple of cases where copies without jackets might sell for £500 and where £10,000 or even £15,000 had been asked for a jacketed copy. I also remarked that young entrants to the book trade were now reluctant to serve any kind of 'apprenticeship' and that many of them learned their job and gained experience at the expense of their customers, the point being that the existence of so many book fairs, not those sponsored by the Antiquarian Booksellers Association or the International League of Antiquarian Booksellers, made it almost too easy for the absolute tyro to get a start.

Publication of the article brought quite a large post bag, mostly from dealers of my own age or older, saying how much they agreed with me. This left me totally unprepared for the vehemence of a letter to AB Bookman's Weekly from Tom Congleton, who trades as 'Between the Covers', whom at that time I had never met. He accused me of being an 'anti-American socialist' and to this day I do not know which of the two epithets those who knew me found more hilarious. Tom Congleton, who is now president of the Antiquarian Booksellers Association of America, and thus a member of the book trade Establishment, went on to say that I had been born, in effect, with a silver book in my mouth, by which he meant that I had inherited the business formed by my father, the implication being that I had therefore had things made easy for me.

I replied that when, after two years at 20th Century Fox and two years national service in the Royal Air Force, I joined my father in 1952, I did indeed have certain privileges. I was given my own set of keys so that I could be sure of being first in in the morning and last to leave at night.

(I made a practice of this so that no-one could point the finger at the boss's son and say that I was doing things the easy way.) I also had the privilege of dusting the books on a regular basis. This proved a very valuable exercise: it not only helped me to know exactly what was in stock but the number of times the book got dusted was a fair indication of what was in demand and what was not. I added that after I had worked at my father's side for fourteen years he had died, leaving me shares in the business, but very little else and that the shares carried with them an inordinate demand for death duties from the Inland Revenue. In fact what I had been left was not money but a machine which, given sufficient hard work, was capable of producing money.

It was true that I had inherited a large stock, a good staff, attractive premises, and a firm with an enviable reputation which my father had established over many years. What I did not add was that I also 'inherited' a number of wonderful friends. By this I mean that as my father's son I had been introduced to many of his friends, men of his own generation, with whom I had formed friendships of my own. I mean such collectors as Rupert Hart-Davis, Simon Nowell-Smith, and George Lazarus; such booksellers as Dudley Massey, 'Dusty' Miller, Percy Muir and, in America, David Magee; and such librarians as Lawrence Clark Powell and John Gordan. I often think that these friends were my father's greatest 'legacy'.

CHAPTER SIXTEEN

ROBERT ELWELL

IN WHICH I MEET A GENTLEMAN

A bookseller's mailing list is rather like a revolving door: people are coming in and going out all the time. I am not quite sure at what point I became aware of a new name on ours, that of Robert Elwell, an advertising executive of New York City. He was in fact Creative Director of a very considerable agency and when someone mistakenly described him as an account executive, he quipped 'Art Directors get ideas, Account Executives get coffee'. Bob Elwell, who turned out to be almost my exact contemporary, became a useful customer, regularly ordering from our catalogues the kind of first editions that I myself would have bought had that not put me in competition with my clients. (A bookseller who is a collector manqué is a fool indeed.) Then in 1962, in company with George and Beryl Sims, my wife and I visited The Netherlands for the first time. Primarily in Amsterdam but also in The Hague we found English books in such shops as Erasmus, the Schumachers' (their building leaning crazily towards the nearby canal), Israel (both Max and Nico) and Menno Hertzberger and his partner Dolf Van Gendt; and in The Hague, Minerva and Martinus Nijhoff. (We found visiting Nijhoff an infuriating business, for one could not browse the shelves but had instead to work through a card catalogue. Anton Gerits, who was to become such a good friend when he and I were elected to the committee of the International League, was working for Nijhoff at that time but alas I did not meet him until twenty years later). In the course of our visits to bookshops, primarily seeking English books, and foreign language editions of English authors, George Sims and I gradually became aware of the quality of Dutch editions of some of the finest English writers, produced under clandestine conditions during the Nazi occupation. The Press of the Busy Bee produced a number of such things. Charles Nypels produced more, but had I been awarding a prize it would have gone to A. A. M. Stols for his work at the Halcyon Press, perhaps for his edition of André Gide's *Le Voyage d'Urien* or his Büchner's *Dantons Tod*. The Gide has coloured wood-engravings by Alfred Latour, the initials and title being by Alphonse Stols. The book was set in Lutetia type and printed by Boosten & Stols in black, red and blue. The Büchner, on the other hand, was set in Garamond, printed in the same combination of colours. The fly-title is a particularly fine example of Stols's design and this is one of the very few books in which he used fleurons.

Back home after a profitable and enjoyable visit, I put in our Catalogue 127, Autumn 1962, an appendix of mid-20th century Dutch printing, both clandestine and otherwise. I wrote just one short paragraph extolling the virtues of these books and later learned that it had been sufficient to strike a spark in Bob Elwell's imagination and to start him on the road to forming one of the great collections of modern European printing.

As I have implied, I was not really aware of what I had started, but I do recall receiving a letter from Bob who, like me, lived by a slightly antiquated code and who, if he could not do a thing stylishly, would not do it at all. My précis does him no justice but in effect this is what he said: 'Dear Mr Rota, It has always been my belief that a man should know his bookseller, and with this in mind I should like you to join my wife and myself for lunch at Brown's Hotel on any day of your choosing during the week commencing such and such when we will be visiting London.' A precise appointment was made and on the due day and at the due hour I presented myself at Brown's and gave my name. The *maître d'hôtel* scurried across the room and whispered to a beautiful and elegant redhead who was sitting by herself. It transpired that she was Bob's wife, the actress Gay Jordan. She quickly gave instructions to the *maître d'* who ushered me across the floor. Gay introduced herself and apologised for Bob who, if I remember rightly, had been having a suit fitted at a tailor who, by a strange coincidence, shared premises with mine, just off Savile Row. Bob turned up a moment or two later and thus began a friendship which became like that of David and Jonathan and lasted until his far too early death at the age of 66 in 1995.

Virtually from that day on the Elwells and the Rotas dined together whenever we were in the same city, be that city London or New York. Bob and I were so exactly in tune with one another that he soon became to me the brother I never had.

He and Gay owned an engaging pedigree poodle. They called it Max. 'I suppose that's after Max Beerbohm' I said (Beerbohm was one of the authors that Bob collected). 'No' he said, 'he's named after *Les Maximes* de La Rochefoucauld.' On another occasion I had sent first a letter giving dates of my impending descent on New York, and then in view of the Elwells' silence, followed it with a rather petulant telegram. Still no answer. From the airport I rang my office and said 'Are there any messages?' My secretary, Anne Prior, replied 'There is a cable from Mr Elwell beginning "*Mea culpa, mea culpa, mea maxima culpa* . . . ."'

There came a time when some previous engagement interfered with our pattern of passing the evenings, so on the day in question Bob took me to lunch at Christcellas where tables were very hard to get and where there was no printed menu. 'I think you will like this', he said. 'It's where the guys from the Round Table at the Algonquin used to go when they were trying to escape from Dorothy Parker.'

In London one day Bob and Gay were our guests at dinner together with two friends of ours who had recently returned from half-a-lifetime's farming in Southern Rhodesia. Our friend, who like Isak Dinesen, 'had a farm in Africa,' gushed at Bob and Gay, 'Are you really American? You don't sound a bit as I expected.' With less time than it takes for a squash ball to come to a stop on the wall at the end of the court and reverse direction, Bob came back with 'Well you see Gay's an actress and I'm just a phoney from way back.'

A diabetic, he had to be very careful about his sugar intake but I always suspected that it was not solely for that reason that he once returned a barman's four successive attempts at making 'a really dry' Rob Roy cocktail in a smart Manhattan restaurant.

As I enjoyed the jokes, the meals and the good fellowship, as Jean and I watched our children grow and become friends of Bob's and Gay's in their own right, the library of fine printing, English, American and continental European was continuing to expand. In America Bob bought largely from Herman Cohen of the Chiswick Bookshop. In London he bought largely from me, and on the continent of Europe he relied on help from Percy Muir and Dr Hauswedell.

A man of strong principle, with a low flash-point, Bob could manage to have a serious row quite quickly. He left the security of one of New York's larger advertising agencies to be part of a tri-umvirate which rapidly headed for the heights as one of the newer and brighter agencies on Madison Avenue. Bob was the ideas man; someone else brought in the clients and the third man provided the capital. One of Bob's major successes was the campaign for Smirnoff vodka, with its particularly witty advertisements. Something about one client displeased him and when his partners would not take the stand that he was prepared to take, he walked out in dudgeon and, apart from some private commissions from Smirnoff, never worked again. He came very near to succeeding as a novelist and as a play-wright but his agency days were over. It was soon after this that Gay started her catering business, its name, 'Gay Jordan, Bespoke Food', being dreamed up by Bob, who was a strong right arm to her in the enterprise.

Year succeeded year and Bob came no nearer finding his own source of major alternative income. As a volunteer he mounted exhibitions for the Grolier Club, and edited the *Grolier Gazette*. He continued to polish and repolish stage plays and television scripts, but nothing actually came off. Then in the spring of 1974, on my last night in New York, on my way back to London after two or three weeks spent touring America, I was having supper with Bob and

Gay in their so familiar but always stimulating apartment on Lexington Avenue. (Gay refused to let me eat airline food, saying quite rightly that it was bad for one's equanimity. If I insisted on taking a night flight home she would say that at least she would arrange that I was properly fed before I embarked upon it). On this occasion as on many others the doorman called up from downstairs to say that my taxi was at the door. I hefted my suitcase and started on the long journey back to Heathrow. Before I had gone two paces Bob said to me 'I'm going to have to sell my books'. '*Now* you tell me!' I countered, 'I'll go home, ring you and arrange to come back next week'. And except for making it a two week delay rather than one week, that is exactly what I did. I barely had time to recover from one attack of jet lag before I courted another. However I did use the time in between to sit with the requisite volumes of European auction records on my lap while I studied again Bob's idiosyncratic, typewritten catalogue of his collection. I particularly liked entries of the kind that he wrote for Stargardt's monumental edition of *The Ring of the Niebelung* designed and illustrated by Joseph Sattler and intended by the State Printing Office as their showpiece for the Paris Exhibition of 1900 (it wasn't finished till 1904). Bob's footnote for this *magnum opus*, which, to judge from its weight, might have been printed on lead and bound in concrete, was 'As influential, as heavy and as ugly as the Kelmscott Chaucer'.

Arrived in New York, not even stopping to drop my bag at Phyllis Gordan's house on East 78th Street (saint that she was, she had kindly agreed to put me up for this sudden unexpected trip to her city), I went straight to Bob and Gay's apartment, just around the corner on Lexington Avenue. Poor Bob had the mother and father of all colds but was determined to rise above it and soldier on. The first and most important task was to complete a financial appraisal of the collection. This meant working our way steadily through some twelve or thirteen hundred volumes, some of which were either so scarce or so *recherché* as to put it outside any one dealer's immediate competence to value every book in the library on sight. Working in the order of the catalogue entries (which appeared to be

by date of acquisition), we looked at each book, considered its auction record and/or its retail record where these were available to us,
put in our respective experience of the particular title (Bob knew
what he had paid, I knew how many other copies I had or had not
seen), and eventually arrived at a retail figure we were both happy
with. Pausing only for dinner, admittedly a good one, we worked
on until 10 o'clock at night (3 a.m. by the time on which my body
was still running). We reassembled at eight the next morning and
worked till ten p.m. once more. On the third day we rose again, and
by about seven o'clock in the evening our task was accomplished.
We got out the adding machine, took into consideration what
should be added to the total price because of the wide range of
the material and the difficulty there would be in trying to duplicate
it, and then deducted what one might call a discount for quantity.
Having arrived at a retail asking price for the collection if sold *en
bloc* we went out for a truly celebratory dinner. We came home by
taxi and Bob and Gay let me out on 78th street at about 11 o'clock,
when the Gordan house was in darkness. In getting out of the cab I
managed to get my thumb caught in the door just as Bob slammed
it to. He offered to call his doctor, who was also his friend, but not
wanting to be of trouble to anyone at that hour of night, and with
the thumb not yet hurting too much, I brushed Bob's offer aside,
said *au revoir* and went into the Gordan house. As the hours went
by the nail blackened and the pressure grew, and I spent most of the
night holding my fist under a cold tap every fifteen minutes or so.

In the morning Phyllis wanted me to see a doctor but I thought
it more important to catch my flight home. 'I'll go to the first aid
room at the airport' I said. After I had checked in (and thank goodness I was travelling business class) I said 'Now I should like to go to
the sickbay please'. 'What?' said the check-in clerk. I explained my
predicament. 'Just talk to the nice young lady in the Executive
Club sir' he replied. I duly did so and she brought me a bowl of ice
and two aspirins.

On the plane I was brought another bowl of ice and yet more
aspirins and I travelled back in the little upstairs cabin with one

hand immersed in ice and the other firmly wrapped round a glass of Bloody Mary, which proved to be quite the thing for washing aspirins down.

At Heathrow I reclaimed my car and drove home gingerly with only one hand grasping the wheel. I arrived just before midnight. My house was in darkness, just as Phyllis Gordan's had been the night before and it was much too late to make a fuss or to call my own doctor out. It was only next morning that I went to the Casualty Department of the hospital, where a nurse took an ordinary common-or-garden paper-clip, straightened it out, sterilized it in a flame and then pushed it through the thumb nail, causing an eruption of black blood on a scale that Vesuvius would have been proud of. Later I lost the nail and the one that grew in its place remains to this day ridged to an extreme degree as compared to its smooth counterpart on the other hand. If I could set the clock back and save the nail but forego the library, I am quite sure my decision would be to sacrifice the nail once again.

But back to the books. Our first hope was to sell them as an integral collection. And with that in mind Philip McNiff, gifted and genial director of Boston Public Library, travelled down to New York to look the collection over. He liked it enormously but found he couldn't raise the price. Bob and I therefore did a little horse trading and arrived at a figure at which I would buy this hugely attractive library and pay him in instalments. Once the books were on their way to London we cleared the shelves in the reserve stock area of our shop, then in commodious premises at 4, 5 and 6 Savile Row. The crates duly arrived and we had a field day unwrapping the books and putting them on the shelves.

We had barely finished this when Decherd Turner, at that time still director of the Bridwell Library at Southern Methodist University, came through London. Decherd was one of that old school of librarians who actually liked books, and he made it his business to handle them on a regular basis. On the morning of his visit to Savile Row I had some of the happiest hours of my professional life as Decherd and I went through the books, each seeking out his own favourites and showing them off to the other, stressing their special qualities and their hidden significance.

The books to which I drew Decherd's attention included the edition of Nietzsche's *Also sprach Zarathustra* designed by Henry Van de Velde for Insel Verlag in 1908. 530 copies of this folio volume were printed in black, red and gold, and were numbered in the press, a conceit very much to my taste, bettered only by editions 'numbered *ad personam*' (i.e. in which the name of each recipient is printed in the colophon of his or her copy). *Zarathustra* is widely regarded as Van de Velde's greatest book, and one of the masterpieces of German printing. An architect as well as a decorator, Van de Velde approached books as architecture, using ornaments as building blocks of decoration. Unlike other designers in the *Art Nouveau* and *Jugendstil* movements, he preferred abstract ornament to the more usual florid designs. The double-page title spread and the four full-page section headings of *Zarathustra*, all elaborate designs in maroon and gold, are quite magnificent.

I also pointed out the edition of *The Song of Songs* designed and printed by Gotthard de Beauclair in 1962. Another folio, this was bound in boards covered with russet silk. The text, set in Monotype Bell Antiqua, was wrapped around (no other phrase will do) by Gerhart Kraaz's exciting lithographs, presenting a perfect marriage of text and illustration. Decherd showed me equally fine things.

All this was done without any sense of rivalry or competition. Neither of us was trying to show how much more he knew than the other: each was merely anxious to share his knowledge in order to facilitate a greater appreciation and hence a greater pleasure. I hope that Dr Turner enjoyed the day as much as I did. I believe it was so.

Of course any number of high spots from the library could have been sold right away, but we were anxious to honour Bob Elwell's knowledge and taste in forming the collection by making a permanent record of it in the form of a printed catalogue. He had kept back just half-a-dozen books, by the way. They included Eric Gill's edition of the *Four Gospels* (Golden Cockerel Press, 1930); Giovanni Mardersteig's edition of *The Holy Gospels* (Officina Bodoni, 1962);

the edition of *The Book of Psalms* put out by the Stichting de Roos (Utrecht, 1947); and *Das Blumenbuch*, 250 flower drawings by Rudolph Koch, cut in wood by Fritz Kredel (Ernst-Ludwig-Presse, 1928-30). This last was a particular favourite of Bob's and he was fond of pointing out that it was this Ernst-Ludwig-Presse edition of 135 copies that was the true first, and not as many people wrongly supposed the three-volume Mainzer Presse edition published by Insel-Verlag in 1929-30.

So we would make a special catalogue. Who was to do the work? Our regular cataloguing staff was already pretty fully engaged. Moreover more than half the books were in German. Most of us could manage French and Latin, and John Byrne, our private press books supremo, still had a quantity of Greek from his college days, but German was another matter. We needed to find a German speaker with some knowledge of rare books. Salvation came from an unexpected quarter. Warren Roberts' daughter Vicki had just finished a course at a German university and was preparing to embark on a career as a German language teacher in her native Texas. She had grown up in the shadow of her father's work in compiling the definitive bibliography of D. H. Lawrence and had been engaged on various tasks around the Humanities Research Center at the University of Texas as vacation jobs while her father was Director there. She agreed to fly to London to help us out for a few months. She began by making each of us a simple vocabulary covering such phrases as 'impression', 'edition', 'handmade paper', 'edited by' and so on. In exchange we gave her a table of book-sizes. Between us I think we managed rather well. Certainly no-one could have worked more conscientiously than Vicki did. It would not have been surprising if she had sought special privileges by virtue of her father's position – he was after all director of the library which was our most important single customer – but if Warren's status affected Vicki at all it was to make her especially punctilious about being early to work, keeping her nose to the grindstone, and being ready to turn her hand to any task, be it making the tea or literally or metaphorically sweeping the floor. At one point she succumbed to a bout of influenza and virtually crawled into work on her hands and knees. We really had to be quite fierce to get her to go back to her digs and take off the time necessary to get herself well again. There were a dozen or more working in the firm at that time and most of us had been part of the team for many years. I can never remember anyone coming in from outside and fitting in so smoothly and with such universal popularity as Vicki.

She, John Byrne and I did most of the cataloguing, which took care of the preparation of the text, but how to present it remained an open question. For an answer we turned to John Ryder, Art Director of the Bodley Head Group, who had been unofficial and, alas, unpaid (save for the occasional case of wine) typographer to the company for some time. The Elwell library, consisting for the most part of well-designed and well-printed books, books moreover which had a relatively high unit value, meant that we could give John Ryder a blank sheet of paper to draw on: we were not obliged to hedge him round with the factors that controlled the production of our regular series of first edition catalogues. We were not committed to a particular format; we had no long-term contract with a particular printer; and there was no great urgency (at least there wasn't when we started). John, whose keen eye and typographical taste influenced the appearance of books of an entire generation, not just those which he himself designed but also those which were designed by people he had trained, by people who had read his books on printing and typography, and by printers to whom he acted as typographical consultant, turned up trumps on this occasion. His chosen printer was McKay's of Chatham, who did a job with which we were well pleased. John chose a page size of 9½ by 6¼ inches and devised a typographical layout based on Bruce Rogers' Centaur type, with Frederic Warde's Arrighi italic. We were able to be fairly generous with illustrations. Because the collection contained a number of *Livres d'Artistes*, and because we were trying to make a point about links between artists and craftsmen, we called the catalogue *The Printer and the Artist*. No. 192, it appeared in the Autumn of 1974. In terms of sales it did quite well and it certainly

John Ryder, *æt* 80

attracted very favourable critical attention. We were proud of it because it was the first assemblage of so many finely printed books from continental Europe, and in particular from Germany, to be catalogued in English. We were able to point out and to demonstrate that in Germany not all the best 'fine printing' came from Private Presses; much came from the house presses of the typefoundries, Klingspor being a particularly good example. Our one disappointment was that most of our sales of the German books were to existing buyers for such things, where we had hoped to carve out a new market. If that was a disappointment I also have a regret: it is that time prevented us (yes, it became a rush in the end) from making an index. Over the long years since the catalogue first appeared I have had several shots at putting that right and in my compilation I have got as far as the letter D. Perhaps I shall be able to complete the job if and when I retire.

A light went out in my world and it became a duller place the day that Bob Elwell died, but I take solace in a thousand memories. I remember how we used to introduce one another to unfamiliar music. He brought me to Walter Piston and I led him to a liking for Mahler. I told him about the big bass drum beat in the 10th Symphony. I remember the year when Bob first had a quadraphonic sound system and played me that drum beat so strongly and so often that the whole apartment began to shake. I remember going with Bob and Gay to a Manhattan gallery on one Saturday afternoon to see a show of drawings – largely erotic – by Hans Bellmer, whom I knew as a book illustrator. This was quite early in our relationship. I feared the drawings would make me blush. I was very glad that Gay was wearing dark glasses so that looking her in the eye was not such a difficult matter after all.

I remember my delight on reading Bob's *Playground*, a play based on *La Dame aux Camélias* and, again, his two-hander called *Lighthouse* which for me summed up the battle between the sexes at least as well as *Who's Afraid of Virginia Woolf?*. I remember my abiding pleasure when Bob sent me copies of his plays inscribed 'From an author who has been fortunate enough to find his audience.'

It was Bob who introduced me to that best of book collecting societies, The Grolier Club, and who in 1971 put me up for membership of that august body. It was there that I saw the first of the three great Grolier exhibitions for which he was responsible, a show of late nineteenth and twentieth century German book illustration. Drawn largely from his own library, the exhibition was arranged to show the development from *fin de siècle* through expressionism to modernism. Even without reading the captions it was easy to see the dividing lines, like two great clefts in the file of showcases, marking the two world wars and their dreadful effects. Bob persuaded the club to break new ground with his second show in as much as it was their first retrospective exhibition devoted to the work of a living artist, Fritz Kredel. I went with Bob to meet Alfred Howell, then Grolier President, to carry books and drawings from Kredel's walk-up studio way uptown to Warren's station wagon for the journey to the clubhouse on East 60th Street. Bob rightly predicted that I would adore meeting Kredel, whom he aptly described as 'an elf from the Black Forest'.

Bob's last Grolier show was styled 'Books as Trouble-Makers'. He invited fellow members to nominate up to three books – and here was the departure from precedent – and write and *sign* the catalogue cards that would sit beside the books in the showcases. Nominations included Foxe's *Book of Martyrs*, 1563, *The Protocols of the Elders of Zion* (the evil forgery designed to whip up anti-Jewish feeling), Marx's *Das Kapital*, 1867, *Mein Kampf*, 1925-27 and Chairman Mao's *Little Red Book*. The exhibition was a huge success, attracting much publicity and a large attendance, but the club refused to publish a catalogue, pleading shortage of funds. I offered to publish it myself, making copies available free to every member, and splitting the eventual profit with the club. In response I had a letter from one senior member of the club council and a visit from another, both saying that I 'was doing myself no good' by proposing this. I think the real fear was that the club might appear to be offering its imprimatur to a list that might come to be thought of as definitive. I made the mistake of telling Bob what had passed and

The Printer and the Artist

**A catalogue of Private Press Books &
Illustrated Books from the United
Kingdom, Europe & America**

Bertram Rota Ltd

The Printer and the Artist, Catalogue 192, 1971
(initials in red; reduced)

he resigned not only from the council, but from the club as well. As an ironic reminder of the affair Bob gave me the catalogue show-cards that had caused the controversy.

Another happier memory is of a Sunday morning in 1971 during the duration of the New York Antiquarian Book Fair. The Antiquarian Booksellers' Association of America held a formal luncheon in the hotel where the Fair was being staged. I attended as a fraternal delegate and made a short speech inviting the assembled company to attend the congress of the International League of Antiquarian Booksellers which was to be held in London later that year. Bill Fletcher, who was also present, reported to the next meeting of the committee of our own trade association that I had spoken, and he kindly said, had spoken well. He concluded 'And because of New York's licensing laws', (alcoholic drinks could not be sold on Sunday mornings) 'he did it stone cold sober!' What Bill did not know was that Bob, all too well aware of the restriction, had furnished me with a truly massive Bloody Mary before I went to the hotel, giving me the Dutch courage he thought I needed before making my first speech from a podium decorated with the Stars and Stripes.

I suppose that, in all, the Rotas and the Elwells were together for a few hours a day on a series of four consecutive days twice a year for some thirty-four years, which is the rough equivalent of living in houses 100 yards apart for perhaps two months out of a lifetime. That is not an awful lot but we made every moment count.

FRANK HOLLINGS : ARRANGING THE STOCK

In 1969 Bertram Rota Ltd purchased the business of Frank Hollings Bookshop as a going concern. Founded in 1892 by Frank Hollings Shepherd, Hollings had become, like my firm, primarily a specialist in modern first editions, but it also had many older books, and books on subjects other than literature among its stock.

Hollings and Bertram Rota Ltd used the same firm of auditors so it was not surprising that when the then proprietor of Hollings, A. T. (Dusty) Miller, reached the age when he wanted to retire, I was asked if I was interested in taking the firm over. I was very much interested, and, in consequence, on the next Saturday morning I went over to Hollings' premises in Cloth Fair, an attractive and historic corner of London, set between St Bartholomew's church, St Bartholomew's hospital and Smithfield meat market. I was accompanied by Ron Taylor, head of Bertram Rota Ltd's antiquarian book department.

The Cloth Fair building comprised a number of small rooms arranged on three floors. All the rooms were crammed with books. On this morning Ron and I wanted to get a rough impression of what we would be prepared to pay for the stock. Pencil and notebook at the ready, I went into a room where I could see a number of first editions in their dust-wrappers. Ron went into the room on the other side of the landing, where calf bindings at first appeared to predominate. After appraising two or three Hemingway first editions and a couple of books by T. S. Eliot I was surprised to find an early theological work. On a shelf below it was a fine colour plate book, a Pomona if I remember rightly. I backed out onto the landing, scratching my head, and nearly collided with Ron, who was coming from the other direction doing the same thing, for he had found modern books mixed up with the works from earlier centuries which were his responsibility.

I called down the stairs to Dusty, who was sitting in front of the only fire that the building seemed to boast. 'Dusty, we are having a little trouble sorting out what is where. Would you be kind enough to come upstairs and explain the system of arranging the stock to us?'

'System?' Dusty responded, and gave the deep slow laugh, which I can only describe as something like a rather loud chortle, which was his trademark. 'The system (and I could almost hear him setting the word in italics) is that if I buy a short fat book I look for a short fat hole on the shelf!'

CHAPTER SEVENTEEN

SOURCES

When my father came back from holiday or from a business trip he would always say 'Don't tell me what you've sold, tell me what you've bought.' He was thus underlining the importance of ensuring the arrival of a steady stream of good things if a bookshop is to flourish. 'Take care of the buying, and the selling will take care of itself.' I don't know if this is a book-trade truism but if it is not, it most certainly should be. By fair dealing and by his unfailingly courteous behaviour towards fellow members of the trade, be they exalted or be they the lowliest newcomer, my father had built up excellent relationships which stood the firm in good stead. I try to keep them furbished.

One source of good books for us obliged us to play by his rules. The son of a bookseller, he had closed the shop when his father died and had taken up a line of work which I imagine he found more profitable. His name was Herbert Jenkins and he lived with his wife and daughter in a semi-detached house in Enfield that was always as neat as the proverbial new pin. Apart from a small glass-fronted bookcase in the drawing-room there was no sign downstairs of the secondary business which took place above. Jenkins, a quiet and gentle, well-built man with a shock of prematurely white hair, apparently toured the country attending auctions of second-hand electric motors and similar equipment. I never did learn the details of his job, but it appeared to leave enough leisure for him to attend house sales and general auctions where odd lots of books were occasionally to be found. With his expenses paid from the electrical business Jenkins's book-buying activities were subsidised to a useful degree. He would bring his purchases back to Enfield in his estate car and then with commendable strength and agility, carry them upstairs onto the landing, and thence by means of an extension ladder, into the storage space he had constructed in the loft.

Jenkins subscribed to *The Clique* and would duly offer specific books from his stock to dealers who advertised for them, but mostly he preferred to deal in wholesale quantities. He sold literature to us and quite possibly, presumably, other subjects to other dealers.

Two or three times a year I would receive a telephone call from him to say that he thought he had enough material to make it worth my while to drive over to Enfield to see him. While Mrs Jenkins served tea, he would clamber up the extension ladder and bring his offerings down to the house's book-lined third bedroom. I think he measured the size of each consignment by its expected wholesale price rather than the number of volumes, but there would typically be three or four hundred miscellaneous books. He had a reasonable understanding of what would appeal to me and what would not and seemed to adjust his asking price accordingly, but I always had to take everything I was offered. Books I really could not abide I virtually threw out the next day but on the whole Jenkins's books were useful shelf-fillers and there were in each consignment one or two books which if not spectacularly wonderful, were still of a reasonably exciting nature. I admired the man's quiet tenacity and I was very sorry when a heart attack carried him off at far too early an age.

Sometimes I fall to musing about the strangest places and the strangest circumstances in which I have bought books. I think of a factory in South London where second-hand sacks and bags were cleaned, repaired and sold wholesale. The managing director and principal shareholder, R. L. Stuart, had a panelled office on the first floor, and there he kept his book collection. He would summon me when he felt it appropriate to cull his shelves. Edging past lorries unloading heaps of dirty, dusty sacks, I would wait in the reception area of the general office watching girls from South London, their patterns of speech short on final 'g's' and preliminary 'h's', painting their finger nails with Gestetner correcting fluid, that being provided by the firm, while nail polish cost money.

I would usually sit for five or ten minutes in the dusty atmosphere, my ears assaulted by the loud clatter of machinery, then Mr Stuart would ring down to say he was ready to see me. Something of a charismatic figure, he was very businesslike and wasted virtually no time on preliminaries. From the glass-fronted bookcases which lined his office walls he would quickly pluck fifty or a hundred volumes, mostly discarding them because his tastes had changed or simply because he needed the space for fresh purchases. Almost all his offerings were in fine condition in the dust-wrappers. Arming himself with a pencil and pad Mr Stuart would then ask me to name my price, volume by volume. If he approved – and his decisions were instantaneous – he would scribble a figure and say 'Right. Next?', pushing me to almost breakneck speed. On occasion he would say 'Not enough'. Sometimes I would increase my offer, but if I did not the book would be put back in the case. At the end of the exercise it took Mr Stuart only a moment to add the columns of figures he had been jotting down and then, while I wrote him a cheque, he would have a couple of workers carry the books down and load them into my car. He didn't sell me particularly valuable books or great rarities but he always had things I was glad to buy. Unusually among English collectors he had a passion for American literature and I welcomed the opportunity to pick up virtually on my doorstep first editions of Fitzgerald, Hemingway, Steinbeck, Updike and so on.

I remember buying a Rex Whistler collection from a veterinary surgeon in Wimbledon and a small but good library of modern first editions from a publican in a desolate area of Wigan, but one of the best purchases I ever made came relatively early in my career when I received a call to the home of a former customer of ours at an address in Surrey which was part of the stockbroker belt. This man also had an interesting occupation – or rather two occupations. First and foremost he was a sponge merchant, importing sponges from the Aegean for the luxury trade in London. As a secondary line of work he manufactured lampshades.

I was summoned to his highly desirable piece of real estate one Saturday afternoon. He was preparing to move to a smaller house and wished to reduce the number of books he had to move. He had bought quite a wide range of first editions of modern literature over the years but the author whose work he seemed to prize most was Peter de Polnay. I suppose I must have sold some de Polnay in my time but I really cannot remember doing so and I do know that I was far from anxious to buy any on this particular Saturday afternoon. Instead I bought a run of Ronald Firbank and various limited editions of the 1930s, and then my eye hit on a book bound in scarlet morocco. All the collector's other books were in their original bindings. What was this book and why had it been rebound? I plucked it from the shelf and found that the minute but exquisite lettering on the spine proclaimed it to be Conan Doyle's *A Study in Scarlet*, the first story to feature Sherlock Holmes. With trembling hands I opened it. Its format suggested to me that it might well be the rare first printing, in *Beeton's Christmas Annual* in November 1887. The story was such a success that the issue was sold out before Christmas. A completely new edition was published in book form by Ward, Lock in 1888. What I had in front of me appeared to have been extracted from the annual's wrappers, and the general title page had been discarded. Thus, without access to reference books and on a Saturday afternoon when the shop was closed and with no help to be had from my colleagues, I had to decide whether I was faced with something of great value or merely a curiosity. My sponge merchant, like Mr Stuart before him, required instant prices. I therefore thought of the largest sum I would ever dream of betting on a horse race, doubled it and quoted the answer to the owner in as matter of fact terms as I could manage. He nodded his agreement and the book was mine. I worked on through the rest of the case, then wrote a cheque and took my purchases away. After a nervous Sunday I went into work on Monday morning and found to my delight that my copy of *A Study in Scarlet* was 'right'. Of course it would have been better had it still been in the original wrappers rather than full scarlet morocco by Sangorski and

Sutcliffe, but no more than twelve surviving copies in wrappers are recorded. I had backed the right horse.

I made several trips to Lancashire to do business with a man we came to think of as the Golden Coalman, a name prompted by his similarity to the Golden Dustman in Dickens's *Our Mutual Friend*. He had retired from a business which sold coal to poor people unable to buy 10 cwt or a ton at a time, and who used to buy a small bagful from our man once a week. In the 1920s and 1930s he had been a keen book collector and he was passionate about condition. He would buy first editions by writers who appealed to him as they were published. He may have read them – I hope he did – but there was never any physical sign of their having been opened. Then he would take two or three volumes and wrap them in a brown paper parcel tied up with string. The parcels were then laid down carefully, like vintage port, in cupboards and trunks.

When I went to see him I was allowed to open as many parcels as I liked, but there was seldom much indication on the outside of which books were within. Any I didn't buy had to be wrapped up again. Needless to say buying twenty books from the Golden Coalman took rather longer than buying a hundred from my sack and bag man.

FOYLE'S

It must have been around 1956 that an enterprising rogue bought books from us on credit (mostly first editions of Hilaire Belloc and G. K. Chesterton) and promptly sold them to Foyle's for cash. This scam came to light when I went into Foyle's Charing Cross Road shop one day and found a sequence of books on the shelf which exactly matched our last despatch to the customer in question. Since he had not paid us, and had sold the books for less than the prices at which he had ordered them, the police brought an action against him.

While waiting to give evidence at his trial I chatted with the head of Foyle's antiquarian department. He told me that when he was interviewed for the job he was only asked one question about his technical competence. 'Can you read Roman numerals?' Christina Foyle enquired.

CHAPTER EIGHTEEN

BROWN PAPER PACKAGES

Rodgers and Hammerstein were respectively the composer and librettist of *The Sound of Music* in which Maria told the von Trapp children in song that Brown Paper Packages tied up with String were among her favourite things. I do not know that every bookseller would rate packages so highly. I confess that I always make a beeline for incoming packages, particularly those without any return address, because of my impatience to see what they contain. Outgoing packages are important too and there are few sights finer than large quantities of them being loaded into the Post Office van in response to orders brought in by the publication of a new catalogue – but the packages have to look right.

My father was not merely being sarcastic when he expressed his gratitude to his uncles Percy and Arthur Dobell for teaching him how to pack well. Brian Harker, our recruit from Quaritch, used to say that if a customer spent good money on rare books it was important that they did not arrive on his doorstep looking like a bundle of washing. I remember Harry Mushlin, the Shaw specialist, telling me that he had a complaint to make about the packer we were then employing. He took me in completely. 'Really Harry' I replied, 'What is the matter? I thought he was doing a good job.' 'Too good' replied Harry, 'It took me nearly twenty minutes to open the parcel he made for me yesterday!'

In contrast to that fellow's excellent work we once had a man we nicknamed 'The Folder' after we gave him a mint copy of a rare pamphlet, quarto in size, at the same time as a crown octavo novel and asked him to send both to the same address. As we soon discovered from the outraged addressee, our man folded the pristine quarto to the size of the smaller book in order to make a neater parcel. It was some little while before we lived that down.

It was Max Beerbohm who said that the world was divided into two classes, those who divided the world into two classes and those who didn't. Be that as it may most of the packers in the firm's history fell into one of two categories: they were either very young men, little more than boys in their teens, or men of retirement age supplementing their pensions with a part-time job. We were never very lucky with those in between, those of middle years who might be described as 'career' packers. I remember one such who, rather surprisingly, had read the English translation of the French novelist he always referred to as 'Prowst', making the first part of the name sound like the front of a ship. His trouble was that he was congenitally lazy, a trait that went down badly among our small but closely knit work-force, a work-force which knew nothing of demarcation lines and whose motto when there was need for a burst of corporate energy was 'All hands to the pump'. If a firm of shippers brought a container-load of books to our door, or if one of us came back to the bookshop in a car forced down onto its springs by its cargo of books (I remember once cramming 1,200 books into a Citroen Safari estate car) word seemed to spread round the firm like wildfire and all the cataloguers, together with the man who kept the accounts, would strip off their jackets, roll up their shirtsleeves and set to, as of course would the head packer (we had two packers in those heady days). His Proust-loving assistant was equally aware of the transport's arrival but *never* made a move until I went to flush him out of the packing department. 'Mr ----' I would say, 'There's a lorry-load of books outside. Can you come and give us a hand please'. 'Yes sir,' he would reply. 'I must just go and wash my hands first'. At this point he would move towards the men's cloakroom like a bolt of greased lightning. The inner door would be heard to shut and there Mr ---- would stay until the danger of having to do some work was safely past.

This habit of dodging the column made him very unpopular with his fellow toilers in the bibliographical vineyard, and it did little to improve my opinion of him either, but I could not very well sack a man for attending to the calls of nature. Imagine the joy that reigned unbounded when one day when I was giving this lazy fellow something of a pi-jaw in my office I finally managed to get beneath his skin. He complained that I was 'always having a go at him' and said in a rash moment that if that was what I thought of him he would quit. Moving as fast as he did when seeking the sanctuary of the cloakroom, I called for my secretary and asked her to come in with her notebook. When she appeared I said 'Please make a note of the time, Anne. It is half-past three on Wednesday, 13 September and Mr ---- has just given me his notice.' Barely suppressing a grin she wrote the memo that would go into the personnel file. Next day ---- came to me and said that he had been 'a bit hasty' on the previous afternoon and that, if I liked, he would withdraw his notice. I thanked him effusively but told him that I had always taken him at his word and that we were now too far down the path, having prepared his leaving papers and booked an advertisement for a replacement. We didn't exactly throw a party when he left but the wreaths of smiles on other employees' faces and the enthusiasm with which they pumped his hand when they said goodbye must have caused ---- to realize that Bertram Rota Ltd was not a firm where scrimshankers were welcome.

In marked contrast to this was the behaviour of virtually every one of the older men that we employed. Whenever I could I engaged people who had worked for the Post Office. This was on the principle of having gamekeepers become poachers. One such that I remember with wry amusement and particular affection was Tom Friend, an old soldier in every sense of the term, who had fought at Gallipoli and survived. He subsequently served in India (about which he told tales that made Kipling's *Soldiers Three* sound like a tea-party). After an honourable discharge from the army he joined the Post Office, this at a time when postmen had to line up for inspection before going out to deliver the letters. They had first to show that the bull's-eye lantern fastened to their belt worked properly. The inspector then walked up and down the line and sent home without pay anyone whose shoes were not polished or whose fingernails were dirty.

Tom used to tell terrible tales of the revenge wreaked by the postmen on customers who were too mean to contribute to the postman's charity collection at Christmas. He told us of one such man who sold wines and spirits and of how two postmen would each take an end of one of his outgoing parcels, and bang it on the corner of a bench until there was a noise of tinkling glass and a satisfying leakage of claret or whisky through the wrapping materials. He said that the man got the message in the end.

Tom was a glutton for work and could pack an amazing number of parcels in an afternoon. I noticed however that he never completely cleared the bench: whether we gave him ten parcels to pack or thirty, I always found next morning that there were two left over from the day before. I realized that this was his way of ensuring the continuity of his employment.

He had another trick. One afternoon I saw him coming back from the Post Office only twenty minutes after he had started work for the day. He went to his bench and filed a fistful of packet receipts, all duly rubber-stamped with the Post Office stamp to acknowledge that the relevant packets had been duly despatched. 'Tom' I said, 'You have only been here twenty minutes, how can you have got all that packing done?' 'Oh I haven't, sir' he replied, 'I like to do the receipts first and get them out of the way! I do the packing later'. 'How do you get the Post Office people to stamp the receipts?' I enquired. 'Oh I don't sir' he said, 'They all know me, so I go round the back of the counter and stamp them myself.' I made sure that I didn't get on the wrong side of Tom Friend.

At the beginning of this chapter I referred to 'brown paper packages tied up with string' and Peter Scott, who joined the firm from school in 1964 at the age of eighteen and is now a much valued associate director, asked if I planned to say a word about the changes I had seen in packing materials. I am afraid I had been in danger of taking them for granted. In the 1950s we kept supplies of three kinds of string. There was thin string for small packages, thicker stronger sisal for large parcels and 'paper' string, a thin yellow ribbon of paper with green borders, overprinted with our name, address and telephone number. This last was used to secure any package that a customer took away from the shop as opposed to having it sent through the mail. I have no idea of how many rolls the firm used to buy at a time but I do know we are just on to our very last one as I write this, and that it is so old that our telephone number still bears the name of the exchange (Regent) instead of merely a row of figures. We use this 'paper' string now for tying up bundles of manuscripts: it does not cut into the edges of the leaves as proper string would.

Of course we used gummed paper tape, too, for a time having that overprinted with our name and address and what I thought was a rather pleasing vignette of Bodley House. The advent of Sellotape and later of huge rolls of two inch wide vinyl tape means that those who do our packing nowadays prefer not to use string at all and in consequence we do not carry any in stock. On a visit to Marks and Co, whose address, 84 Charing Cross Road, Helen Hanff made famous, I was surprised to find Mark Cohen, Ben Marks's partner and the 'Co' of the punning name, saving the string from that day's incoming parcels, no matter how long it took him to unravel the knots. It seemed to me to be a waste of the great man's time; now I am amused to find that I sometimes follow Mark Cohen's example, for I hate to be without any string at all during my occasional stint at the packing bench.

The basic packing for all our outgoing parcels used to comprise the following three or four layers: first, a reasonably thick wrapping of newspaper, then a strip of corrugated paper, next, in the case of books which were large, fragile, rare or any permutation of these qualities, stiff cardboard, possibly in the form of a ready-made box; and lastly a sheet of stout brown paper. Did we use newspapers because that was a habit we had got into when all paper was in short supply during and after the war? Certainly we continued to wrap books in newspaper for many years after the war ended and as recently as ten or fifteen years ago I regularly collected papers from family and friends. Some overseas customers obviously enjoyed the extra reading matter that they got in this way and one or two even asked if we would make a point of always using say, *The Times*, or perhaps *The Daily Telegraph*, in their parcels. Today the ink from almost all British newspapers comes off on one's hands. A friend who manufactures printing ink tells me this is because the newspaper proprietors will not pay the price of a high quality, completely fast ink. Perhaps it was this tendency for the ink to stray from the place where it was intended to remain, i.e. on the newspaper, that caused us to start buying blank newsprint by the ream.

We still use corrugated paper and cardboard but the advent of bubble wrap (clean, light, and easier to cut to size) has brought a welcome change to the packing bench. A less happy invention was the Jiffy bag. The notion of a padded envelope is all very well but these bags lack rigidity. They may be just about acceptable for mailing single copies of mass-distribution paperbacks which can be easily replaced if something goes wrong, but I shudder at even the thought of rare pamphlets being sent through the post in them. Now that some envelopes are lined with bubble wrap they can at least be opened hygienically: pulling the tape to open the bags that are padded with recycled shredded paper etc. can cause a veritable snowstorm, leaving a mess on the bench and an unhealthy cloud of particles hanging in the air. Visualising just such a cloud I sometimes fall to wondering what the next development will be. Now that computer can talk to computer, and can respond to customers' enquiries for books with a near-instantaneous offer, reinforcing the bald description and price with a coloured reproduction of the binding or of an illustration, can it be long before the customer's response 'I'll take it' triggers, not just the automatic e-mailing of an invoice, and five minutes' work in the packing room, but a kind of electronic transfer of the book itself? Like watchers of *Star Trek* on television, will we see, not people this time, but a book dissolve into a cloud of particles which spin faster and faster before disappearing only to reassemble and materialise elsewhere – on another planet in *Star Trek* perhaps, but more probably in California in the case of a book? The catch phrase 'Beam me up, Scottie' might even be imagined to be coming from somewhere between the covers.

In 1930 the Cresset Press brought out a two-volume folio edition of Gulliver's Travels with illustrations commissioned from Rex Whistler, then a young artist who had only just left the Slade. 205 copies were printed and the book was a big success. Throughout my bookselling career it has always been in demand. By 1999 a fine copy might have sold for four thousand pounds. When I joined the firm it was engaged in selling a Rex Whistler collection which included one of the ten copies printed on vellum, one of about five to have an extra suite of the plates, also printed on vellum. We had recently sold the original sketches for the murals in the Tate Gallery restaurant, and one of my first cataloguing tasks was to list an almost complete set of books illustrated by Whistler, or with dust-jackets by him.

With this background I was much interested when the original copper-plates for the Cresset Press Gulliver came up for auction in London in 1968. Bidding for them started quietly and I thought I stood a good chance of buying them, until Keith Fletcher, a bookseller whose family owned an important personal collection of Whistler, joined the race. Eventually Keith went past my limit and bought the Lot. The following year his father, Bill Fletcher, telephoned me and said that he had obtained permission to have the twenty-six illustrations reprinted from the copperplates, but without the text, in an edition of 100 copies presented in green morocco-backed boxes in the style of the binding of the Cresset Press edition. Who, Bill enquired, should he ask to contribute a preface? I put up a name. 'No,' said Bill. I tried another. 'No,' came the answer. I had a third shot. 'I don't think so,' Bill replied. 'In fact you have failed to persuade me to ask anyone but you!' I have never been good at avoiding challenges or refusing requests for help and so it was that when H. M. Fletcher's edition of the plates appeared in 1970 it had a short foreword by me. Looking back thirty years later I am staggered by my presumption in tackling the writing of a critique of this major work of Whistler's from the shaky platform of my inadequate knowledge of the history of book illustration. The score would have been Whistler : 5 – A Lilliputian : 0 had it not been for one thing : in *the 1930 edition the plates were coloured by hand, not by Whistler, but under his supervision and I happened to have in my possession proof pulls of two or three plates as submitted to the artist for his approval of the colouring. The proofs bore Whistler's detailed comments and I was able to state that he had 'softened the effect the colourist had sought to achieve, and had made less apparent the distinction between adjacent masses of colour'.*

Perhaps I can count the final score as Whistler : 5 – A Lilliputian : 1.

CHAPTER NINETEEN

LAWRENCE DURRELL

ALAN THOMAS HELPS HIS OLD SCHOOL FRIEND

Alan Thomas cut quite a figure in book trade circles in more ways than one. In later life he sported a deerstalker hat and an Inverness cape. On high-days and holidays he tended to wear a richly embroidered waistcoat which once belonged to William Morris. These garments, together with his long beard, made him as distinctive as his taste, erudition and flair made him distinguished. The sight of that beard always put me in mind of the old man in Edward Lear's poem

> Who said, 'It is just as I feared! –
> Two Owls and a Hen,
> Four Larks and a Wren,
> Have all built their nests in my beard!

His catalogues were a joy to read, not least for the footnotes, which frequently comprised witty expositions of a right-wing political philosophy. Alan used to specialize in illuminated manuscripts, and then in books on architecture but he claimed that rising prices in a market that he himself had helped to make eventually forced him out. In 1958 when he was president of the Antiquarian Booksellers Association he made a most eloquent and inspiring speech of welcome when the ABA entertained the Grolier Club in London. He said that antiquarian bookselling was virtually the last calling in which a man could be master of his own destiny: what he got out of it was in direct relation to what he put into it. Furthermore one could chose those with whom one wanted to do business. If a bookseller did not like a book or a subject then there was no compulsion for him to deal in it.

Alan had been a school friend of Lawrence Durrell's when they were both living in Bournemouth and the two remained close all their lives. Apart from my professional concern with Durrell's writings I had a collecting interest in him as well and this was one of the links in the friendship that Alan and I forged. He would often ring me with a question about a possible bibliographical variant in the Durrell cannon or to ask the going price of one of Durrell's first editions. I did not in the least mind him doing this but he did have a bad habit of telephoning me at home on Sunday mornings. On one such occasion he rang to tell me that Larry had decided to sell his archive, which is to say all his extant manuscripts, typescripts, corrected proofs and correspondence files to date. He had asked Alan to act for him and Alan wondered if I would be willing to provide a valuation. I said that I would but I would of course need to charge a fee. Alan asked how much I would charge and I said that for making the valuation, cataloguing the material and then finding a buyer for it I would look for a 10% commission. Alan replied that he would not care to ask Larry to pay that much. I do not think he could have realized quite how much work would be involved. As it was he said that he thought it would be better if I told him the net sum that I thought I could get for Larry, taking my remuneration from the other side. This suited me rather better, because the percentage I had quoted had been a *prix d'amitié*.

A couple of months later I went to the United States armed with a descriptive catalogue of the papers. I made my way to the University of Southern Illinois at Carbondale, the town's name deriving from the strip-mining industry which disfigured much of the land around it. My friend the poet Kenneth Hopkins was teaching a creative writing course at the University at the time and kindly put me up in the bungalow the University had made available to him as part of his remuneration. In fact Kenneth gave a very good party for me there. Next day I met the genial Director of Libraries at Southern Illinois, Ralph McCoy and sold him the Durrell archive on mutually satisfactory terms. This was in 1969.

Almost thirty years later the London bookseller Bernard Stone was offering another 'Lawrence Durrell archive'. Of course what it comprised was the manuscripts from the last two decades or so of Durrell's life. The price was much more than that of the earlier archive, even though the exact figure seemed to differ from month to month. Bernard proved unable to find a buyer and before long the material turned up in a Sotheby auction catalogue. It included some books from Durrell's library and duplicate copies of some of his own later writings. The estimate was on the high side. I discussed it with Shelley Cox, now Rare Books Librarian at Southern Illinois and she decided not to bid. In the event I was not the only dealer to sit on my hands and, unsurprisingly, the Lot failed to reach its reserve price and remained unsold.

At this point I had another telephone call from Alan Thomas. Whether it was on a Sunday morning I do not recall but its burden was that Larry was very disappointed at the turn of events and Alan would be grateful if I could help. I said that the material, having been offered widely at varying prices (and with its exact composition varying somewhat too) and then having failed the attempt at selling by auction, it would be difficult indeed to place it at an advantageous price in the near future, but, perhaps because I welcomed the opportunity of succeeding where Sotheby's had failed, I agreed to have a shot. I confess I took what I am sure was a wholly regrettable degree of pleasure in sending a van to collect the material from Sotheby's and transfer it to our own warehouse.

Once we had the material under our own control we removed the multiple copies of some of Larry's own writings, added one important typescript (an early version of *Reflections on a Marine Venus* that was half as long again as the published book), and then made a completely fresh catalogue description. Armed with this I went back to Southern Illinois, offering the material at a price with which both they and I felt comfortable. Obviously it made good scholarly sense for all the papers to be together and I remain delighted to have helped to bring this happy union to pass.

A SORT OF BOOK PANDER

At the party that Kenneth Hopkins gave for me in his quarters at Southern Illinois University I met members of the English faculty, library staff and some of Kenneth's students, chiefly from his Creative Writing programme. They were for the most part a very pleasant bunch, although they included a rare books librarian who almost literally took the University to the cleaners. This worthy had bought a dry-cleaning business in Florida and in anticipation of leaving the university's service he had persuaded a gullible graduate assistant to wrap and post to the dry-cleaning shop sundry books and manuscripts selected from the rare book department's vault. Happily the luckless innocent who was doing the packing finally smelled a rat and when the mail-man delivered the final parcel the Director of Libraries and the campus police followed him into the cleaners.

But all that was in the future. On the evening of the party I had something else to think about. A mature student from the Creative Writing class, uncertain exactly why she had been invited to Kenneth's party, cross-examined me closely about my work and my reason for being in Carbondale. Eventually she said: 'I see. You're some kind of book pander!'

CHAPTER TWENTY

GEORGE LAZARUS

WHO KNEW WHAT HE LIKED

One morning in 1926 a young man who was destined to become one of the great book collectors of his generation walked into my father's tiny shop in Davies Street. He gave his name as George Lazarus and said 'I have just had a row with that man [Percy] Muir down the road. Will you be my bookseller?' From that day until his death in 1997 at the age of 92, George Lazarus bought no book or manuscript except from or through my father or, after 1966, me.

When he first came to us George Lazarus was just down from Caius College, Cambridge, where he read modern languages, and had gone to work on the London Stock Exchange as a member of his family firm, Lazarus Bros, who were the leading jobbers in gold mining shares. He went on to become senior partner. The time and energy he put into his career in the City meant that he had little opportunity for visiting bookshops, perusing catalogues or attending auctions, three of the archetypal collector's prime passions. To build his library, his collection of Dutch paintings and his equally impressive holdings of Imperial jade he followed one principle: find the best dealer that you can and then work through him. For jade George relied on Spink & Son. John Mitchell in Bond Street was his agent when he bought paintings, and he turned to us for books and manuscripts. Do not be misled by his seeming reliance on the professionals: each collection was very much his. He may have leaned on the advice and expertise of his chosen dealers, but the decisions were emphatically his own. Where his library was concerned he laid down the criteria; he set the limits of auction bids; and he said 'Yes', or 'No, that's too much', if he thought someone who knew of his interest was trying to exploit it.

He began collecting books while he was still an undergraduate but in 1926 he set about building a collection based on the mainstream of the English novel in the 20th century. There were two basic rules: to be included an author had to have produced work which gave George pleasure, and left him with the conviction that it would be of permanent value. This was to be an intensely personal collection. Fashion and general critical opinion were totally disregarded.

One of the first authors whose first editions George bought was John Galsworthy. The names of H. G. Wells and then D. H. Lawrence were soon added. By the mid 1950s some thirteen novelists were represented including E. M. Forster, Aldous Huxley and Somerset Maugham. Women writers were not neglected: Elizabeth Bowen, Constance Holme, Mary Webb and Virginia Woolf were added to his library. Among Irish writers he chose Sean O'Casey, Frank O'Connor and Sean O'Faolain. From America he purchased William Faulkner and John Steinbeck. It is worth making the point that George began buying books by most of these authors before their reputations were firmly established. His first aim was to build complete sets of the first editions of every work in the author's canon. He insisted on fine condition but paid no heed to dust-jackets. Indeed in the early days he would have thrown them away had my father not persuaded him to keep them in a drawer, even if he would not tolerate them on his shelves. George then reinforced the printed works with letters and manuscripts wherever he could find them. In this he was decidedly ahead of the field.

He was a good-looking man, always well groomed, giving off a faint scent of an expensive toilet water. He could be charming, and was a most generous host, but, dreadfully impatient by nature, he refused to suffer fools gladly and his wrath when aroused was a frightful thing to see. Yet he loved quiet pursuits, was devoted to his garden where, in retirement, he would work alongside his gardener, taking great pains as he strove for perfection. He was also an avid follower of cricket. His opinions were always black and white: there were no shades of grey in his critical vocabulary. Thus Mike

Gatting, the tubby captain of Middlesex, was 'the best b----- bats-men ever to play for England'. Lawrence Durrell on the other hand, whose books I had been faintly praising 'couldn't write for toffee'.

George Lazarus, in his eighties,
with Lady Hookway and Alan Cameron

As the scope of the Lawrence collection grew, gradually encompassing American first editions, foreign language editions, periodicals with contributions by Lawrence, books about Lawrence and so on, so other author-collections had to go in order to make room on the shelves. George told me to offer three manuscripts by the near-forgotten and highly unfashionable novelist R. H. Mottram to Norwich County Library, Mottram being a Norfolk man. George said I was to ask £150 each for them. The Librarian replied that he would only pay £50 each. George said 'Tell him if he will buy the first one for my price, I'll make him a present of the other two!' Face was saved; the manuscripts ended up in the right place; and George had done his good deed for the day.

He was as astute when it came to disposing of good things as he had been when he was buying them. My father had acquired for him at a charity sale in New York in 1937 the manuscript of William Faulkner's novel *Absalom, Absalom!*, 1936. It was a bargain at the equivalent of £50, but this was before Faulkner's reputation was firmly established. When the time came in the 1960s for the Faulkner shelves to be cleared to accommodate yet more Lawrence, George instructed us to sell his set of the books, plus the *Absalom, Absalom!* manuscript. We suggested what we thought was a pretty good price for this last, but George pooh-poohed it, and insisted on our asking £6,000 – almost twice as much as we had proposed. Dr Ransom, to whom we offered it first, bought it for the Humanities Research Center at George's figure, apparently without turning a hair.

The Lawrence collection was by now manifestly the best in private hands. It included 138 autograph letters, some very early, some to his sisters, others to agents, publishers and reviewers. The Lazarus manuscripts began with Lawrence's first novel, *The White Peacock*, and continued with the complete version of *Sun*, the play *David*, sundry short stories and many poems. A manuscript of a translation of Leo Shestov's *All Things Are Possible*, attributed solely to S. S. Koteliansky, is written entirely in Lawrence's holograph, thus demonstrating Lawrence's involvement in the final text of the translation. Some of these pieces were bought at auction and some from the catalogue of Lawrence MSS put out by the Californian dealer, Jake Zeitlin; I purchased *David* in a Los Angeles hotel room in 1974; an early three-part article, 'Flowering Tuscany', was discovered in a file at William Heinemann's Surrey headquarters when my firm was making an appraisal of the Heinemann archive.

The Lazarus collection of printed books by Lawrence is particularly rich in presentation and association copies. There are books inscribed to Lawrence's sister, Emily, and to his brother, George. There is a copy of *Love Poems and others*, 1913, inscribed to Ford Madox Hueffer. *Psychoanalysis and the Unconscious* is inscribed to S. S. Koteliansky. Then, too, there are books inscribed to Pino Orioli, publisher of the first edition of *Lady Chatterley's Lover*, although the only inscribed copy of that title in the collection is 'the author's unabridged popular edition' of 1929, a year after the first printing.

George Lazarus's disdain for dust-jackets has already been mentioned. Thank goodness he was persuaded not to discard the jacket for his copy of the first (suppressed) edition of *The Rainbow* or that for the first American edition of the *Boy in the Bush*, the only jacket designed by Lawrence's friend, the painter Dorothy Brett.

The collection includes all three issues of the Beaumont Press edition of the poems issued as *Bay*, one of the 120 copies on handmade paper, one of 50 copies on cartridge paper (actually far scarcer than the numbers imply, because of an accident during production which meant that only half the issue survived) and one of the 30 copies on Japanese vellum. Perhaps the scarcest Lawrence text in the collection is the *Letter to Charles Lahr*, 1930, which bears the statement that it is one of only six copies. Helping to build the Lazarus collection was one of the most satisfying tasks that bookselling gave me. On George Lazarus's death the collection passed by bequest to the University of Nottingham.

JUSTINE

One morning the exotic girlfriend of a customer of George Lawson's came in and asked George for help in finding a suitable birthday present for her man. I do not know to this day whether George suggested it or whether she stumbled on it for herself but the book selected as a birthday gift was the rare (and expensive) first edition of the Marquis de Sade's Justine, 1792. *George had the book wrapped for her and as she took it out of the shop she said 'Charge it to ---'s account, will you?' To the pains described in the Marquis de Sade's pages this ingenious mistress had added the exquisite one of making her beau pay for his own present. We later heard that the gift had proved acceptable in every way.*

CHAPTER TWENTY-ONE

DAVID MAGEE

MID-ATLANTIC MAN

Before air travel made the world so much smaller many American booksellers formed the habit of coming to England by Cunarder each summer on a buying trip to replenish their shelves. One such annual visitor was the San Francisco dealer, David Magee. He was in fact not American but everyone's idea of the quintessential Englishman. He was educated at Lancing, where he was two years junior to Evelyn Waugh. A grandson of a former Archbishop of York, he was one of the eight children of the vicar of St Mark's church in St John's Wood, just a few minutes walk from Lord's, the world's most famous cricket ground.

David left Lancing with no formal academic qualifications. Admonished by his father to 'Go West young man, go West', he set out to seek his fortune as a farmer in California. He got as far as San Francisco and decided to become a bookseller instead. He was one of the best of his generation.

On his visits to England he scarcely moved outside London during the three or four weeks that he was on our side of the Atlantic. He tended to stay at Brown's Hotel, scarcely two hundred yards from our Vigo Street premises, and, skipping the hotel breakfast, would come to us for coffee at half past nine each morning. Some dealers visited us with narrowly focused wants ('What first editions of Hemingway do you have in the dust-wrappers?' is a fair example of this.) David Magee's approach was very different. One day my colleague Ron Taylor followed David's deceptively casual circuit of the shelves and said to him 'What exactly are you looking for, Mr Magee?'

'I don't know, but I shall recognize it when I see it,' replied David.

He spoke truly too, for he had a phenomenally sharp eye for a good book, whether in his own field or out of it.

He also had a wicked facility for coining nicknames. There are no prizes for guessing which Marylebone bookseller, now gone to his rest, David dubbed 'Mr Doublespeak', nor for identifying the two California dealers he called 'the Katzenjammer Kids.'

In his entertaining book of memoirs, *Infinite Riches*, David tells how he bought from us a collection of William Morris material. This was a transaction that gave me a special pleasure for two reasons: the first was the perhaps ignoble one that the material concerned had been consigned to one of the two major London auction houses before the owner sought my opinion, but once he had heard my view of what the collection was worth and how it should be treated, he withdrew it from auction and sold it to me; my second reason for gratification was that David nominated the transaction as the one which had given him the greatest pleasure and satisfaction of any in his career.

One morning in the late 1960s David came into my office for his routine morning coffee. As we were chatting his eye lit on a water-colour propped against the wall. From the other side of the room he correctly identified it as a Burne-Jones. He asked if it was for sale and I told him that it was part of a much larger lot. He promptly requested an option on the entire collection. A few days later he came round to inspect it all. In *Infinite Riches* he describes the scene: 'I could scarcely credit the state of confusion that reigned in that room. The floor was knee-deep in what looked like rolled-up maps or samples of wallpaper. There were portfolios bulging with draw-ings, framed watercolours, tiles, pots and a heap of books.' David asked me what the rolls were and I replied that they were cartoons for stained-glass windows, many of them twenty feet long. They were the work of a man called Dearle, who was one of the managers of Morris, Marshall, Faulkner & Co., the firm headed by Morris that made the famous chairs, tapestries, wallpaper, stained-glass windows and much besides. The material came down through Dearle's family and it was from one of his descendants that I bought it. David spent a couple of hours looking through it – the drawings, sketches and watercolours by Burne-Jones, Rossetti and others; the designs for tapestries, wallpaper, tiles, etc.; a dye-book including many samples of textiles with instructions as to processes; letters from Burne-Jones, Morris and Rossetti to Dearle about work in progress, and even the company's Minute Book.

Let David take up the story again : 'I sat down in a chair and in a quaking voice enquired the price. When I had been restored to life with strong spirits I heard myself say : "I'll take them".' David later arranged for them to be sent to San Francisco where he sold them to Sanford Berger, the great William Morris collector, almost as quickly as he had bought them from me. The collection is now one of the jewels in the Huntington Library's crown.

Over a period of several years David bought from us a number of books which were later to grace the pages of his monumental three-volume catalogue of Victoriana. In fact during that period he bought from us pretty well every fine, bright first edition of Victorian literature that came our way. It later transpired that while the catalogue of 2,049 items was being printed, David sold the collection intact to Brigham Young University. In an amusing prefatory note he dedicated the catalogue 'to the other members of the D M Club, Dudley Massey and Dusty Miller [two of the more colourful London booksellers of the period] without whose enthusiasm, encouragement & advice this catalogue would have been finished in half the time.'

It was natural that when I made my first visit to San Francisco, several years after my father's death, I should begin by turning my footsteps towards David Magee's shop, which was then on Filbert Street. David said that he was determined that the visit should be a success for me and at once proposed a generous discount which would apply to anything I purchased, right across the store. If I saw books that I wanted that were still too expensive I was to tell him. Then he produced from a cupboard the holograph manuscript of Conan Doyle's historical novel *Sir Nigel*, not an unimportant book, and a highly desirable manuscript; I am sure David could have sold

Chap XVII

The Spaniards on the Sea.

Day had not yet dawned when Nigel was in the chamber of
Chandos preparing him for his departure and listening to the last words of
advice from his noble master. That morning, before the sun was
half way up the heaven, the King's great Philippa with the
greater part of those who were present at his banquet set its
sail, adorned with the lions and the lilies, and turned its
brazen beak for England. Behind it went five smaller cogs
crammed with squires, archers and men-at-arms. Nigel and
his companions lined the ramparts of the castle and waved their
kerchiefs as the burly vessels, with drums beating and trumpets
clanging, a hundred knightly pennons streaming from their decks
and the red cross of England over all, rolled slowly out to the open
sea. Then when they had watched them until they were hull down
they turned with heavy hearts to the preparation for their own more
distant venture.

"Cheer up your heart, friend" said Delves,
the rough squire, striking Nigel on the shoulder...

It took them four days of hard work ere their
preparations were complete for many were the needs of a small force
in a strange country. Three ships had been left to them, the
Cog Thomas, the Grace Dieu, and the Basilisk, into each of
which one hundred men were stowed, besides the thirty
seamen who formed the crew. In the hold were forty horses,
amongst them Pommers, much wearied by his long idleness and
homesick for the slopes of Surrey where his great limbs might find
the work he craved. Then the food and the water, the bowstaves and
the sheaves of arrows, the horseshoes, the knives, the axes, the
ropes, the vats of hay, the green fodder, and a score of other things

A leaf from the MS of
Sir Arthur Conan Doyle's *Sir Nigel*, 1906 (reduced)

it to a collector or a librarian with ease, but he said he wanted me to have it. He charged me the equivalent of £5,000 (this was in 1975), a price which was on the generous side of fairness. I took it back to England with me and gloated over it for some little while. It is now in the Pierpont Morgan Library.

Although David remained a very English Englishman, with a passionate love of cricket and a habit of peppering his speech and his letters with the language of his public school and phrases from his beloved P. G. Wodehouse, he was perfectly assimilated into the San Francisco scene. Together with his wife, Dorothy, he entertained royally at the Saint Francis Yacht Club, and at Jack's celebrated restaurant; known as a two martini or even a three martini man, he had perfected the small circular movement of his hand, the forefinger extended, which brought the yacht club steward with a tray bearing another round of drinks.

David was a member of the Bohemian Club, and wrote a number of 'entertainments' for performance there. His two-volume bibliography of Grabhorn Press books is in itself a fine memorial to his life and work. With his customer Elinor Heller he covered the years from 1915 to 1940 and with Dorothy's assistance he later dealt faithfully with the years from 1940 to 1956. All in all he was the sort of bookseller who makes me proud of my calling. He was moreover a hugely likeable man, and if I seldom saw him without a glass in one hand and a cigarette in the other, it is certain that I never saw him without a smile on his lips. He gave a start and encouragement to several generations of young booksellers in California and when he died I doubt that he had an enemy in the world.

When I talk to lay audiences about the pleasures of working with rare books I always stress that it is a physically tiring affair and no job for weaklings. Books printed on clay-coated art paper can be deucedly heavy. Buying them from houses where it is difficult to get a car or van close to the door seems to involve more carrying of substantial weights than the law of averages would suggest. The desire to keep sets of books intact, even in transit, causes us to overfill cardboard boxes so that when the time comes to lift them they seem to be nailed to the floor.

Closing up the books on a shelf to eliminate gaps, thus making thefts easier to spot and leaving room to introduce new stock, can cause havoc, not least because of the differences in size that one encounters in the world of books. It is true that most atlases are either quarto or folio, and that most duodecimos are verse, but a row of novels selected at random from the output of the last hundred years can show differences in height of three inches or more. This can make for difficulties when it comes to taking a row of books from the top of one bay of shelving and putting it on, say, the bottom shelf of another. The trick about moving a row of perhaps twenty books at once, stretching up to take them, then bending to set them down in their new location, is to keep them under great pressure from each end. If the new shelf is not uniform with the old one and the top of just one volume catches, the compressed row can explode and all twenty books can end up on the floor, probably with a few corners bruised and a hinge split to boot. My father's first assistant (i.e. the first helper he ever hired) who became his First Assistant (i.e. his manager, and supervisor of other staff), came to us straight from school around 1927 and stayed until he was called up for war service around 1943. His name was Percy Lauder. He was a lugubrious character. I never saw him evince the least interest or excitement when would-be sellers, private or trade, brought books to offer us. It wasn't that attractive rarities failed to interest or excite him, it was just that he thought a show of enthusiasm on his part might raise the price against him. It is not surprising that Lauder saw a lot wrong with the book trade, nor that he had a number of absolutely hopeless remedies for the conditions that offended him, but he felt particularly strongly about the shelving problems caused by the differences in book sizes, the back problems caused by the weight of books in conventional bindings and the damage that a trainee could cause by spilling an armful of books on the floor. His consequent pronouncement was the saying of his that I liked best : 'If I were king, I'd make two laws: all books would be octavo in size and bound in aluminium.'

CHAPTER TWENTY-TWO

HILAIRE BELLOC

OR THE CASE OF THE BLOODSTAINED ARCHIVE

Those who think they see a pun in the subtitle of this chapter could very well be right.

I have always maintained that the best people to sell contemporary archives (e.g. all an author's papers, or the files of a publishing house) are reputable dealers in rare books and manuscripts with an established track record in this field, and certainly not auctioneers or literary agents. (*'He would say that, wouldn't he?'*). Their business methods work very well if a single manuscript of a well-known published book comes onto the auction block, or if an agent conducts a private auction to see which publisher will pay a colossal advance for a typescript that might appear to have the qualities that make a best-seller, but the methods which work for important individual pieces simply cannot be carried over into the market for entire archives.

For one thing auctions of this nature require the potential buyers to make too large an investment of time and money in discovering exactly what papers are present, what their market value might be and how that figure relates to their worth to the purchasing institution. I say 'institution' because archives are hardly ever bought by individuals: the cost and the bulk of major archives both work against private collectors. Once a library has made up its mind about how much it is prepared to pay it has to set about finding the money, for few institutions are able to buy sizeable archives out of their normal budgets. Fund-raising can be quite a lengthy business and it is my experience that librarians are unwilling to undertake it, or the rest of the series of tasks I have outlined, unless there is some assurance, firstly, that the actual price will be in line with the general consensus of opinion about market value, and secondly, that if they are prepared to meet that value then they will be allowed to complete the purchase. Let me report how things turned out in one specific instance.

On a morning in the spring of 1980 the post included an envelope from A. D. Peters, a distinguished firm of literary agents who had represented, amongst others, Evelyn Waugh, Graham Greene and Rebecca West. Hilaire Belloc had been another of their authors, and looking after the interests of his Estate remained one of A. D. Peters' responsibilities.

When I opened Peters' envelope, out fell an attractively printed eight-page brochure announcing the sale by tender (effectively a postal auction) of Hilaire Belloc's surviving archive and library. I knew that Belloc had sold some manuscripts in his lifetime but the original material (*viz.* manuscripts, typescripts, proofs and so on) for a large proportion of his published work was here, and the brochure listed many of the titles. It then spoke of the correspondence files, which were extensive: I later discovered that there were in excess of 160,000 pieces in the files. It seemed that Belloc had scarcely thrown away an incoming letter or failed to file copies of the letters that he himself sent out. We were told that there was a summary listing of the letters that could be made available for inspection. Lastly there were the books in Belloc's library – approximately 10,000 of them.

A covering letter went on to say that this description was being circulated to about 120 libraries in the English-speaking world, including all the major research libraries known to be buying twentieth century literary material, the British Library, and the University of Texas at Austin among them. Most of the other addressees were Jesuit colleges and universities. I not infrequently represented the University of Texas in matters of this sort but in the present instance they told me that they were not very anxious to have the material and would not therefore get involved. This left me free to represent another valued client, the Burns Library at Boston College, which is of course a Jesuit foundation. Interested

Part of Hilaire Belloc's library at King's Land

parties were invited to make an appointment to view the books and papers and the brochure indicated that each bidder would be given either a morning or an afternoon to make their examination. I wrote to Peters on behalf of Tom O'Connell, who was overall Director of Libraries at Boston College. I said it was preposterous to allow us only half a day to inspect such a huge collection and had a charming reply from Sheila McIlwraith, a young agent in the Peters firm. She graciously said that since half a day was insufficient I could have a full day and I could moreover take a colleague with me. I turned to George Sims who, following our purchase of his business, was now officially a consultant to Bertram Rota Ltd. George and I had worked together, and traded with one another often enough for each to understand the other's scale of values. Moreover George had bought and sold some of the Belloc manuscripts that had come onto the market in the author's lifetime. We made a date to go down to Belloc's house, King's Land in the village of Shipley just outside Horsham. The house was dominated by a fine example of a smock windmill. Belloc used to write at a table in the mill and some of his papers were still housed there. In fact everything seemed as Belloc had left it. Nor did the books appear to have been dusted since his death. I saw more dead spiders on Belloc's shelves than I can recall seeing in any other library. Belloc and his wife, Elodie were very close and it is said that if his work took him away from home or he was absent for any other reason they exchanged letters every single day that they were apart. When Elodie died in 1914 Belloc left her things exactly as they were and then closed up her room.

Apart from the signed and annotated copies of a number of his own books, Belloc's library was not particularly exciting. It was useful as a scholarly resource in as much as it showed what he had read and what had influenced him. One of the books I liked best was *Ann Veronica* inscribed by its author, H. G. Wells, 'To Hilaire Belloc, who *can* write prose, from H. G. Wells, whose case is more doubtful.' I was also amused to see an entry in the brochure for 'The first thirteen volumes of *The Yellow Book*': only thirteen volumes were ever published.

The manuscripts included the final draft of *The Path to Rome* and much of Belloc's verse, some of it very heavily corrected. Also present were the original drawings by 'B.T.B.' (Lord Basil Blackwell) for *Cautionary Tales for Children*.

The letters were particularly hard to assess in the time available to us. Apart from a long series of family letters, there were good correspondences with Shaw, Buchan, Wells, Bennett, Father Knox, Yeats, Galsworthy and other literary figures, as well as letters from various members of three families with which Belloc was closely connected, the Herberts, the Asquiths and the Chestertons. There were business papers galore, not to mention drafts of Belloc's parliamentary speeches, family photographs and Belloc's diaries and engagement books between 1891 and 1939. We had a busy day.

Travelling back to London on the train I asked Sheila McIl-wraith, very politely and I hope not too pointedly, what experience she had of buying and selling archives. She laughed and told me that this was her first case. Her boss, Michael Sissons, managing director of A. D. Peters, had given her the task of selling the Belloc books and papers and when she asked how she should go about it Sissons tossed across the desk to her a recent back number of the journal of the Society of Authors which contained an article on that very subject by (have you guessed?) one Anthony Rota. In it I listed twelve questions which I felt needed to be answered before a valuer or appraiser could set a justifiable figure on any manuscript or archive. Those who would like to see them will find them print-ed in Appendix II.

In the course of the badinage that followed Sheila pretended to rebuke me for having insisted on extra time to view and then using only a small part of it. I told her that if I couldn't have two *weeks* then five or six *hours* would take me as far as seven or eight.

Next, Sims and I prepared notes of the things which each of us had seen, as well as those *not* seen, (almost as important). We valued item by item some of the things we had had time to examine and made projections to cover things we had not been able to study closely. We took due account of the two contradictory *dicta* which are the cornerstones of the archival valuer's creed. The first is 'The whole is greater than the sum of the parts' and the second 'The longest purse gets the best bargain'. The first of these states the blindingly obvious: a complete collection, or even a large one, usu-ally gains in significance by virtue of assembling material in one place. If each item were valued separately the total might come to, say, £10,000, but the value of the *toute ensemble* is almost certainly higher than that. Indeed one American valuer I knew, and whose body was eventually found floating face down in the river with a bullet in the head, once told me that in valuing collections he al-ways added up the individual parts and added an automatic 40% to the total! One reason why he was wrong to do this is what I shall call the 'longest purse syndrome'. It is an undeniable fact that as the selling price increases, the number of potential purchasers, and thus the competition, becomes smaller. A great many people would like a single manuscript poem by Belloc and strong bidding might well move the price up to as much as £250, but that is not to say that a thousand pages of manuscript poems would bring a thousand times as much, i.e. £250,000.

I prepared a long report for Tom O'Connell. Instead of giving a precise figure I gave him a range of prices, saying that I could not see that the archive was worth less than so many thousand pounds, (we were in fact talking in five figures sterling) or more than thus many thousand pounds, (now we were into six figures). I thought a bid somewhere in the middle should secure the archive. Tom was the ideal client in this sort of situation. Each of us had complete faith in the other and he accepted my figures without question. He told me how far I could go in my opening bid – I called it that because we hoped to get one more in under the wire. It was a good bid, a bold bid, but not an extravagant bid.

Now began a cat and mouse game in which my objective was to get our bid in as late in the day as possible without having it ruled out of time. I didn't want it to leak back to any of the other bidders who might then find it easy to go just a fraction higher. Somehow or other – in fact it can only have been from Sheila – I learned that the serious contenders were now down to a short list of three. Only a handful more had expressed serious interest on receiving the brochure, which underlines my point about this not being the best way to go about things. As it was the three left in the race were the British Library (whose representative was said to like Belloc's verse but to find his prose not of the highest order), Boston College itself, and Georgetown University, another Jesuit institution. I was content to do battle with the British Library for I knew their bid would be soundly based: like Boston they had sought a commercial valuation from experienced professionals. Georgetown worried me. They were relying solely on opinions within the library and although the people giving them were highly competent professional *librarians*, they just did not have, at least in my view, enough experience of buying and selling archives month in month out for many years. They therefore represented something of a wild card – their bid could be much too high or much too low.

Much nail-biting ensued and then we heard from Sheila that our bid was the highest and had been accepted.. She and I joined forces to get an export licence and I made the necessary shipping arrangements. A team of us from the bookshop would go down to King's Land, together with Sheila, Philip Jebb, who was Belloc's grandson, and a colleague from Jebb's architectural practice. We would take packing material with us and have all the books and all the papers neatly stowed in cartons in the course of one long day. The following morning the shipping company would bring a container to the door. It would be filled with the pre-packed cartons and taken straight to Heathrow.

If everything was to be ready for the crew to load into the container on the second day an enormous amount needed to be done on the first. It was interesting to see how quickly the two architects filled their allotted cartons: they had some kind of concept of space which enabled them to know instinctively which twelve or twenty of the wide range of large and small packets would fit into a box, while we booksellers were still working by trial and error. By half past twelve the troops were visibly tiring and Philip Jebb, his wife and I took them all off to the village pub for a cold lunch in the garden. Getting them back to work as soon as I decently could, I tried to demonstrate the urgency of the situation by 'leading from the front', charging up one staircase and then leaping across a little landing to the next flight of stairs. All would have been well had I not failed to see a beam half way across. I cannoned into it, saw stars and was quickly reminded in the most forceful way of the extent to which scalp wounds bleed. Jaqi Clayton my secretary had joined the packing team and she and Sheila McIlwraith vied with each other to show the world at large how good they were at first aid. Accordingly they took it in turns to apply soothing swabs, and then assorted plasters to my scalp. Still seeing stars, but feeling much better, I bent down to continue the packing. Quite literally this move proved disastrous for as I bent forward pressure came on the wound and then on the plasters and blood began to drip on to the papers. We mopped up as best we could but time and again over the next hour or two a sizeable blob of blood would fall onto an otherwise immaculate manuscript. What will future scholars make of these bloodstains? Will they think that Belloc literally 'sweated blood over his manuscripts?'

Eventually my wound healed. Next day the container came, was filled and taken away and everyone was left rather happy. Discussing it all over a celebration lunch I could not resist – I never can – telling the other side, in this case Sheila McIlwraith, how they had got everything wrong. Not unnaturally Sheila demurred. I responded by saying that if I had been selling the collection by private treaty I would have got the Estate some 25% more than in fact they received. Sheila riposted at once, saying that the Estate would have accepted even one or two pounds more than the next best offer, but in fact the bid from Boston College was almost half as much again as the second best bid. Between Sheila and me honours were perhaps even but there is no doubt in my mind that on this occasion the real winner was Boston College, which had secured a rich archive at an eminently reasonable price.

Prominent among the American dealers who came to London on buying trips regularly each summer through the fifties and sixties were the New York booksellers Phil and Fanny Duschnes. They had elegant premises at a smart Manhattan address and displayed a good stock of fine books, mostly from the nineteenth and twentieth centuries. They probably carried a greater representation of the publications of the Limited Editions Club than anyone else in the world. In England they had the reputation of being tough buyers, always trying to beat prices down. I met them early on in my bookselling life. When the third summer of our acquaintance came round they made their annual visit to us (we were still in Vigo Street) and, conferring and complaining, made their selection from our shelves.

'How much would those be to me,' Phil asked. I did some quick sums and named him a price. 'Why, that's only ten per cent,' protested Phil, naming exactly the discount that British dealers almost universally extend to one another as a courtesy. (In America the reciprocal discounts tend to be a little higher). I pretended to check my calculations. 'Yes, that's right,' I said, assuming surprise but not suggesting a better rate. At this stage Fanny joined in: 'Ten per cent! Ten per cent! Do you know what it costs us a night to stay at The Dorchester?' I was dying to recommend a cheaper hotel, but discretion prevailed.

However I was reminded of this episode when the following summer I paid one of my regular calls on Harry Mushlin, who makes various fleeting, but always welcome, appearances in these pages. Although still to some extent a 'runner', he now had a little eyrie of an office at the top of three or four flights of stairs in Bond Street, almost opposite Sotheby's front door. There he kept a small but select stock. I bought a few things and looked at more. As I was leaving Harry said 'Do you have plans for lunch?' When I replied in the negative he told me that his wife had made him more sandwiches than he could comfortably eat and invited me to share them.

So it was that I went back a couple of hours later, to find Harry's glass-

topped display case covered in piles of books, with flakes or crumbs from a soft eraser lying thickly beside them. As I went in Harry erased the price from a book and pencilled in another. It did not take a psychologist to realise that if the old price was rubbed out the new price must be higher. 'What's this Harry,' I asked, tongue in cheek. 'Do you really think the market's going up?' 'No,' that clever man replied, 'but I've got Mr Duschnes coming this afternoon. He likes a big discount and I'm arranging things so that I can give him one.'

CHAPTER TWENTY-THREE

LAURIE DEVAL & BOB FLECK

IN WHICH WE SAY GOODBYE TO AN OLD FRIEND
AND MEET A NEW ONE

Towards the end of 1981 members of the antiquarian book trade in Great Britain, and not least my wife and I, were much saddened by the lamentably early death of Laurie Deval, who was for many years Percy Muir's partner in the firm of Elkin Mathews. He died of a brain tumour. He was only fifty-eight.

We had always regarded Laurie as a popular figure and were not surprised that the book-trade was well represented at his funeral service, which took place at a relatively early hour on a bitterly cold morning in a crematorium on the outskirts of Chelmsford. Hylton Bayntun-Coward came all the way from Bath; George Sims made the early morning journey from Reading; and several of the book-trade's octogenarians turned out. What we did not expect was to see the entire population (or so it appeared) of the village of Takeley where Laurie had both his business and his home. We then discovered what should have come as no surprise to us: Laurie had been active in the village cricket club, the amateur dramatic society, the campaign against noise from nearby Stansted airport, and so on. His wife Mary and his daughters also played a full part in the life of the village.

I suppose that Jean and I first got to know Laurie and Mary because we were part of a set that gravitated together at the annual dinners of the Antiquarian Booksellers' Association. Rodney and Sonia Drake were part of the group as were Boris and Jean Harding-Edgar and Hylton and Charlotte Bayntun-Coward. Laurie was most people's idea of the quintessential Englishman, red of cheek, firm of hand, quick to laugh and slow to bear a grudge. Hailing from

Laurie Deval

Barking, he affected Cockney slang much of the time and if he wanted more beer in a public house he would call out for 'two more jars of bitter please'. When I telephoned once to ask if I could call in on my way home from Cambridge he told me that he had a badly inflamed nose by declaring 'I've got a bug in m' hooter'. He was a good trencherman and a generous host. I have left till last the most important thing: he was a first-rate and very shrewd bookseller. He had a particularly good knowledge of typography and the printing arts in general, and often seemed more concerned to have the right book go to the right place than to secure every last penny for it.

When the attitude of some of those who were then the ABA Establishment caused some of us to lose patience with them over such matters as promoting book fairs and fighting auction rings, a group of men at the dinner table I have described put themselves forward for election to the committee. We were variously dubbed 'The Ginger Group' and 'The Young Turks'. The first year that we stood not one of us was elected. In the second year I won the place previously held by Frank Hammond, an unashamed apologist for the ring. After that I could propose resolutions but I had enormous difficulty in finding a seconder, but in the third year Laurie was elected to sit alongside me and we worked together happily and, I like to think, effectively.

In Takeley Laurie had a cottage at one end of the village and Percy Muir a house at the other end. In the grounds of Percy's house were two long wooden buildings with a cross-piece joining them together. They looked as though they might have been left over from an army camp but rumour had it that they were once chicken houses. From these buildings Elkin Mathews carried on their business. This was fine in the summer months but decidedly chilly in the winter. Takeley was just a few miles down the road from Bishop's Stortford to Dunmow, which made it a useful stopping-off place when I was going to buy books in Cambridge, or to visit Boris Harding-Edgar in Buntingford. There were always good things to buy (I remember a day when George Sims and I found a bundle of portrait drawings by Will Rothenstein and greedily snapped up all the representations of authors). There was always coffee or tea as well, and I cannot remember ever visiting Elkin Mathews without learning something useful about books and their makers from either Percy or Laurie. Percy moved away and went into semi-retirement in 1970, dying in 1980, just a year before his much younger colleague. When Mary decided that Laurie's business had to be closed down and sold. I was proud to be asked to give her advice and help in this sad undertaking. Various divisions were made. Some of the better typographical items and the children's books went to auction. I bought much of the English literature, but the reference library and the stock of bibliography I offered, on the advice of Nicolas Barker, to Robert Fleck of Oak Knoll Books who had started bookselling comparatively recently and whom I had never met. Bob flew in from Delaware to see the books for himself. I took to him right away because he showed a proper concern for Mary's feelings as well as behaving in an honourable way and making her a fair price. I introduced him to Mary, showed him the arrangement of the stock, pointing out a number of the better things, not because I thought he would miss them but so that he should be aware that I knew they were there and that I would be looking for their value to be reflected in his final offer.

The preliminaries over, I left him to his task and for the next couple of days he tackled it most diligently. Then he rang to tell me he thought he would be ready with his figures on the following afternoon. He asked most particularly that I should go down to Takeley to be with Mary when he put his total to her. He also said he would like to explain to me first just how he had arrived at it. And he said that if I was not happy with it he would not put it to Mary at all. He added that if all went well he would like to take Mary and my wife and myself out for a quiet celebration dinner at which the business could be put behind us. He asked me where we might eat and I suggested the Foxley Hotel on the outskirts of Bishops Stortford. It was a hostelry much favoured by the partners in Elkin Matthews when they were entertaining and it was, coincidentally, the hotel where Bob was staying. 'Was it convenient for me?' Bob asked. I said that it was only an hour's run from our house but that since I didn't want to drive backwards and forwards through the traffic that crowded London's northern rim more often than was strictly necessary, I would bring my wife when I came to collect Bob in the afternoon and would leave her to read quietly in a corner of the lounge until we came back with Mary some hours later.

When we arrived at the Foxley next day I introduced Jean and Bob briefly and then discovered that the lounge was being used by a convention of salesmen and that there was nowhere else downstairs to sit. Bob at once offered Jean the use of his room. He took her up, settled her in a chair, showed her where the telephone was and invited her to order a tray of tea on his account whenever she wanted one.

Then Bob went through his figures, section by section. Some he had put a little higher than I reckoned, others a little lower, but the final answer was more than satisfactory. Indeed I thought it would come as a pleasant surprise to Mary, and I would be able to recommend it wholeheartedly. Bob and I drove on to Takeley and went through everything again with Mary and with her brother, a bank manager, who was one of Laurie's executors. They both professed themselves well satisfied and Bob and Mary shook hands on the deal. By the time we had made arrangements for packing and shipping it was not too soon to be heading back to the Foxley for dinner.

'Had everything been satisfactory?' Bob asked Jean.

'Well' said Jean. 'At four o'clock I thought a cup of tea would be welcome so I picked up the phone but couldn't get anyone to answer it. So eventually I went downstairs, found the reception desk and asked if I could have a tray of tea upstairs. 'Certainly madam, what room?' came the reply. At this point Jean realized she had no notion of Bob's room number. 'I'm afraid I have no idea'.

'Well what name is it?' asked the receptionist. And suddenly Jean heard herself saying 'I only know him as Bob!'

HARRY NORTH
DEMONSTRATES AN UNUSUAL TECHNIQUE

After a successful jumble sale in aid of a charity, I was helping several friends to clear the hall and dispose of the unwanted leftovers. Among them was a motley collection of fifty or a hundred books on a variety of subjects.

'Anthony, you know about books, will you deal with this lot?' the chairman of the organising committee asked.

'Certainly,' I said. 'I'll take them down to Harry North.'

Harry North ran a little second-hand bookshop in Green Lanes, Palmers Green. He was something of a character. He swam in the council's open-air pool every day of the year, regardless of the weather, and nearly every week he had a letter in the local paper on some issue or other. His bookshop was clean and tidy and his books were modestly priced. When my father still lived in Palmers Green he was a regular visitor to Harry's shop and over the course of my school years I myself spent a great deal of my pocket money there.

So it was that I was not a complete stranger when I staggered in just before Harry closed on the Saturday evening in question, carrying two heavy bags of miscellaneous books. 'Hello Anthony,' Harry said. 'What have you got there?'

'A pretty miscellaneous lot, I'm afraid,' I said, 'but I want to sell them to you.'

'Hmmm' Harry said, rummaging through the contents of the bags. After three or four minutes he straightened up and told me :

'Here's what I am going to do : I am going to offer you thirty shillings for the lot and hope you don't take it!' This was an unusual buying technique but it certainly convinced me that I was unlikely to get more for the books and certainly not from Harry. I have been circumspect about using this particular form of words in my own dealings with those offering me books.

CHAPTER TWENTY-FOUR

HARRY CAHN

WINSTON CHURCHILL,
AND LARGE PORTIONS OF CAVIAR

I have already made brief mention of the Churchill collector,
H. A. Cahn, but he deserves more elaborate treatment in this book.
Mr Cahn had been a customer of ours for some two years when I
first became aware of him. He was formally correct in everything
that he did and although we became close friends, speaking to one
another at least once a week for twenty or thirty years, he never
called me other than 'Mr Rota', nor did I ever address him except as
'Mr Cahn'. This became singularly odd when his wife Clementine
began to call my wife and me by our first names and even invited us
to use the short-form of her name, Tiny, which is how she was
addressed by her family.

Harry Cahn was born into a merchant banking family in Frankfurt. He once told me that before Hitler came to power, directors of
his bank sat on the boards of twenty of the thirty largest companies
in Germany. As a bachelor he occupied a grand apartment on
the top floor of the building which housed the bank. The bank
provided staff to take care of all his domestic chores and he even
had the luxury of a valet. Then, as the Nazis tightened their grip on
Germany, life became more and more difficult for the Jewish
community and those who could began to leave the country. Harry
himself did not get away until 1938 when he managed to get to
England, but only by leaving almost everything he possessed behind him. He was beginning to make a life for himself in London
when war broke out and he was interned as an enemy alien. When
he was eventually released he served in the Pioneer Corps of the
British Army.

'When the war was over', he used to say, 'I found myself in a foreign country, a banker without capital. What was I to do?' He solved the problem in two ways. First he looked after the investments of a number of German emigrés, some of whom had had more good fortune than he in getting their money out of Germany. Then, more unusually, he set up as a banking consultant. He would match his clients to banks – and more importantly, bank managers – who were exactly right for their needs and their particular situation. He would endeavour to see that the personal chemistry between client and manager was good. He would then advise the client on all aspects of the relationship with the bank. This would include basic advice about how to dress when visiting the bank, even down to the sort of shirt that would be appropriate; and instruction in wise practice. I remember that he used to say 'If there is bad news, be sure the bank hears it from you first'. Then he would review balance sheets, look at business plans and so on, suggesting how undisputed facts could best be presented to win the required response from the bank.

Once we had become friends he invited me to make use of his services, without charge, whenever I felt the need. I remember going to him once with a particular proposition and getting advice for which I have always been grateful. Through a contact of my colleague George Lawson we were offered access to a considerable capital sum which would only be available to us for investment in North America. For example we could start from scratch a subsidiary business in Toronto or New York, stocking it to a large extent with books supplied from our London-based business. Alternatively, we could buy an existing North American bookshop. This would enable us to hit the ground running. I telephoned Mr Cahn and reported all this to him. He asked if he might look at the figures and review our detailed plans. The next day he came back to me and said 'Mr Rota, I have looked at these proposals. I have no problems with the arithmetic – indeed the figures are good, but I am going to advise you not to go ahead'. 'Why not, if the figures are right?' I asked. 'Mr Rota', he said, 'I know you too well, I know the way you run your business, I have been inside your home, I know your wife and I know your children. I know that you would keep a close eye on New York and that the moment there was any serious problem there, you would jump on a plane and go to do something about it. Believe me, serious problems would arise, they always do. And you would soon be living on aeroplanes between London and New York. You would earn more money, yes, but at what a cost.' For a while I was very disappointed, but I followed his advice and soon came to realize how sound it was.

Our business together had begun quietly when, probably around 1960, Mr Cahn wrote to us to ask for catalogues, saying that he was interested in collecting first editions by Winston Churchill. I later discovered that his book collecting centred around Churchill because of his admiration for Churchill's successful struggle to defeat Hitler.

Buying from catalogues was not building up Mr Cahn's collection quickly enough, so he came to us at Bodley House to see what Churchill we had in stock and to learn how progress might be accelerated. I remember to this day the impression he made on that first appearance. Then as always in the future he was immaculately turned out. When he raised and removed his bowler hat not a single grey hair was out of place. His moustache was neatly trimmed. His suit well cut. His velvet-collared overcoat, his gloves and his glistening shoes, all spoke of a man who took trouble to present himself well. At this first meeting I learned something about the present strength of his Churchill collection and about the criteria Mr Cahn had set for its development. It transpired that he wanted to range both widely and deeply, taking in books to which Churchill contributed a foreword or a preface, books about Churchill and books about Churchill's times which made significant mention of the man. Mr Cahn also wanted advance proof copies, inscribed copies and foreign language editions. He insisted on the highest standard of condition.

Over the next six or twelve months I sent him quotations of four or five items. Each time he responded quickly, coming in to the shop to look at the books for himself. Each time he tried to get the price down; drawing air in through his teeth, he would say that the price seemed very high. Was that really the lowest that I could take, he would ask? Could I not do a little better for him? He was not a particularly rich man, and so on. At Bertram Rota Ltd we had never favoured the tactics of the Persian market and always quoted figures which we were confident were fair and eminently attainable. So it was that when Mr Cahn complained in due course that we were not offering him very many things I explained our pricing policy to him and pointed out that for the best Churchill material the demand far exceeded the supply. I said that even though he had developed the habit of paying our price in the end I found it distasteful and time-consuming to have to defend our figures on every single occasion. If another customer did not make me go through that rigmarole then it was possible that he or she might get first chance at particularly good material. Mr Cahn saw the point at once and never questioned a price again.

And he knew about prices. He kept a meticulously compiled card index on which he noted the price brought by every copy of a Churchill item he saw in dealer's catalogues or sold at auction. He also developed the habit of enquiring of me before he bought Churchill material from other dealers or from the private sources that he cultivated.

In his collecting he went as far as to take the publications of the Political Warfare Executive – leaflets that were dropped over occupied Europe for propaganda purposes. These made much use of Churchill texts. Harry Cahn had made contact with a telephone operator in Hamburg who used to ring him when working the night shift to tell him of any PWE leaflets that he had recently discovered. There were more of these than Harry really needed, so he came to pass his duplicates on to me. This was a very useful source of supply.

Although I have now dropped into the habit of referring to Mr Cahn as 'Harry', I still did not call him by that name to his face. As our friendship developed we began to exchange hospitality. Harry and Clementine Cahn lived on the top floor of a block of flats in Hampstead with a terrace giving splendid views over London. The problem was there was no lift to get one up to that top floor and on our first visit my wife and I marvelled at Harry and Clementine's fitness (they were no longer young) in bounding up those seemingly endless stone steps. We visited them in their home countless times. Until she was comfortably past her ninetieth birthday, Tiny gave glorious dinner parties, often cooking and serving an entire salmon. From his days as the heir apparent to the merchant bank in Frankfurt Harry was accustomed to drinking good wine and he certainly served such. Tiny's first husband had been an antique dealer and he left her lovely china, glass and silver. In the living room was the nursery furniture, two little chairs and a table, which had been used by the little boy who became Kaiser Wilhelm, the 'Kaiser Bill' who ruled Germany during the First World War.

Perhaps best of all were the special invitations we used to get two or three times a year. One satisfied investment client used to express his thanks by sending Harry a large tin of caviar. Then we would get a phone call: 'Mr Rota, we have some caviar and we have some champagne and the question is, how soon can you be here to share it with us?' Even then the quality of the accoutrements added to the perfection of the occasion. Caviar spoons and the knives for spreading the black treasure on points of toast were, of course, made of horn so that metal should not affect the flavour, but the best part of the evening for us was hearing Tiny and even Harry reminiscing about the old days in Frankfurt. Occasionally a sombre note would be injected as when Tiny's mind ran forward a few decades to the time when, as she put it, 'you were reluctant to call the police if you had had a burglary lest worst things should befall you.'

By now whenever Harry went away for more than a few days at a time (he and Tiny would sometimes visit his sister in America) he would say to me 'Mr Rota, you have *plein pouvoir*' and I found this a most awesome responsibility. I tried to explain to him that it was easy to spend thousands of pounds on my own account, knowing that if I made a mistake or an error of judgement, I could balance it out on the next transaction. When I was spending *his* money things were wholly otherwise.

The collection had now grown to a fearsome size, utilizing every inch of shelf space in his study and filling cupboards all over the flat. Virtually all the 'A' items in Woods's bibliography of Churchill were present, in uniformly fine condition and often with dust-wrappers where such existed. Not every scarce pamphlet was there, perhaps because Harry had not succeeded in finding copies in satisfactory condition, although the almost impossibly difficult twopenny edition of *Mr Brodrick's Army* was one of the high spots of the collection (see page 134). There were presentation copies galore, including some to Churchill's private secretary, Sir Edward Marsh. There were two mint copies of the limited edition of *Marlborough*, the morocco spines of each four-volume set completely unfaded and matching perfectly, a rare combination. There were Advance Proof Copies, the text differing substantially from final publication. The roll call of books to which Churchill had contributed was virtually complete. Periodicals with contributions by him abounded. Books about him were well represented, as were books in which he was discussed at any length at all. There were books from Randolph Churchill's library, there were foreign language editions of Churchill's own writings and, thanks to that German telephone operator, the collection contained a fine array of the propaganda leaflets. I confess I found it mildly amusing that Harry used cellophane shirt-bags from his laundry to keep the slimmer volumes and the pamphlets in pristine condition.

Inevitably there came the day when Tiny died. Thereafter Harry was like a fish out of water. Her family tried to keep him in good spirits as did his friends, but it was an uphill struggle and not very long thereafter Harry succumbed to cancer. We had lost two good friends.

The last service I could do for Harry was to sell his Churchill collection for the benefit of his heirs. With George Lawson I made the trip back to Hampstead and we set to work on the melancholy task of making an appraisal of the value of the Churchill material if sold *en bloc,* (which was the fate Harry wanted for it.) Going through the entire collection piece by piece I came to admire anew the pertinacity and energy of the man who had assembled such a monument to Churchill, his hero, the man who had defeated Hitler.

We learn in this life to beware of people selling gold bricks at bargain prices but I have been the beneficiary over the years of several instances of people knowingly selling me books for far less than they were worth. One lady invited me to her house in the country in order to buy back from her the collection of books by Lawrence of Arabia that we had helped her to build up over the preceding decade. I was able to offer her quite a decent profit on her original investment but she said to me, 'No, Mr Rota. I am a sick woman and I haven't very long to live. I don't need that much money for the books. I will take £1,000 less because I want you to have them to pass on to other people at affordable prices.'

The motives of the owner in the second instance I shall quote were not laid out so explicitly. When I joined the committee of the Antiquarian Booksellers' Association in 1959 I found myself, as I have told, in the embarrassing position of being in a minority of one. Such awkwardness as I felt was mitigated to a large degree by the kindness and consideration of the then president of the ABA, Harry Pratley, of Hall's Bookshop in Tunbridge Wells. Harry was a saintly man, loved by all who came to know him. Harry was well known in the town; indeed he was almost too well known, for when walking through the streets of Tunbridge Wells with him one could not hold a conversation because it seemed as though every third person stopped to greet him and wish him well as he passed.

In his business dealings he treated sympathetically widows and those obliged to sell books they would rather have kept. He was a pillar of his church. He organised the giving of baskets of groceries to every pensioner in the district each Christmas time. He was totally selfless in the work he did for our trade association.

At a book fair in London one year he sought me out and invited me down to Tunbridge Wells to look at a collection he had just bought. 'Anthony,' he said. 'I have just bought a lot of inscribed copies of books from Wilfrid Scawen Blunt's library at Crabbet Park. I would like to sell them as a lot and I would like you to have first refusal of them.'

A few days later I went down to Tunbridge Wells by appointment and Harry took me to a little room in the basement of his shop where 150 or 200 literary first editions were laid out on shelves. They included some books (verse and diaries) by Scawen Blunt himself. Harry named the price that he wanted. It was low in three figures. Before leaving me to look at the books and make my calculations he added that he did not want to argue about the figure. I was either to take it or simply decline. Harry went upstairs and I began to work along the shelves that he had indicated. Before I got to the end of the first one (there were four in all), my running total had already passed the figure he had given me. At first I thought I must have made a mistake so I added the figures again: the result was the same. I wondered what to do. I decided that a bookseller of Harry's long experience knew perfectly well what a bargain he was offering me. I stayed in the basement long enough to make it look as though I had given due weight to the price of each book on the four shelves and then went upstairs, thanked Harry warmly. I wrote a cheque and took the books away. Harry said to me later that he had bought the books reasonably and was delighted to have had the chance to offer a friend (in this case a young friend and a new friend) an opportunity to share his good fortune. The world would be a better place if there were more people like Harry Pratley.

CHAPTER TWENTY-FIVE

THE SITWELLS

Over the years my company transacted a good deal of business with members of the Sitwell family, mostly buying manuscripts from Edith, Osbert and Sacheverell Sitwell on behalf of the University of Texas. My father used to visit Edith at the Sesame Club, where she lived when she was in London, Osbert at Renishaw, and Sacheverell at his home at Weston in Northamptonshire. After my father's death in 1966 I had the very real pleasure of looking after our business with Sacheverell, as well as working with his younger son Francis, who had inherited Dame Edith's surviving papers.

Sir Sacheverell (he had inherited the baronetcy on Sir Osbert's death) was a gentleman in the finest sense of the word. Tall, slender and by this time rather frail, Sachie, as he was almost universally known, never failed to think of the comfort and convenience of others and to put them ahead of his own.

In the course of assessing the fair market value of some of his manuscript notebooks, I discovered that they contained many unpublished poems. With due diffidence I asked whether Sachie might allow me to bring out a selection of them in a limited edition. He readily agreed and sent me three groups of poems which he particularly favoured. Most of them I liked very much but there were two or three which I felt did not stand up to the level of the others and I asked, in the most polite terms I could find, whether he might substitute others for them. He was furious. He told me in effect if not in terms that my job was to be a publisher and not a critic and he insisted that I return all the poems to him. He remained upset for some little while.

That is how things stood when, following Sir Osbert's death, Frank Magro, his valet and companion, and effectively his male nurse after he was crippled by Parkinson's disease, inherited a life-tenancy of an apartment in the Castello di Montegufoni, the family's house and estate in Tuscany. Wanting to sell Osbert's last manuscripts and various inscribed books which were also bequeathed to him, Magro approached the University of Texas, and Warren Roberts, director of the Humanities Research Center there, asked me to go to Italy on his behalf to list and evaluate what was available. Although Magro had been wonderful in his support for Sir Osbert, I knew that the family were not pleased that he should have inherited as he did. Not wanting to make matters worse between Sir Sacheverell and myself, I telephoned Francis and explained my predicament. He said that he was quite sure his father would understand my position and would not take umbrage if I did the University's bidding. As it happened Sachie was in residence in Montegufoni when I arrived. He was out to dinner when I called on him so I left my card with his housekeeper. Immediately after breakfast next morning this polite and considerate man, in advanced years and in poor health, with only one lung, climbed the long steep stone staircase to Frank's apartment, knocked at the door and asked to see me. Then he apologised profusely for not having been at home to receive me the previous evening. He enquired about my health, wished me a pleasant stay and bade me good morning. It was clear that our editorial quarrel was over.

Six years later we published not a selection of Sachie's poems but a symposium edited by Derek Parker in Sachie's honour. It included contributions by Cyril Connolly, Raymond Mortimer, Kenneth Clark, William Walton, John Piper, John Rothenstein, Lady Diana Cooper and Hugh MacDiarmid.

But I am getting ahead of myself. In October 1969 I flew out to Pisa and instead of taking the fast bus along the highway to Florence, took a slow, stopping train made up of antiquated but beautifully finished carriages. It wound its way through vineyards and through market gardens full of ripening crops of giant tomatoes, corn-cobs, marrows, pumpkins and melons. At our approach old women in aprons ran out of their railway-workers' houses to close the gates of level crossings against road traffic.

Healthy looking chickens scratched around only inches from our wheels. In due course we arrived at Florence where Frank Magro met me. Maltese by nationality, he was of average height and stature and very neat in his appearance. He had hired a Mercedes and driver to collect me from the station and take me out to Montegufoni but first he said we should take a cup of tea on the terrace of a cafe opposite the Michelangelo statue of David, rather too many, I thought.

The sun was setting as we left Florence and wound up into the hills for our journey of perhaps twenty kilometres to Montegufoni itself. As we turned into the castello the light had practically gone. The sky had turned the darkest of dark blues. Bats flitted to and fro in the courtyard. Some beast of burden, memory tells me it was an ox, brought in a cart loaded with grapes to make the Montegufoni wine which was for a long time marketed under the label of 'Sir Baroni Osbert Sitwell'. (The white was better than the red, I found, although both were eminently drinkable.) Two old women, kerchiefs over their heads, sat on low chairs against a wall, cleaning bottles with a mixture of sand and water. It was a magical moment.

Frank pulled out an enormous key and opened the door that let on to his private stair. When, breathless, we arrived at the top, he shut the apartment door, itself some four inches thick, behind us and said 'Now we are alone, we can do what we like. We can laugh. We can sing. We can even dance!' I hastily declared that 'My wife always says I am a terrible dancer', giving emphasis to the first two words. Letting the implication float past him, Frank prepared a pleasant meal for us, flirting mildly the while.

In the morning I did my work with the books and manuscripts before Frank showed me round Montegufoni. It was fascinating to see features of it which I only knew from the descriptions and illustrations in Osbert's *Great Morning*. At lunch time we walked down the hill between rows of vines to the village *trattoria* where Frank had booked a private room and ordered a veritable feast of Tuscan cooking. I felt stuffed like the proverbial turkey-cock as I was eventually loaded onto the plane for London.

I have to thank my old friend John Pearson, author of *Façades*, the composite biography of the Sitwells, for introducing me to opportunities to handle still more Sitwell autograph material. I bought some from the lady who typed Sir Osbert's manuscripts for him, and rather more from David Horner, who was Sir Osbert's companion (in this day and age one might well say 'partner') for many years. There was irony in the cruel trick which Fate played on Horner. As Sir Osbert was more and more disabled and confined by Parkinson's disease, so Horner flew the coop to flirt at various continental spas. Then came a night when he, Osbert and Edith were all staying at Montegufoni. They were sitting in the salon after dinner, drinking and listening to music. First Edith went to bed, then Frank Magro carried Osbert upstairs, leaving David Horner alone to continue listening to the gramophone and, it is suspected, to continue to drink. Eventually he switched off the music, switched off the light, left the room and turned towards the stair. Unhappily he turned the wrong way and instead of ascending pitched headlong down a flight of stone steps. He broke a number of bones, did something ghastly to his spine and knocked himself out. He lay in a pool of blood until one of the servants found him the following morning. First the doctors said he would not live, then that he would not walk again. The first prediction was wrong but alas the second was all too true and when I met him he was confined to his bed, except for an hour or so each afternoon when he was carried to a chair in the living room of his elegant apartment in York House, the mansion block near the foot of Kensington Church Street. I believe that Osbert paid the rent at York House but David Horner's days of visiting continental spas, whether to flirt or purely to take the waters were definitely over.

In the circumstances I thought he remained remarkably cheerful. He was a wonderful gossip and full of mischief. His eyes would gleam as he demolished this person's character or that one's reputation. Before each of my visits he would fill an attaché case with good things: letters to Osbert from his father, Sir George; manuscripts of poems by Osbert; letters from Edith and Sachie to himself; the typescript of an early version of *Miracle on Sinai*; a letter from Edith to Osbert; letters he had received from Osbert and so on. He would pull these things out of the case one by one, like a conjuror producing a succession of rabbits from a particularly commodious top hat. Sorry though one was for his condition, visiting him was in no sense a depressing experience. I was sad when his death, doubtless a happy release for him, deprived us of his company.

Visits to Weston to see Sachie were always a pleasure. His housekeeper, Gertrude, who had been a maid at Renishaw, was kind enough to say she welcomed our visits since my wife and I always cheered Sachie up and even led him to take a little more food than the minuscule amount that had become his wont. As Derek Parker has recounted in the foreword to the Symposium, to a background of Scarlatti, there might be talk of Liszt, Tiepolo, Modigliani, Torcello and much more – and then Sachie might ask if he might turn on the television and watch some all-in wrestling.

Towards the end of his life Sachie seemed to think that everyone was of the same generation as himself and had had the same opportunities to travel. If one mentioned Vienna and *Sacher-torte* he would say 'Did you know Frau Sacher?'. 'You've met Modigliani of course?' would be the introduction to a string of stories. That our visits to Weston sometimes resulted in a little business was a bonus. Each meeting with Sachie was a delight in itself.

PAUL SCOTT

In 1967 I took over the firm's dealings with the writer Paul Scott, whose Raj Quartet was beginning to win him much praise, and the television adaptation of which was to bring him fame. We were engaged in selling his manuscripts and other literary papers and, admiring the Quartet as much as I did, to say nothing of liking the earlier novels that I had read (and especially The Chinese Love Pavilion, *set in the time of the Malaysian troubles) I found my new task very congenial. I went to see Paul in his study in his home in Hampstead Garden Suburb, and had lunch with him several times in Soho. We got on famously. I learned that he and I had grown up in the same North London suburb, Paul being twelve years my senior. We talked about his work as a literary agent, a subject which fascinated me. Through the literary agency, David Higham Associates, he had had dealings with William Collins & Sons when my wife worked for them some years before. I suggested that Paul and his wife and Jean and I should go out to dinner together one night. This seemed to be a popular idea and we arranged a date.*

Came the day and Jean and I went over to Hampstead to collect Paul and Penny. We had a drink at their house and then went to the restaurant, where the four of us shared one bottle of wine, Paul taking only one glass. We all enjoyed the evening and on the way home I said to Jean, 'What did you think of him?' 'He was fine,' she replied, 'but he was "sloshed".' 'How could he have been drunk?' I responded. 'You saw him: he only had two drinks all evening.' 'I don't know about that, but he was drunk' Jean insisted. 'Didn't you notice how slurred his speech was?' 'It's always slurred', I countered. 'Then he must always be drinking,' Jean said.

Alas she proved right. Paul had a form of writer's block which he could only get through by keeping a tumbler of gin on his desk. He would start sipping it at ten in the morning and not stop until he had finished writing for the day. In personal terms this was a tragedy, for the medical evidence suggests that the illness that carried him off in 1978 at the age of 58 was certainly encouraged and probably brought on by the heavy drinking.

CHAPTER TWENTY-SIX

BEWARE OF
LITTLE OLD LADIES

When I entered the book trade in the early 1950s the prevailing morality about buying seemed to be that it was all right to play catch-as-catch-can when dealing with fellow booksellers, and to be as tough as you liked when making purchases from owners or executors who were themselves hard-headed businessmen, but a special standard of conduct was called for when dealing with the proverbial 'little old lady,' the kind of person aimed at by advertisements for the Scottish Widows insurance people. That was the received wisdom, but in my own case I have consistently found that the little old ladies can look after themselves very well indeed – and are often far tougher than their young male counterparts who are supposed to be blessed with the ability to drive a hard bargain. Such was certainly the case when I went to Columbus, Ohio in 1986 to talk to the collector Lloyd Emerson Siberell's widow about her late husband's quite outstanding Powys collection.

English literature boasts a number of prolific families, the Brontës and the Sitwells among them, but I doubt if any of them surpassed the Powys family in the number of family members who wrote and published books or in the total number of works they produced. Mention the name of Powys and one thinks first of John Cowper, primarily a novelist, then perhaps of T. F. renowned for his whimsical short stories, and of their brother Llewelyn, whose philosophical essays still enjoy popularity. In addition there were A. R. Powys, Littleton Powys, (and his wife Elizabeth Myers), Gertrude Powys, Philippa Powys and Marion Powys, who wrote about lace-making. Lloyd Siberell collected them all. He was moreover John Cowper's bibliographer and for some titles his publisher too.

He did much to promote John Cowper's interests in America and not unnaturally the two men became good friends. Thus it was that the Siberell collection was unusually complete, contained many presentation copies and included lengthy series of letters.

After Lloyd Siberell's death, his widow, his second wife, younger than he, retained his book collection for some years, but in 1985 (when I would judge that she was in her mid-seventies) she decided that the time had come to sell it. She therefore wrote to the heads of the more obvious research libraries that might have been interested in buying such a collection *en bloc*, the Humanities Research Center at the University of Texas being one of them. Her asking price, I heard over the grapevine, was $60,000. None of the librarians she approached rose to the bait, one telling me privately that he thought $40,000 would be a more appropriate figure. It was at this stage that Mrs Siberell first wrote to me.

That first letter, like all that followed it, was a model of old-fashioned courtesy, and seemingly of diffidence too. Her husband had bought many of his books from my father, and later a number from me, she said, so it was natural that she should turn to us. Would we, she wondered, be interested? Of course we would, we replied: was there any sort of catalogue or list that we could see? Yes, came the answer, there were handwritten catalogue cards and Mrs Siberell had heard that there was now a machine which could copy these. She 'thought' it was called the xerox. She wasn't very good at mechanical things but if she could get the hang of it she would make me a set of the slips. But how, she asked, could she get it to me? Finding this seeming naïveté rather charming, I explained about air mail and about courier services. Here, I decided, was one of those 'little old ladies' who needed special care and help.

The catalogue duly arrived (I seem to remember that I got landed with the courier's bill) and I began to make a rough appraisal. I decided that in the prevailing climate the collection could not be sold as one lot but would have to be divided. Its worth to Bertram Rota Ltd I set at something between $25,000 and $30,000 depending on such factors as the condition of the books, the warmth of the inscriptions and the contents of the letters – things impossible to gauge from the catalogue entries.

I communicated my findings to Mrs Siberell as gently as I could. She replied very graciously, confessing disappointment and saying that she could not take less than $40,000 – after all, the xeroxing had cost quite a lot! I said that my wife and I would be in the United States quite soon and would be very happy to call on her to examine the books and to try to negotiate a compromise. 'If you are prepared to be flexible,' I wrote, 'I am optimistic about our chances of reaching agreement.'

Back came the reply: 'I will bend but I will not break.' In addition there was a good deal of helpful if rather simplistic travel information and advice. We arranged to fit Columbus into our itinerary.

When the day for our visit finally arrived our plane was delayed and we were a couple of hours behind schedule. The instant we got to our hotel I rang to explain that we would be late. We would just grab a sandwich and jump into a taxi. 'Oh, you poor dears,' said Mrs Siberell, 'Wouldn't you prefer to lie down for a couple of hours to recover from your journey? Please don't distress yourselves on my account.' I said we were anxious to be with her at the earliest possible moment, so she told me to make sure the cab driver didn't try to take us the long way round, something, she warned me, that they were prone to attempt with strangers.

Forty minutes later we were at the foot of the elegant apartment block which was now her home. We made our way up and the door was answered by as sweet an old lady as we had pictured from her correspondence and telephone calls. After renewing her expressions of anxiety about the supposed strains of our journey she said in a stage whisper 'Mr Dainton is here.' I looked at my wife and raised my eyebrows in question. She raised hers in reply. Who was Mr Dainton? Something in Mrs Siberell's manner led me to imagine that he was a widower from the apartment across the hall, that he was lonely, very fond of Mrs Siberell and had perhaps dropped in on the pretext of borrowing a cup of sugar. How wrong can one be? Two minutes later we were introduced to a man in a business suit who passed me his card and introduced himself as Roger Dainton, of Dainton, Perks and Dainton (or so we will call them). 'I am this lady's attorney' he said. So the weak and defenceless widow was not defenceless after all. For the first time in my life an owner had her lawyer on hand when I called to view a private library.

Mrs Siberell showed me where the books were. If one included periodicals and letters there were several thousand items, many of them by their nature unique. After ten minutes Mr Dainton said 'Well, sir, what is your final offer?'

'I haven't the remotest idea yet,' I replied

'Oh. I'll give you a few more minutes.'

'A few more minutes won't be enough, I'm afraid. I expect to spend the next two or three hours looking at everything carefully.'

'Hmmh! Well I suppose you know your own business best.' Turning to his client he said 'Mrs Siberell, you don't need me here for this. I am going back to my office. Call me when Mr Rota is through.'

Three hours later he was back. I had seen enough to know that the figure at the top of my bracket was appropriate, i.e. $30,000. Mr Dainton seemed favourably impressed, but Mrs Siberell was implacable. 'Flexible' or not, she wanted $40,000 and not a cent less. Mr Dainton despaired of mediating and very decently, and perhaps shrewdly, asked us all to join him as his guests for dinner at his club.

The club, all dark wood, highly polished, with soft lights, and liveried staff speaking in hushed tones, could have been anywhere in St James's. Towards the end of a good meal Mr Dainton turned to me and said 'Mr Rota, if you were to sell this collection for more than $60,000 would you be prepared to divide the excess equally with this lady?'

'Certainly. You have my word on that,' I countered without even pausing to think.

'Mrs Siberell,' Mr Dainton continued, 'the speed and assurance of this gentleman's answer convince me absolutely that he *knows* he is not going to get as much as $60,000. My advice to you is to take his offer here and now. If you don't you will have a couple of rooms full of books, but you can't pay the rent and buy the groceries with books. Here's your best chance to turn them into money.'

And, very reluctantly, Mrs Siberell agreed, but the supposedly naïve little lady had proved much harder to do business with than the tough attorney. Mr Dainton asked me to 'drop by the office' in the morning to 'sign a little bit of paper.' At 10 am next day I presented myself and proceeded to sign my life away, at least to the extent of agreeing to a schedule of payments with horrific penalties if it was not adhered to. Then Mr Dainton said 'I'd like you to meet my son. He is the senior partner now and will look after Mrs Siberell when I'm gone.' We walked down the hall to a room with superb views over the city of Columbus, and Mr Dainton duly introduced me. Then he said 'John, this gentleman is going to . . .' (He broke off and suppressed a giggle.) He tried again 'is going to give Mrs Siberell . . .' It was no good, he had to pause to choke back a guffaw. 'Is going to give Mrs Siberell $30,000 (pause for a gale of laughter) for a heap of old books!' Unable to contain himself any longer he rocked with laughter, clearly convinced that I was quite mad. Of course it is nothing new for the uninitiated to find it hard to take the world of old books seriously. I remember that when George Sims put a brass plate on his gate, bearing the simple caption 'G F. Sims – Rare Books', the village policeman asked what it meant and on being told asked 'And is there a living in that?'

Who had the last laugh with the Siberell Powys collection? The attorney was clearly amused and probably thought he had earned his fee quite easily. Mrs Siberell marketed some of her assets very successfully and presumably enjoyed the role-playing she had engaged in. My wife and I met a charming lady who turned out not to be as naïve as I first thought and so saved me the moral dilemma of trying to buy to the best advantage while watching out for the interests of the supposedly weaker party. I ended up with just about the best Powys collection in private hands. Manuscript material, including 1,800 complex pages for John Cowper Powys's major novel *Wolf Solent* went to the National Library of Wales and I published a Powys catalogue (No. 244, 1987) that I remain very proud of.

It did quite well, but the bookseller Margaret Eaton, a good friend, was selling her own Powys collection at the same time and had had a head start. Moreover I bought the collection formed by Kenneth Hopkins which came onto the market very soon after. Three Powys collections (of which I owned two) was an awful lot for the market to absorb and today, more than a decade later, I still have some Siberell books on my shelves, but please don't tell Mr Dainton: I wouldn't want to give him the satisfaction.

Helene Hanff's book 84 Charing Cross Road *and its adaptation to stage and screen made Marks & Co's bookshop and its London address famous throughout the English-speaking world and perhaps beyond. The book's hero was Frank Doel (played on screen by Frank Finlay) who was first assistant to Ben Marks and Mark Cohen, the 'Marks & Co' of the firm's title.*

Frank was a gentle, unassuming man, with an incredibly wide knowledge of books and booksellers. He had an amazing memory: he not only knew points and prices but the whereabouts of every copy currently on the market.

If in the 1950s I needed a standard set of an author's works I would always begin by telephoning Frank.

'Frank, it's Anthony. I need a Bradenham edition of Disraeli. Can you help?'

'A Bradenham Disraeli? I sold one last month. Let me see now: twelve volumes, black cloth. Being who you are I suppose you want one in the dust-wrappers? Tom Thorp has one but one of the dust-wrappers is a bit torn. I think your best bet at the moment would be Foyle's. As you come out of the lift on the second floor, turn left and it's in the third bay on the right – somewhere around shoulder height. The first volume's got an ugly bookplate in it but otherwise there's nothing wrong with it, and they want £125 for it as far as I remember.'

This prodigious feat of memory and many others like it were at the disposal of all Frank's friends, absolutely free of charge. What a loss it was when, thinking a severe and chronic pain in his stomach was cancer, he avoided going to the doctor and died of peritonitis which could have been avoided had he sought help in time.

CHAPTER TWENTY-SEVEN

THE JOHN GAWSWORTH MEMORIAL SERVICE

In 1971 a number of us gathered in the private chapel of a large house in Kensington to say farewell to 'King Juan I of Redonda', a crown John had inherited from M. P. Shiel, the science fiction writer. I say 'John', but John Gawsworth was itself a pseudonym, picked, the uncharitable said, because it could easily be confused with 'John Galsworthy' and perhaps result in extra sales. 'John' was actually Terence Ian Fytton Armstrong. He was born in 1912 and soon displayed a passion for literature. He became a fine lyric poet and a good editor. As King of Redonda he 'ennobled' people who had helped M. P. Shiel, but later, when he was in his cups, which was all too often the case, he would draw his sword and lay it on the shoulder of virtually anyone who would buy him a drink. In short he became a tragic figure. The chaotic service in June 1971, on his birthday, was attended by many book trade figures and a number of minor writers. Here is an account of it taken from a letter I wrote at the time to Albert Sperisen, book collector, typographer, and linch-pin of the Book Club of California.

'Yesterday I went to the Gawsworth Memorial Service with Dusty Miller (late of Frank Hollings), and Winnie Myers, the auto-graph dealer. Alan Thomas was there and remarked that a really 'liquid' dinner would have been more appropriate. It was held in a large private house in Kensington. After ringing the front door bell, we were ushered into a dark, panelled hall which was rapidly filling with incense billowing out from the Chapel. At the appointed hour we made our way towards the source of the smoke and took our places in the pews. The Chapel was richly appointed and seemed strangely at variance with the curiously assorted congregation. At least two of Gawsworth's wives were present, but luckily there was no scratching or hair pulling. At least 20% of the congregation appeared to be in a chronic state of inebriation. One man from this faction, wearing a particularly horsey tweed suit, had to be frowned at very hard before he stubbed out the cigarette he was cheerfully smoking in the front row. A server, who looked like something out of Firbank, and who was making eyes at some of the male members of the congregation during most of the service, lit the candles and we were away.

The priest, a mild little man who proved never to have met John, began the Invocation. He had got no further than 'In the name of the Father' when there was a noise like a herd of wild elephants on the rampage. Three or four heavily shod mourners were making their way up the bare wooden steps. The priest paused to let them take their places and began again. Once, twice and three times more he was interrupted in a similar fashion. Boldly he carried on.

He got to the Homily. He said a little about John, and then dropped what was for me the bombshell of the evening. He tossed it in casually as an aside. 'Although John Gawsworth was nominally a Hindu . . .' he said. A Hindu? John? Whoever told him that? When I picked myself up, I could not but smile at what could only have been one of John's more tongue-in-cheek pronouncements. The priest, somewhat nervous by now, went on to comment on the aptness of Mr Francis Fytton's description of John as 'a pacifist-in-arms'. For reasons that will become apparent, I never did get to hear Mr Fytton explain this singular phrase. Neither of my companions could shed light on it afterwards, and George Sims and I worried at it like two dogs at a bone for half-an-hour yesterday. I am sure John disapproved of war – who doesn't – but that's not the same thing as being a pacifist, let alone a pacifist-in-arms.

We came to the Prayers and Requiem. All knelt for the Prayers, including, as well as the Catholics, a Jew, several members of the Church of England, a number of atheists and at least one Methodist. The priest than said 'I am now going to say a short Requiem. You may resume your seats if you wish, although some of you may prefer to remain kneeling.' I regret to say that the entire congregation scrambled back into their chairs, some with sighs of relief.

The next item on the agenda was scheduled as 'Appreciation spoken by Francis Fytton, Esq.' The priest called for Mr Fytton but answer came there none. I met him outside afterwards: he had mistaken the hour. In his absence the priest invited Oliver Cox to read something that Lawrence Durrell had written about Gawsworth. At that point up jumped Sir John Waller, Bt., who also appeared to have taken drink, although as Derek Patmore remarked afterwards, he was if anything more sober than usual. 'If Francis has not come, Oliver, I will say a word' he began. 'Sit down, John' Cox hissed in a stage whisper. 'Not now'. Reluctantly, Waller resumed his seat while Cox completed his reading. As soon as he had concluded, Waller leapt to his feet again saying it was now his turn. He made a rolling progress down the aisle, stepped through the communion rail and looked round for somewhere to put the armful of books he was carrying. The altar was handy, and he dumped them there. This sacrilege was too much for the priest who insisted on their prompt removal. Unabashed Waller began again: 'I remember John...'. Cox wasn't having this. 'Not now John, we are in the middle of a service' – and he literally dragged the protesting baronet the length of the aisle and down the stairs and out of the chapel. The noise of their going gradually vanished into the distance. The priest was obviously glad that the end was in sight. I can't swear that he shrugged and said 'Oh well' but that was what he clearly wanted to do. He certainly did continue 'The service is nearly over anyway' and at a brisk trot he led us into the final Prayers and Benediction.

I ought to have stayed for the poetry reading afterwards but my two companions were too utterly depressed and would have none of it. As they had left things in my car, and as I had promised to drive one of them home, I followed their example, folded my tent, and silently crept away. On reflection afterwards, I could only conclude that this rather sad but tragicomic service was absolutely appropriate to celebrate John's life, which in itself had had so many elements of tragedy and comedy intermixed.

232

TACTICAL SEATING

I have enjoyed almost all the time I have spent at committee meetings of our trade association, but never more than the two or three years when Anton Zwemmer served on the committee with me. Founder of the art bookshop in Charing Cross Road and the gallery in Lichfield Street, which still bear the Zwemmer name, he was one of the most distinguished members of that circle of booksellers of a previous generation to whom my father introduced me. I think I was still in short trousers, spending a day of the school holidays with my father, when he had to see Anton on a matter of business before taking me to see a show. As far as I remember the business meeting was to tie up our sale to Zwemmer's of a complete set of books from William Morris's Kelmscott Press. Anton, with his white hair, his commanding height and gracious bearing, cut an impressive figure but he was not the least intimidating.

I was very pleased when, some twenty years later, he was persuaded to stand for election to the ABA Committee and was successful at his first attempt. I went to his inaugural meeting early but did not take my place at the table until Anton had arrived and chosen his. With almost indecent haste I took the place next to him, starting a habit that held good on the second Wednesday of every month (traditionally the day for ABA meetings) while Anton remained on the committee. My unashamed purpose was to have Anton's company and conversation during the tea break, for he had a fund of stories, particularly concerning his dealings with artists, of which I could never hear enough. He had after all published works illustrated by Maillol (Horace's Odes *and* Daphnis and Chloe*) and he seemed to have met everybody who mattered in the world of art.*

My favourite story was of a friend taking him to meet Matisse in the latter's studio. Anton was still a young man with his way to make and was much in awe of the famous artist. The studio was full of canvases. Nervously, almost reduced to a stammer by the great artist's presence and the magnificence of the paintings all around him, Anton blurted out his admiration. Matisse shrugged and moving his hands through 360 degrees to encompass all the pictures in the studio, said to the young man

'*Mille francs au choix*'. *I cannot imagine that anyone made Anton a more generous offer throughout his long life and I know that it was his eternal regret that at the time he received it he was not in a better position to take advantage of it.*

CHAPTER TWENTY-EIGHT

SPEAKING UP

I suppose I have always been fond of the sound of my own voice. I suspect that I developed a liking for it at my kindergarten, where I was frequently called to the headmaster's study to read to parents of prospective pupils. When I had made my way through several easy sentences the headmaster would say 'And the little fellow is only four!' My father took a poor view of this whole process for he had taught me to read before I ever went to school.

In my early teens I revelled in taking part in the meetings of my grammar school's pompously named Society for the Discussion of International Affairs. Hours spent in these naïve school debates proved useful when I came to take a more active role in politics a few years later, but in between came National Service in the Royal Air Force. For two years my 'public speaking' was restricted to issuing stentorian commands such as 'Squa-a-a-d Halt!' on the rare occasions when I had to take a drill parade of the Headquarters staff in preparation for the annual inspection by the Air Officer Commanding-in-Chief; and to shouting 'Sir, 605' when my name was called at the weekly Pay Parade.

By the time I was demobilised in 1952 Clement Attlee's Socialist government had given way to the return of Winston Churchill and the Conservatives, but I had found the Socialist era so irksome and frustrating that I joined the Southgate Branch of the Young Conservative movement in order to meet like-minded people and to work for the Conservatives' continuance in power. Ours was an active branch with almost 1,000 members. At one time no fewer than five people who had been through our ranks were sitting in the House of Commons. At Borough, County and National elections we sent teams of workers from our own safe, Tory seat to work in marginal constituencies. We raised our quota of funds for the

Party's central organisation and, save for a short break in the summer, we organised a series of weekly political meetings. These drew an average attendance of 100 people. Many were addressed by celebrities, but speaking competitions, model parliaments and so on provided opportunities for home-grown talent.

Later, when I was Divisional Political Secretary, it was my responsibility to arrange speakers for fifty consecutive weekly meetings, and if I learned nothing else from that experience I learned that being a celebrity or being the acknowledged expert in your field was not enough: if you did not know how to put your material across you might as well stay at home. Personally I would rather hear a good speaker read the London Telephone Directory than listen to a bad speaker, even if he were the greatest living authority on, say, marginal decoration in 14th century French illuminated manuscripts.

I took to this new world like a duck to water, and was soon being asked to propose votes of thanks, then to introduce speakers, and to take part in debating competitions and the like. On one occasion when I was teamed with my friend Michael Thomas, a trainee barrister who later rose to be Attorney General of Hong Kong, we came third in the national finals of the Debating Competition for the entire Conservative Party, not just the Youth section. After that I was invited to join the Party's panel of voluntary speakers for the Home Counties North Area, which covered the whole of Middlesex and Essex. The better to prepare for this I did what I always did when faced with a problem: I bought a book about it, in this case a splendid little work called *Public Speaking and Chairmanship* by Frederick Mills.

This gave useful instruction about employing 'Alliteration's Artful Aid,' varying the length of sentences, varying the speed and tone of delivery and so on. Published at 7s. 6d. in 1953 it was one of the best investments I ever made. Then I was invited to take a Central Office course in public speaking. From it I learned a great deal from an admirable tutor, many of whose words sing in my head even as I write this.

He taught us how to ensure that no members of the audience fell asleep while we were speaking, how to deal with hecklers and what to do if an unfriendly audience started to sing 'The Red Flag'. It is many years since I addressed a political meeting, and I have never had to try out his tactics in the matter of 'The Red Flag' but on hot afternoons on campuses in the southern states of America I have been grateful for the tutor's advice about those likely to nod off.

Other words of his came back to me some ten years after I heard him utter them. I had flown from London to Madison, Wisconsin, on the first leg of a three-week tour of North American libraries. I was met at the airport by Lloyd Griffin, nominally Chief of the Reference Division of the University of Wisconsin Library but who actually filled three jobs there and was the hardest working librarian I had ever met. As he drove me to my hotel I reminded him that he had not said if he and his wife were free to join me for dinner that evening as I had asked. He replied that I had arrived on the day of the annual dinner of the Library's Friends and that he and Rachel had bought a ticket in my name, hoping I could join them. If I felt too tired from the journey they would understand. A couple of hours later I found myself sitting between Lloyd and Rachel at a catered dinner in the Library. When the plates were eventually cleared away Lewis Kaplan, the Director of Libraries, introduced the speaker, Joseph Rubinstein, an academic who had become a dealer and who had just issued his third rare book catalogue. At the end of a stimulating address Dr Kaplan rose again and began welcoming specific guests by name. My mind raced back to Central Office speaking classes and lesson number one. Our tutor had said he was going to ask each of us in turn to speak for one minute about 'Why I am a Conservative'. Then turning to one lady he had said 'You madam, you begin'. When we had all finished he said 'Thank goodness I do not have to instruct you in politics but only in how you talk about them.' He proceeded to tear apart our various performances. The lady who had spoken first was quick to protest. 'I am no good at impromptu speaking'. 'Impromptu? Nonsense!' roared our tutor, 'You had nearly a minute's warning!'

237

I have never forgotten that comment and the advice that it carried and, sensing where Dr Kaplan was heading, I prepared an opening sentence and a closing, just as I heard Dr Kaplan say, 'Many people have come a long way to be here tonight, but none further than Anthony Rota, who has travelled from London. Anthony, would you care to say a few words and comment on Mr Rubinstein's remarks?'

Oddly enough it was through the Conservative Party and my work on the speakers' panel that I began to lecture on rare books. Obviously most of the speaking that members of the panel were asked to do concerned politics, either talking on general topics such as current affairs or foreign affairs, or on specific issues such as capital punishment, the Landlord and Tenant Act and so on, but in addition we were invited to declare our readiness to speak on one or more non-political subjects. Long before I would have dared to face an audience of book-collectors, librarians or fellow booksellers, I ventured to put 'Rare books' down as a 'recreational subject' on which I was prepared to address Conservative Party audiences the length and breadth of Essex and Middlesex. I was not altogether surprised when I found that this subject went down rather better with the audience than did, say, my rather naïve thoughts on 'The Suez Canal'.

I have quite lost count of how many times since then I have spoken to book-collecting societies, groups of library friends, and assemblages of booksellers and librarians, but only once have I spoken to the accompaniment, albeit the involuntary accompaniment, of a piano. This was in the elegant Green Pastures restaurant in Austin, Texas, where the private room in which we bookmen were dining was not soundproof and the strains of a cocktail piano could be heard very clearly from the bar next door.

Speaking to a piano accompaniment was one thing but at the University of North Carolina at Chapel Hill I had another unique experience. Whenever I am to speak for more than five minutes I always ask for a glass and a plentiful supply of water to be within easy reach. This is partly because my throat gets dry and partly because taking a sip of water provides a pause which can either be used to heighten dramatic tension or to enable the speaker to collect his thoughts. At Chapel Hill my request for 'a glass of water' brought consternation: it was evening, no janitorial staff seemed to be about, and no glass could be found in or around the lecture theatre. When I expressed a reluctance to begin without having some sort of drinking vessel to hand, a desperate search produced an empty Dr Pepper can. This was washed out and then filled with water in the cloakroom before being placed, discreetly out of sight of the audience, behind my portable lectern. When I needed to take a drink I raised the can to my lips and as those in the front row saw the familiar Dr Pepper packaging, they began to giggle. I had to make a quick readjustment and use the sipping technique when I thought it was time for a laugh rather than time to increase the tension. From that day on I have always put in my request for a glass rather earlier in the proceedings.

On another occasion I had to give a paper on changes in the book trade to an audience attending the International Book Fair which followed the 1990 Congress of the International League of Antiquarian Booksellers in Tokyo. The arrangements were made by the indefatigable Mitsuo Nitta, head of the Yushodo Company in Tokyo. I was surprised when, a couple of months before I was due to speak, Mitsuo asked me for a copy of my text. I replied that I was reluctant to define the text so early and asked him in his turn about the degree of understanding of English I could expect from my audience. He answered me by saying 'About half'. On further enquiry I found that this did not mean that they would understand half what I was saying, but that only about half of them would have any English at all. Clearly something had to be done. Mitsuo's preferred solution was to have me read a sentence from my script, which would then be translated by a Japanese interpreter. I would read another sentence. The interpreter would repeat it in Japanese and so on. I thought this would kill any hope of spontaneity, or rapport with the audience and Mitsuo therefore arranged for the Japanese listeners to be given parallel texts in their language and mine for use at the time of delivery. Thus it was that I eventually stood in front of a cosmopolitan assembly comprising 100 or 150 Japanese book collectors mixed with dealers from the twenty or more nations that make up the International League. It felt strange to see the Japanese earnestly following my text, tracing their path along the lines with their fingers. I must say though, that they laughed in the right places and we all finished at more or less the same time.

After-dinner speaking is one thing, and lecturing is another but teaching is 'something completely different'. Strangely enough my first two invitations to teach came in the same year, 1987. The first was from Terry Belanger, who invited me to teach a one-week course in Building Twentieth Century Literature Collections as part of the programme at that year's Rare Book School at Columbia University. The second was from Tom Staley, then Provost of the University of Tulsa, offering me a Distinguished Visiting Fellowship for one semester in order to teach a post-graduate class on any theme of my own choice that was based on special collections in the University Library. I decided to see how the intensive week at Columbia worked out before committing myself irrevocably to the longer haul in Tulsa.

Terry gave me fair warning: 'I must tell you, Anthony' he said, 'That most of my instructors go home after a week here and spend 48 hours in bed.' The schedule was certainly a punishing one. I arrived during the hottest July New York had known for forty years. My course was to begin on the Monday morning but I was instructed to report for a semi-social gathering on Sunday evening in order to meet the students, mine and others', as well as the rest of the faculty. There were lectures on at least three evenings and all students and faculty were expected to attend. My students, at least, had papers to write and I had to find time to mark them. Early each morning, before class, the faculty were required to be on hand when coffee and muffins were served, and many of the students seemed to have their breakfast. Typically this was the time when other people's students would come up and say 'Oh Dr Rota' (I hold no

doctorate but confess that my only protest was a silent one) 'I wanted to take your course but so and so's was what I finally decided to
sign up for. But could you just tell me about . . .' If you were not
careful there was a clear risk of teaching the course twice, once in
the classroom and once outside it.

In most of the eight or ten courses that were offered in any one
week of the four week Rare Book School the instructors worked in
tandem, their classes running morning and afternoon, save perhaps
for one or two library visits during the course of the week. Terry
Belanger suggested to me that I should follow the same pattern,
working with an American librarian. This suggestion was not without appeal, but it seemed to me that it would be very difficult to
make a seamless garment out of the two halves and to ensure that
there were neither gaps nor overlaps, unless my fellow instructor
and I could spend at least a couple of days together two or three
times over the months leading up to the course itself. Since the
Atlantic Ocean put a very expensive obstacle in the way of this
counsel of perfection, I opted to soldier on alone. This meant that,
never having taught before, I was faced with the need to fill three
hours of classroom time every morning for a week, just with the
sound of my own voice, plus of course any contributions I could
wrest from the class.

The students were all graduates. In fact the first three to apply to
take my course held ten degrees between them, an intimidating
thought. The average age of the class was probably something close
to 35 or 40. Some of the students had ten or twenty years experience
as librarians in special collections departments and all of them were
paying $450 (in later years it rose to $650) in tuition fees, to say
nothing of transportation and living costs. These figures made me
feel my responsibilities, and to say that I was nervous on the first
morning of the course would be the understatement of the year.

That day I thought that the bell for the coffee break would never
ring. After ninety minutes I had used up the notes I had drafted
for the whole day and had started on the morrow's. I began to
think that we would reach the end of the course by noon on the

241

Wednesday. Next morning things began to take a different turn. As the class and I grew used to one another I found ways of encouraging them to contribute. By asking carefully phrased questions I found I could elicit quite long answers which the rest of us could discuss with profit. Half way through the Thursday morning session I had to say to the class that if they didn't keep their contributions brief, we would be there all weekend.

In the middle of the week I got the School Commissariat to provide a cold lunch for the class. We all sat round one big table and I invited William Matheson to be our guest. Bill was an old friend and the one man I would have chosen to work with had I gone down the tandem route. Bill's experience as a private collector, as Head of Special Collections at Washington University in St Louis and then as Chief of Rare Books at the Library of Congress enabled him to answer wisely the students' carefully thought out questions.

In the afternoons the class went on various excursions. On one day they had to visit the current exhibition at the Berg Collection at New York Public Library and write a report on every aspect of it. Was it well publicized? Once in the building was the exhibition area easy to find? Was it easy to get a catalogue? Were the captions apposite? Were they easy to read or did one have to bend down and use a magnifying glass? Were the exhibits well selected? Were they arranged in a logical sequence? Did they tell a story? Were conservation and security issues properly addressed? Later we went through the various reports in class and after that we had all learned a lot about how to mount a good exhibition – and how not to.

On another afternoon we visited the current exhibitions at the Grolier Club, and there met Professor Jack Hagstrom who had built a 17,000 item collection of Robert Frost material and then donated it to Amherst College. Jack and I had what I believe is called a 'structured discussion' about the methodology of building such a collection. All this was done over a little liquid refreshment. After that the students were given a tour of the club's outstanding bibliographical reference library. The next afternoon Jack Hagstrom had us up to his apartment to see the collections he was working on currently and to discuss changes in the bookselling scene and the effect that they would have on the building of collections in the future.

Terry was right: I went home tired – but happy.

I have said that I accepted Terry Belanger's invitation to teach at Rare Book School at Columbia in 1987, and that it involved a 'voluntary' (Miss it if you dare!) appearance to meet the student body at a reception on the Sunday night preceding the course. I duly presented myself at the appointed hour and I was very glad to see the familiar face of Dr Steven Corey, Rare Books Librarian at the Gleeson Library in the University of San Francisco. Steve bore down on me and said 'When you've done your duty rounds come and join a crowd of us for supper'. Steve had taught a class in fine printing and private press books the week before and said he had stayed on just to see me, but I knew of old what a tease he was.

After half-a-dozen of us had been out to dinner in a San Francisco restaurant some years before, Steve had invited me to try a very special cognac which he had at home. His expertise in these matters was to be taken seriously, so I accepted the invitation. Half an hour later I was standing in Steve's drawing room sipping the excellent brandy and listening to his friend and house-mate play the piano. Suddenly I felt myself swaying. I tried to focus on the chandelier but it appeared to be swinging. Making for the safety of an armchair I spoke of what I had just experienced. Steve wickedly said that the brandy was indeed very strong. It was only when the next morning's newspaper reported that the city had been the subject of some relatively mild earth tremors that Steve confessed that it was the room *that had in fact been swaying.*

Steve was a great joker. He was also of what used to be coyly referred to as 'a certain persuasion', a fact that he tried to use to have fun at my expense at a library conference in Texas in 1983. The occasion was the last day of the Association of College and Research Libraries pre-conference, which was always held just before the annual jamboree of the American Library Association. The scene was the conference hotel in Austin and more than 200 librarians were present, including some from the Humanities Research Center, my most important institutional customer.

The theme of the pre-conference was 'Collecting the Twentieth Century' and I was to be the third of the day's speakers. I was sitting in the front row right opposite the podium. Richard Landon, from the Fisher Library in the University of Toronto, made a brilliant presentation, and then, as the applause died away, the chairman, Alan Green from the Library Company of Philadelphia, dismissed us for our twenty minute coffee-break. At this point Steve Corey came up to me and said that he had been sharing a room with a friend who was heading off to Dallas right away. Steve had arranged to share with somebody else that night but his host had not yet arrived. Steve therefore asked if he could put his bags in my room in the interim. Of course I agreed to this but when Steve asked if I would help him move them then and there, I explained that, as Steve very well knew, I was the first speaker after the interlude and that I just wanted to sit quietly for a few moments to collect my thoughts and to take a last drink of water. I therefore gave Steve my keys and invited him to make free of the room. Steve went off and ten minutes later Alan Green suggested to me that I should take my place on the platform, as he banged his gavel and invited the audience to resume their seats. With devilishly precise timing Steve re-entered the room and minced (there is no other word for it) down the aisle until he stood immediately opposite the table behind which I was seated. He smartly slapped a large bunch of keys down in front of me (which of course drew everyone's attention) and then said in the loudest of stage whispers 'Here are your keys, Anthony, and thank you, thank you for a wonderful night!'

At the time I was furious, but later saw the funny side as I reflected that those who knew me would be aware that, should my eye ever wander, it would wander in a diametrically opposite direction. Steve and I laughed about it all over a drink at Juan Goldstein's Champagne and Caviar Bar on Austin's 6th Street, a hybrid establishment where the first words on the bill of fare were 'Shalom, amigos'.

CHAPTER TWENTY-NINE

TULSA, OKLAHOMA

'ONCE YOU CROSS THE RED RIVER
IT'S ALL DESERT!'

On one of my regular visits to the University of Texas at Austin I was chatting to that most urbane and civilized of men, Jenkins Garrett. A former Regent of the University of Texas, he has probably done more than anyone to advance the cause of rare books and libraries in the State of Texas. He asked me where I was going next and when I told him that I was on my way to visit the library at the University of Tulsa in Oklahoma, Jenkins said 'What are you going there for, Anthony? Once you cross the Red River it's all desert!' I knew I was being teased but even on that first brief visit I came to like Tulsa very much. None the less, I confess I looked down a little apprehensively as my plane carried me north across the river that marks the border between Texas and Oklahoma.

Tom Staley met me at the airport and drove me into town in an open car. As we went along the bank of the Arkansas River we passed the Phillips oil refinery on the other side . Quite unpleasant fumes were thick in the air. 'Do you smell that, Anthony?' asked Tom. 'Let me tell you that to you that's Chanel No. 5!' Tom was of course referring to the fact that it was wealth from such enterprises that provided the money for the university library's expansion.

Going back to Tulsa in 1988 to take up my Visiting Fellowship I suffered from no apprehension at all, or none at least for any reason of geography. My wife and I had both travelled extensively in America but never for longer than three or four weeks at a time, almost always staying in hotels or with friends. Actually living there for three months, doing the marketing instead of the shopping, keeping the yard tidy instead of the garden, getting to know the neighbours, arranging to have the car serviced, all these would be new experiences.

While I was teaching at Tulsa, preparing over six days what I was to say on the seventh, I was in regular touch with my office in London, helping and advising those who were running the bookshop in my absence, as well as dealing with matters that came my way in my new role as President of the International League of Antiquarian Booksellers. On top of all this, with the encouragement of the university administration, I gave lectures at nine other institutions. I found it all quite a handful and gently chided my friend Mark Reed, a member of the English faculty at the University of North Carolina in Chapel Hill. 'Mark', I said, 'didn't you once tell me that teaching was a sinecure?'

He chuckled and replied 'Oh but it is, Anthony, just as soon as you have contempt for your subject and contempt for your students.'

That was the trouble: my subject was English Literature and my students were very bright. How could I have contempt for either?

The Fellowship was for me rather like a sabbatical. I had been selling rare books and manuscripts in the same firm for thirty-six years and was ready for the challenge that the offer from Tulsa represented. My students all had bachelors' degrees in English and were reading for their masters' degrees. I was allowed to choose the subject that we were to study, having a free hand as long as it was relevant to the work of the English department and as long as it drew on the strengths of the library's special collections. In addition to the two-hour class every Tuesday afternoon, I was expected to be in my office at posted hours on each Wednesday – presumably to explain to any individual students who cared just what it was that I had been trying to say on the previous afternoon. In addition to my office in the English building I had a carrel in the special collections department of the library. I also had a stack pass by courtesy of Sid Huttner, head of Special Collections. This was of great assistance to me when I sought material to illustrate points I wanted to make in class.

Unlike the carrel, my office had no outside window and its bare walls were decidedly bleak. My neighbour across the corridor, Professor Manley Johnson, took pity on me and brought me two potted plants, a selection of prints and pictures, some picture hooks and a large hammer: between us we soon made the place more like home. Then I put two books on one of the empty shelves, reminding myself that books breed like rabbits. I stood back for a short gestation period and lo and behold there were three volumes there. By the end of the week there were seven. By the end of the term I had three large cartons to send home by bulk post. Where all the books came from heaven only knows.

My subject for the course, by the way, was what one could learn about economic history, social history and in particular the history of publishing, from studying the physical characteristics of books, even before beginning to read what lay between the covers. I called the course 'Apart from the Text', the title I gave to a book which I subsequently based on my classes.

Although I made my students work quite hard, I think we all enjoyed our Tuesday afternoons together. We were fortunate enough to meet in the rare book room, where we sat round a refectory table. One week, instead of being in the room ahead of them to greet them by name as they came in, I waited until they were all seated and then made an entrance pushing a library trolley loaded with carefully selected volumes. 'Today we are going to get physical', I said, noting with pleasure that eyebrows began to go up all round the room. 'Working together', I continued, 'I want you to arrange these books in chronological order. When you have finished you may go home. Good afternoon'. I turned on my heel and began to leave the room. 'Oh, there is just one thing', I said. 'You are not allowed to open any of them'. Of course I didn't leave. I stayed near the books and watched as the class reasoned out for itself a fairly logical sequence. Asking why they had put X before Y and not vice versa led to some surprising theories. I will confess now that I had prepared a couple of elephant traps by using bindings which were themselves anachronisms. I felt a little bit mean about this.

On other occasions I had the class working in pairs to produce small exhibitions, complete with catalogue descriptions, to illustrate various points that I was trying to make. Sid Huttner agreed to put the best of these exhibitions on display. One pair made a very good job of laying out and describing some twelve editions of a Graham Greene novel. Apart from the first English and American editions, translations into ten other languages were represented.

These foreign language editions were drawn from the author's own file, a very extensive one, which I had sold to Tulsa a few years before. Studying enough of them enabled the students to draw certain general conclusions, some of which may seem elementary to book-collectors, booksellers and librarians but which may still come as a surprise to those who merely read books for their text, and who seldom travel abroad. The students quickly noted that the vast majority of French books are published in printed wrappers rather than in cloth. They observed that Spanish and Italian editions made lavish use of illustration on the covers in order to promote sales. They found that the order in which Greene's books were published varied from country to country. The presence of new editions and paperback editions indicated in which countries his sales were greatest and so on. These were hardly earth-shattering discoveries but at the end of the exercise the class had learned something, or, to be more precise, had taught themselves something, which is probably more valuable.

My last class before the Christmas vacation and my return to London took the form of a quiz. My wife had cleared out the larder in the lovely lake-side house which we had rented and I made my way to the English department weighed down by a large carrier bag full of packages. 'Name two ways in which the spread of railways throughout Victorian England had a major influence on the book trade,' I said. At the first correct answer I slid a pound of Windsor Red cheese down the table to the student who had won it. A can of grapefruit segments went to the first person to give me the year which saw the first recorded use of a dust-jacket and so on. This being a temperance campus I was not able to use bottles of wine as prizes but we managed to find a good home for those we had left over, none the less.

At the end of the class I took the students just off campus to a diner where I had lunched once or twice a week throughout my stay, usually with Darcy O'Brien, a full-time member of the English faculty, a Joyce scholar, a novelist and a most entertaining companion. The people at the diner had laid out bowls of things to nibble and things to dip into and I had arranged for there to be an open bar. I was surprised how very modest the students were in their drinking.

Twelve months later I received in London a postcard which read 'Come back, Professor' [a title given out of respect, I assumed, for I was not entitled to it]. 'All is forgiven. The nights grow cold and our larders grow empty.' It was signed by all the class.

Enjoyable though our time in Tulsa was – and it was very enjoyable indeed – the trips that the university encouraged us to take outside the city and outside the state were both entertaining and instructive. Driving through rural Oklahoma and through Kansas and Arkansas we saw a great deal of middle America, and we liked what we saw.

GAINESVILLE

A few winters ago I was honoured to receive from Jake Chernofsky, editor and publisher of AB Bookman's Weekly, *an invitation to give the keynote address at one of the intensive seven day courses he organised for new entrants to the book-trade. I was to talk about ethics and etiquette, two subjects close to my heart. The course was to take place in Gainesville, Florida and Jake offered me a round-trip ticket from London, bed and board for the whole week, a small honorarium and the promise of another speaking engagement (at a book fair in St Petersburg, Florida) the following weekend. I was flattered and I accepted.*

When I arrived at Gainesville I was met by Dr Margaret Knox Goggin, a retired librarian of boundless energy and enthusiasm, who was co-director of the school. 'Do you know the school faculty?' she asked. 'Most of them,' I replied. 'I see.' she said, 'They won't go to supper till you arrive!'

The faculty comprised Jean Parmer of Parmer Books, who had at one time worked for the Internal Revenue Service and was therefore well placed to advise on tax matters; Jennifer Larson of Yerba Buena Books; Michael Ginsberg, specialist in Americana; Ed Glaser from Sausalito, specialising in early science and medicine; Alan Stypeck from Second Story Books in Washington, D.C.; and Steve Mauer, a computer expert. Altogether they made a formidable team – and, yes, we had a good supper.

It appeared that, because I was giving the keynote address, I counted as faculty and was required to attend a pre-school faculty meeting to be addressed by Dr Goggin. She laid down some simple but quite strict rules. She reminded us that we were there for the benefit of the students, not to indulge our egos. She said that faculty members making in-jokes to amuse their cronies would be asked to leave at once. At mealtimes and during coffee breaks faculty were not to sit together. Indeed there was never to be more than one faculty member at any one table. Privately admiring this rather severe policy, I joined the regular faculty for a book-scouting expedition to Gainesville's bookshops before our work began. Our specialisations were reasonably complementary and between us we pretty well covered the spectrum. All of us found something to buy.

In the evening the students assembled and after dinner I addressed a hundred or so people drawn from all over America. Most were in their fifties or sixties and were looking to bookselling for a second career, but there were some younger folk present also. I based my talk on two quotations. The first was from the Latin: 'Quis custodiet ipsos custodes', ('Who shall guard the guardians?'). The point I was trying to drive home was that to a large extent booksellers made the rules of book collecting and if they themselves cheated, the whole thing, not just their livelihood but their lives, would be totally without meaning. My second reference was to Mrs Doasyouwouldbedoneby from Charles Kingsley's The Water Babies. I stressed that etiquette was really a question of good manners and consideration for others. The acid test of any proposed action was how you would react if you were in the other person's shoes.

Jake apparently liked all this for he said to me at the end of the evening: 'You've done your job. You have your return ticket and your bed and board are paid for for the rest of the week. What you do now is up to you. If you want you can go and sit by the pool. Equally if you like to row in with the faculty we would be very glad to have you.' I chose the latter course, which proved to be hard work but very rewarding. For the lecture sessions all the faculty sat on the platform facing the students while the lecturer gave forth. Alas it wasn't safe to drop off to sleep because each lecturer in turn had the habit of looking round and asking one or other of his colleagues for confirmation, or for an alternative point of view. As the only foreigner present I was frequently the subject of such questions as 'Is that how they do it in England, Anthony?' In addition I had a role to play in a mock-auction, and acted as a faculty adviser in workshop sessions devoted to cataloguing and pricing books. Nobody could pretend that this course alone, intensive though it was, could turn a tyro into a highly professional dealer, but I am sure that those who have been through it, or something like it, are better booksellers for the experience.

When the school was officially over Dr Goggin and Jake gave the faculty a very grand dinner in a private room at Dr Goggin's club, but we could not entirely relax even there, for the prize Lot at the mock-auction was a pair of tickets for the otherwise exclusive faculty dinner!

CHAPTER THIRTY

AUCTIONS

Back in the 1950s the book room at Sotheby's (and for that matter the sale room at Hodgson's in Chancery Lane, which was exclusively devoted to book sales) was not laid out like a theatre, with the seats in rows facing the auctioneer, even though the events were sometimes highly theatrical. Instead the auctioneer sat on the rostrum at the head of a pound, or inverted horseshoe. A porter would hold up each book, or a representative item from a Lot, as it came to be sold, and would then walk slowly round the pound, silently offering to show the book to any of the dealers seated at the tables that formed the boundary of the enclosure. Places at those tables were taken by the regulars in strict accordance with custom and protocol. Indeed places could be said to pass from father to son, rather like the privileges that went with a porter's badge at Billingsgate fish market.

Under the auctioneer's left hand sat the head of Quaritch; like Maggs opposite him he was there to buy the rarest and most costly items; next to him somebody from Francis Edwards, perhaps Charlie Harris, or his son 'young Charles'; then Thomas Thorp, perhaps Tom himself with his distinctive bottle-bottom spectacles, or perhaps his first assistant Wally Harris, his huge dome of a head crammed with book-lore; and after Thorp either Stanley Sawyer or his brother Raymond. At the end of the pound one would find Dawson's, Alan Thomas, Charles Traylen, and Harry Mushlin. Going up the other side were Marks, Joseph, Dobell, Pickering, Maggs and lastly, just under the auctioneer's right hand, H. M. Fletcher. My father used to sit facing the auctioneer, somewhere between Sawyer and Alan Thomas. Part of the fun of this arrangement was that it allowed for eleventh hour viewing. Dudley Massey of Pickering and Chatto, who must have grown very tired of hearing himself described as looking like Voltaire in profile, was a past master of this technique. Perhaps he had not viewed the sale at all during the posted viewing hours, or perhaps he had simply not looked at the Lot which was now on the auction block. In either case some instinct seemed to tell him that a bargain was about to be knocked down, so he would snap his fingers to attract the attention of the porter and, while bidding with his left hand, would use his right to collate the book in question and to weigh up its condition. A volume might rise in price by several hundred pounds during this performance and Dudley might well withdraw before the final bid in any case. If on the other hand he joined in the bidding from the very beginning he was virtually impossible to shake off, usually keeping on and on, past any formal limit he might have set himself, until he became the victor in the end.

Up the table from him Ernest Maggs's white beard would wag like a demented signal flag when there was something rich enough to appeal to his firm's appetite, something that caused his head to nod to signal his bids. In between, Mark Cohen, of Marks and Co, and his Charing Cross Road neighbour, Jack Joseph, sat staunchly side by side through the whole of every sale, snapping up any unconsidered trifles that the other players let fall. Jack was the wag of the auction room. Between them Mark and Jack would buy every copy of the *Encyclopaedia Britannica*. If three sets followed one another as successive Lots and Jack bought the first for, say, twenty pounds, when the auctioneer called the next Lot Jack would shout 'Same as the last, sir' and would very probably have the Lot knocked down to him without another bid being offered. This was regarded as fair enough and a useful timesaving tactic, but Jack would also cry out the same text if the next Lot were not the 13th edition of the *Britannica*, but, shall we say, a Nuremburg *Chronicle*.

To shake off Dudley Massey when he seemed intent on buying regardless of price, my father would often interrupt the carefully programmed incremental steps in the bidding which are by law at the discretion of the auctioneer. If the bid against us was £400, the next regular bid would be £450 and after that £500, £600, £800 and

£1,000. Instead of £450 my father would perhaps call '£700, sir' and, often enough to make the game worth while, the gambit would succeed and the Lot would be knocked down to us. This was not necessarily an extravagant gesture for we could be pretty sure that had the bidding rose in smaller increments it would have reached this point and perhaps gone past it: by making a large advance we attempted to demonstrate that we were keen on the Lot and would not readily let it go. Our competition would get no bargain. Moreover the irregular increase was often sufficient to break the seductive rhythm of the bidding which could carry our opponent past the limit he might well have set himself.

My father used to speak of 'playing a bid', rather as an angler might 'play' a fish. Certainly he brought home from the auction rooms some very fine catches indeed. We bought some of our greatest bargains at auction, when, for example, other bidders seemed not to have noticed some subtle hidden attraction of a particular lot and we were able to buy it on or around the figure at which the auctioneer opened the bidding, a figure which we might not have had the effrontery to offer the owner by private treaty, lest we be thought to be robbers. Nowadays alas auctions do not offer bargains as frequently as once they did. Two lots I especially remember were a large quantity of books and pamphlets from the S. Dominic's Press, and a portfolio of sketches and drawings from Max Beerbohm's studio at Rapallo. The S. Dominic's Press under the direction of Hilary Pepler published books written or illustrated by Eric Gill and David Jones, among others. The press runs were comparatively short and editions were bound up in small batches, one batch often differing from the others in binding style. A lay brother who worked at the Press as its only true professional once told me that every time the bell rang for another service, the amateur printers would troop out to the chapel only to return with new revisions in mind. Thus it is that the variants in S. Dominic's Press books are practically without limit. Certainly in our bargain lot we found almost as many variants not described in Evan Gill's bibliography of his brother's work as we found actually listed.

The Beerbohm portfolio came to us by an interesting route. My father had spotted it in the catalogue quite late in the day and hadn't had time to view it thoroughly. Our friend Harry Mushlin was bidding on it and seemed set to go a long way. Instead of opposing him, my father let him buy it. I think £650 was the price. After the sale my father drifted over and congratulated Harry on his advantageous purchase. Harry swelled with pride. My father asked him if he had a ready buyer for it or if he was going to split the collection,. Harry said he had no one waiting for it. 'How much would you take for the whole portfolio?' my father asked. '£850' said Harry, counting a £200 profit a good reward for holding the lot for only an hour. 'Done!' said my father, who would have had to pay much more if he had chosen to try to outbid Harry in the saleroom. We lived off the contents of that portfolio for several months.

JONAH – LUCKY FOR SOME

Percy Muir, my father's friendly competitor, was once called to Lady Ottoline Morrell's house in Garsington in tandem with my father to offer for some books culled from the Library. They decided to make a joint offer and to divide the books between them afterwards, each picking alternately volume by volume. It mattered very much who was to start, for what they both wanted most was the very rare pamphlet of verse called Jonah *by Aldous Huxley, who was a regular visitor to Garsington.* Jonah *was issued in 1917 in an edition of only 50 copies. A coin was tossed to decide who should have first pick, and the winner went straight to the copy of* Jonah *and plucked it from the shelf in triumph. Then Fortune smiled on the loser, for a second copy, which had been inadvertently concealed inside the first, fell out, and both booksellers went home in a warm glow and not one, but two collectors were able to fill a serious gap on their respective shelves.*

CHAPTER THIRTY-ONE

THE RING AND THE BOOK

WITH APOLOGIES TO THACKERAY

'Writing your memoirs?' people asked, 'I bet you won't say anything about "The Ring"'. Being unable to resist such a challenge has
cost me dearly in the past. Nevertheless here I go again.

Let us be quite sure we understand what is meant by a 'ring' or
'knockout'. A ring is a clique of bidders, usually trade buyers, who
make an informal agreement not to bid against one another at a
public auction in the justifiable hope that their *ad hoc* syndicate
will thus be able to make purchases at artificially depressed prices.
They then hold a second auction among themselves (the knockout)
and divide between them the difference between the prices realized
in the public sale room and the higher total obtained in the secret
auction. Book auction rings are what we are concerned with here
but it certainly used to be the case that rings were prevalent and far
more blatant in many other trades. For example it was once reported that dealers in oriental rugs held their knockout on the steps
leading down from Sotheby's gallery to the street, and
the legislation which finally outlawed rings is alleged to have been
prompted by the indiscreet behaviour of a ring of scrap-metal merchants bidding for a surplus battleship.

To understand the attitude of the booksellers who continued to
participate in the ring, many of them otherwise honourable and
certainly law-abiding citizens, some of them representatives of the
finest and most powerful firms in the trade, it has to be remembered that until the passing of the Auctions (Bidding Agreements)
Act of 1927 rings were not illegal. Dealers saw them as a defence
against the malpractices of some auctioneers (e.g. inflating prices by
taking imaginary bids from the chandelier or off the wall – to this

day booksellers personify the non-existent or phantom bidder as 'Major Wall'), and what was regarded as the greed of owners who would not sell directly to a dealer but instead expected not just one, but a number of experts to make a free gift of their expertise. Dealers who enjoyed friendly relations with one another did not see why they should be 'forced' to bid against one another. Of course they were not 'forced' at all, but when they put their case to me I understood what they meant, and even felt that there was a grey area here. If two friends, one, say, a specialist in natural history and the other in atlases, found themselves at the same sale, and a run of Curtis's *Botanical Magazine* was not attracting much bidding, there would be no obligation, legal or moral, for the specialist in atlases to bid on the natural history Lot just because it was going cheaply. Let us suppose the natural history specialist buys it for a low price and realises that his friend had refrained from bidding. When an Ortelius atlas comes onto the block he returns the compliment and allows the atlas specialist to get a bargain too. There seems nothing wrong in that. The trouble comes when there are not two Lots at issue but several hundred, and when there are not just two dealers in the room but twenty or more. Then instead of a system of unspoken favours, those in the ring resort to a second auction and a division of the cash spoils. That is certainly a contravention of the law and hardly morally acceptable either.

I have spoken of a second auction, but sometimes there was a third and even a fourth. One hears of such divisions as 'Town *v.* Country' and 'Charing Cross Road *v.* Bond Street.' Often the 'little men' would be paid off after the second auction (first knockout) and sent home with a small but useful cash 'dividend' burning a hole in their back pockets. The big firms would then put the best books up for sale again. I have to confess that my great-uncle Percy Dobell complains in his diary of his irritation at having to sit through three sales of the same books in the space of two days. What was going on is all too clear.

I have never taken part in a knockout in my life, but that is easy for me to say because I came into the trade at a time when the culture was changing. *The Times* had got its hands on the marked catalogue of a disaffected ringer who, to his fury, was eliminated after the first round of illegal bidding. The paper was threatening to publish the annotated catalogue, showing just who bid what at the illicit sales, and the whole subject became one for public debate. At this point a group of younger dealers, including Laurie Deval (Elkin Mathews), Rodney Drake (James Bain Ltd), Boris Harding-Edgar (Charles Rare Books) and I, pressed our trade association to take its head out of the sand and lead a reform movement. Eventually it did so. It is impossible to eliminate ringing, just as it is fruitless to attempt to eliminate original sin, but ringing today is not the grievous problem and open scandal that once it was.

My father used to tell the story of his first attendance at an auction sale, which must have been around 1919 or 1920 when he was sixteen or seventeen years of age. He had been sent to a country sale by his uncles, Percy and Arthur Dobell, his catalogue marked with the limits up to which he was to bid. When the first Lot marked came up, he took a deep breath, looked up at the auctioneer and opened his mouth to call out. Suddenly he felt an excruciating pain in his foot. He looked down and found that one of the Joseph family was standing on his toe. 'You do your bidding in the public house afterwards, young man, and if you're lucky you'll get a poached egg on toast for your tea,' said whichever representative of the house of Joseph still had his heel resting on my father's little toe.

I did once experience for myself what made ringers reluctant to give up the practice. I was one of a group of five booksellers who saw an array of really fine books at exactly the same moment. The books were priced by supposedly knowledgeable owners, themselves professional bookmen, but some of the volumes were marked at figures way below their true worth. We could have stormed forward and scrummaged for the bargains, but cooler heads prevailed and we bought the books between us and then proceeded to share them out by holding a private auction between the five of us. I came to admire if not the ring at least the mental agility of the participants.

In our case I had to remember when bidding that if I made a successful bid of £150 that was, let us say, £100 above the £50 that a book had cost the syndicate, thus giving rise to a 'dividend' of £100, my bid was only costing me £130, not £150, because as one of five sharing in the distribution of the excess, I would receive a dividend of £20. Be that as it may, that afternoon I went back to my father with a bundle of notes burning a hole in my back pocket. It seemed an easy way to make money: no wonder some of the old lags were reluctant to give it up.

Had I been a member of the ring I would have been upset by the thought that some of *my* money might be used to pay off the relative minnows who only went along for the dividend, and had neither the knowledge to buy, nor the expectation of being allowed to buy, any of the best books.

Where the law was concerned the climax came in 1919 with the notorious Claygate sale. Arthur Freeman and Janet Ing Freeman tell the story admirably in their book *Anatomy of an Auction*, 1990. At Claygate books from the Foley Family Library were sold several times, first in public and then in as many as three successive 'settlements' and some booksellers took home from the knockout as much as a senior assistant would earn in a year.

It has been remarked that a competent auctioneer ought to be able to stop the ring in its tracks but the Lancastrian bookseller Eric Morten used to say that to his certain knowledge some provincial auctioneers used to benefit from the ring by making their offices available to the ringers to hold their settlements in, in exchange for a £10 note left under the blotter. Whether this was true or just a good story I do not know, but I am sure that human greed is at the root of most auction room troubles.

I remember the Birmingham bookseller, Frank Hammond, saying to me once that it was wrong that our trade association should try to tell him how he should buy his books. As a result of that exchange I was particularly pleased that it was his seat on the Antiquarian Booksellers Association committee that I captured when I was first elected to that body. When I eventually served a term as president of the association I had to think what I could do to reduce the power of the ring, even if I could not abolish it. The difficulty lay in securing a conviction, because, however much some of us disliked the practice of ringing, taking the witness stand to see old friends sent to prison was nobody's particular wish. What I did therefore, during my presidency and in those that followed mine for some years, was to arrange private meetings with those I suspected of illegal bidding and swear to them by all that I held holy that, should evidence of malfeasance by no matter whom come to my attention, I would call a meeting of the Association's standing committee on auctions and pass the results to the police, regardless of who got hurt. I certainly cannot claim to have stopped the activities of the ringers but I do believe I gave them serious cause for thought and reduced the effectiveness of their operations.

THEN AND NOW

Every so often in the late 1950s my wife and I used to get in the car and take a two or three-day swing around the SE corner of England on a buying trip. Leaving London at five or six in the morning we would have breakfast in Sevenoaks or Tunbridge Wells, buy a few books from my cousin, John Dobell and from Harry Pratley at Hall's Bookshop, go on to see Gilbert Fabes (author of Modern First Editions; their points and values*) in his shop in Rye before calling on Gilbert's daughter in the converted bus they both lived in at Winchelsea; Mary Ranger at Seaford, Howes bookshop at Hastings and Glover and Daughter at Eastbourne were all regular stops. Then to Brighton (Holleyman and Treacher and George Sexton), Worthing, Horsham and finally back home, the car weighed down on its springs by our purchases. 'That was then and this is now,' as they say, and I doubt that the same trip made today would yield enough good books to fill one modest-sized carton, let alone a car.*

CHAPTER THIRTY-TWO

'THE LAW IS A ASS'

DAVID JOSEPH BRASS
v. THE ANTIQBOOKS LTD PARTNERSHIP

Thus Mr Bumble in *Oliver Twist.* In 1990 David Brass, a descendant
of the founding fathers of the great firm of E. Joseph & Co. found
times a little hard, as did most of us in the antiquarian book trade
that year. Some of us tightened our belts and, to mix metaphors, cut
our coat according to the available cloth, but David had particularly heavy overheads to meet and felt a more drastic solution was
called for. He knew that a hard-nosed set of American money men
(alas for him he did not know just how hard-nosed they were)
had enormous sums of money available and wanted to buy an antiquarian book business in London. They were said to have plans to
combine it with one in California and another in New York but
those plans came to naught. David was introduced to an accountant called Richard Bergman who was said to be an associate of
Michael Milken, who went to prison for doing strange things with
bonds. Mr Bergman effectively bought out Joseph's for a substantial
sum of money. He retained David to run the firm on a very comfortable salary. Mr Bergman's interests were put in the name of a
company called Antiqbooks Ltd which was represented in London
by another accountant, one Jerry Schneider. I think David believed
that he would be allowed to run the company as he always had but
that he would be able to benefit from virtually unlimited capital
and from contacts and systems made available to him through Mr
Schneider. Unhappily the relatively bad times in the book trade did
not disappear overnight just because Messrs Milken and Bergman
had made an investment, and soon David's American masters were
unhappy with the return on their capital. They instructed David to

take certain measures to alter the situation. He thought some of them unwise and others unfair to loyal staff and did not implement them. He thought Mr Schneider in breach of his duty and Mr Schneider thought the same of David. A battle royal was in prospect. The future of one of the great names of late 19th and 20th century bookselling was in danger.

Against this background I received a telephone call from David Brass when I was at home one Saturday morning. He sounded quite overwrought and asked if he could come to see me right away. We were due to go out but arranged to postpone our journey. I should say here that at that point David and I were acquaintances rather than friends. Neither of us had been in the other's house before and, being of different generations and different philosophies, we did not go out together although we might find ourselves at the same table at trade functions. When David reached us he was in a very distressed state. I calmed him as best I could and asked how I could help. He said his lawyer had requested him to get some authoritative trade opinions in answer to a short list of questions. Would I be prepared to answer them? I said of course I would and took the first step on a slippery path.

First I was asked how I would regard a practice of automatically increasing the prices of unsold stock by a uniform percentage at fixed intervals, say every six months. I said that this was a nonsense. Some unsold stock might already be too dear while there might be a few pieces that could be doubled in price. Uniformity and antiquarian bookselling went badly together.

Next I was asked what would be the result of banning all buying for, say, three months. I said that it could be nearly fatal to a firm. Regular customers would soon notice that nothing fresh was appearing on the shelves. Those who offered books and found that no buying was taking place would immediately think there was something radically wrong with the firm's credit and damaging rumours would spread through the book world like wild fire. There were a few more questions of a similar nature.

David seemed pleased with my answers. Then he asked me if I

would be prepared to write a letter to his lawyers saying much the same that I had said to him. Here was a man in great distress, a recent past president of my trade association and until recently the head of a respected firm with which my family had had dealings for seventy years. Of course I said I would write the letter he wanted.

A couple of weeks later he rang to say that his counsel had asked if I would be prepared to talk to them. I thought to myself 'In for a penny, in for a pound', and made an appointment for early one evening. In chambers we went over much the same ground and eventually I was asked if I would be prepared to be an expert witness. The questions seemed to me to be so open and shut that I scarcely hesitated. I duly went before a commissioner of oaths and swore my affidavit, hoping that the case would be settled out of court without my being called. Meanwhile Mr Schneider and his side were, through their lawyers, approaching other booksellers to give expert opinion to counter mine. They could not find anyone. Just before the case was due to start David came to me and said that because the opposition had failed in this, they were going to attack my competence to run a whelk stall, much less a bookshop. They would do this on the basis of the admittedly poor trading results for our last two financial years. David warned me that the situation would get very unpleasant and very personal. I could of course have withdrawn at that stage but had I done so I could never have looked myself in the face again.

I was called to the witness box towards the end of the six-week trial and David's counsel took me through my affidavit – all twenty-one pages of it. As I re-read it now, eleven years after the trial, I see no reason to change one syllable of my evidence. I will not pretend that my cross-examination by Michael Burton QC, whom 'Driff' Driffield in his book about the case, *Not 84 Charing Cross Road*, called a 'pit bull terrier with bad breath', and who cross-examined me for something like two hours, was anything but an unpleasant experience. I thought the day went well for David's side, as did his solicitors, Paisner & Co., and his counsel. We were all shocked when a few days later the judge, Judge Paul Baker QC, found against David. This verdict was reversed on appeal but by that time the harm had been done. A good firm had gone to the wall, the book trade had attracted some unfavourable publicity, David was out of work, and was faced with a bill for costs of gargantuan proportions. The fact that he quickly landed a good job in California is beside the point.

I have implied that if the same situation occurred today I would act exactly as I did before. I will just add one rider. I do not know that I would have been so ready to rush to David's defence had I known that he had told his American employers that it was entirely normal for the head of a bookselling business in Great Britain to earn £120,000 a year at the time in question. In the first place I would take issue with that as a matter of fact and in the second place such a salary would have been a huge compensation for some of the things that David complained about.

HOW WRONG CAN YOU BE?

I once had through my hands a manuscript notebook of Ian Fleming's in which he had jotted down various thoughts. On one memorable page he had written : 'Scrambled eggs and coffee, the only two things that never let you down!' If he had said : 'Scrambled eggs and coffee, at their best a feast for a king', I might have agreed with him but I have eaten too many overcooked, lumpy scrambled eggs in hotel breakfast rooms, and have been served too many cups of weak and watery coffee, much of it in America I am sorry to say, ever to accept that Fleming was right. (The notebook is now in the Library at Eton. I haven't tried scrambled eggs at Eton but I can vouch for the excellence of the rest of the food – and of the coffee.)

CHAPTER THIRTY-THREE

THE JOHN RODKER
ARCHIVE

At the time when I was still cutting my bookselling teeth, and for a few years afterwards, Marianne Rodker, John Rodker's widow, was carrying on the rump of her late husband's publishing business from an apartment in Manchester Square in London. Gone were the heady days of Rodker's Egoist Press, which published the first English edition of *Ulysses* (albeit printed in France), and of his Ovid Press, which brought out Eliot's *Ara Vos Prec*. No longer did the Rodker imprint publish such attractive and seminal material as the early cantos of Ezra Pound, magnificent in their scarlet vellum bindings sixteen inches tall, but Rodker's Imago Publishing Company continued to operate, and was still engaged on the vast enterprise of publishing the entire canon of Sigmund Freud's writings.

I had several dealings with Marianne Rodker, as did others of us at the modern end of the rare book trade. Although both attractive and charming, Marianne had the reputation of being a difficult woman to do business with and indeed she seemed to want prices which would have left the dealer with a scarcely adequate return. Certainly she had good things to dispose of.

I went to see her one weekday afternoon in 1961 and came away with two piles of books and a wood-carving which was a portrait bust of Ezra Pound cut by Henri Gaudier-Brzeska. I conveyed my purchases from Manchester Square back to Vigo Street by taxi. The bust of Pound comprised a piece of wood about two inches square and three feet long. The carving consisted of a few nicks and slashes that might have been made by rather careless axe blows. I remember to this day sitting in the cab and using my left hand and both feet to try to prevent the piles of books from falling over as we went round corners, while grasping the wood carving firmly in my right hand. I was terrified that if I let go of it I might forget it and leave it in the cab. I was sure that if I did so either the next passenger or the driver would fail to recognize its significance and it would end up by going up someone's chimney as firewood.

I did get it safely back, and was pleased to pass responsibility for it to my father. He never admitted to being as nervous about its possible misuse as I was but I noticed that he passed it on very quickly, selling it to John Hewitt, a dealer who normally dealt in antiquities. It is now in the University Art Gallery at Yale.

This episode came to mind when in September 1984 I heard from various sources that, following Marianne Rodker's death in retirement in France, her children were minded to sell the books and papers which she had inherited from John Rodker, being file copies of Egoist Press publications, correspondence with authors, business files and so on. I received this intelligence from various sources and was soon in touch with Marianne's daughter, Dominique Tiry.

Dominique was a delight. Having raised a family she had now gone back to teaching drama in a school on the outskirts of Paris. Her husband, Philippe, had a job that many of us would regard with envy. It was his task to dispense money from the state to French performers and theatrical companies who wanted financial help to tour abroad, and to decide which overseas actors and companies who wanted to perform in France should be given a subsidy. He was a kind of one-man Arts Council. He told me, only partly in jest, that he saw ten or twelve shows or performances of some kind every week of his working life. For weekend relaxation he cooked, and he was a very good chef, as I was to discover. Meanwhile I addressed myself to Dominique, who with her brother, a musician, had inherited the Rodker archive and library.

The best letters and manuscripts were now in the Tirys' apartment on the rue de Vaugirard, and these pieces I set to work to appraise on a Friday afternoon in late October. I began by working my way through a file of no fewer than forty-five letters written to Rodker by the painter David Bomberg, a founder-member of the

London Group, of whom Rodker said in 1931 'Of the young men painting today, he is perhaps the most important.' In so far as his own finances permitted, Rodker was a patron to Bomberg and he did all that he could to promote his cause. Then I looked at ten unpublished letters from James Joyce, of which more anon. Next came correspondence exchanged between Rodker, various French writers and Marianne Rodker's mother, Ludmilla Savitzky (née Bloch), who translated into French Joyce's *Portrait of the Artist as a Young Man* and *Stephen Hero*, to say nothing of such writers as Pushkin, Virginia Woolf and Aldous Huxley. The manuscript of her translation of *Dedalus (i.e. Portrait of the Artist)* was one of the treasures laid out for me on the dining room table – which was why Dominique and I ate in the kitchen.

On the table too were letters from Richard Aldington, Havelock Ellis (fifty-eight letters, mostly concerning his editing of Restif de la Bretonne's *Monsieur Nicolas*), Ford Madox Ford, Wyndham Lewis (Rodker published Lewis's *Fifteen Drawings* at the Ovid Press in 1920), Ezra Pound and Isaac Rosenberg, the poet whose life was so tragically cut short in the trenches of the Western Front in 1918.

Also set out for my delectation were the setting copy for the American edition of Ezra Pound's *Lustra*, together with the author's annotated typescript of poems omitted from the English trade edition but included in the American text. A note in Pound's hand said that the omission was made because of the pusillanimous nature of the English publisher and printer. He added 'Ça vous donnera une idée de l'imbecilité anglais et la pudique célèbre'. Next there was Pound's heavily corrected typescript of his book *Hugh Selwyn Mauberley*. Material by Rodker himself included a series of more than three hundred letters written to Marianne over a period of thirty years. In addition there were autograph manuscript and typescript drafts of Rodker's controversial book *Memoirs of Other Fronts*. I had a busy day.

But the material in the Paris apartment was not all: in the family farmhouse near the village of Lestiou in the Loire valley were the remains of Rodker's library, together with his business papers.

We went to see these the following day, when the weather had turned much colder. Philippe and Dominique drove my wife and me down from Paris. The countryside was covered by a thick white frost. I knew we were nearing our destination when we crossed the bridge over the Loire at Beaugency, the bridge that features in Joyce's story for children *The Cat and the Devil*. Lestiou itself looked like something from a film by Renoir and indeed the villagers could have come straight from the set of *Partie de Campagne*.

After pausing at the baker's to buy wonderful buttery croissants still warm from the oven, Philippe asked us what we would like for lunch. I asked if we could have 'Something local'. Philippe just grunted but when we eventually got to the table, a table groaning with good things, he announced that everything set before us, whether to eat or drink, had come from not more than five kilometres away. But that was a treat in store, as my Latin master used to say of a declension we had yet to learn. The immediate problem was to open up the house which had been shut down since the end of summer. We swung back the shutters on their rusty hinges while Philippe made a fire in the big stone grate. The house was close to the river and the damp cold seemed to be eating into our bones. The Tirys lent us oversized boots, fleece-lined jerkins and the like to put on over our town clothes, and, after breakfasting on freshly brewed coffee and warm croissants, we finally set to work.

The books in the library included a presentation copy from Jean Cocteau; Eliot's *Ara Vos Prec* (Ovid Press, 1919); Ludmilla Savitzky's working copy of Joyce's *Portrait of the Artist*; a copy of Rodker's edition of *Ulysses*, inscribed to Ludmilla and her husband by Joyce; Wyndham Lewis's *Fifteen Drawings* (Ovid Press, 1920); Pound's *Draft of Sixteen Cantos* (Three Mountains Press, 1925) and *Draft of Cantos 17 to 27* (Rodker, 1928). There were other rarities and association copies too numerous to mention, but what was to take most of our time was the task of cataloguing and appraising Rodker's business papers, being chiefly the surviving files of his various publishing enterprises. We estimated that these files contained approximately fifteen thousand pieces: they occupied some thirteen linear feet of shelving. The papers were stored in outhouses even colder than the farmhouse itself so, clumping along in our clumsy boots, we carried the files in, an armful at a time, and worked on them on a table we dragged in front of Philippe's blazing log fire. Our way from shed to dining table passed through the kitchen, where Philippe was busy at the stove. Wonderful smells floated up as he browned onions, made sauces and baked an apple tart. I cannot now remember every dish that we ate but I did note in my journal that we were served home-made terrines of duck and of rabbit; local ham; saucissons with an onion vinaigrette; rillettes of pork; boudins blancs with sautéed mushrooms, potatoes (were they boulangères or sarladaises? memory fails me); three local cheeses; and an apple tart. All this food was washed down with excellent local wines beginning with a sparkling Crémant de Loire, followed by an Orléanais rosé, an Orléanais rouge, and ending with a pear liqueur made by the Tirys' neighbour from fruit that they supplied to him from trees in their garden. I ate so much at lunch time that for one of only three occasions in my lifetime I chose to go to bed without supper. Eventually we returned to Paris, tired but happy, and needed no rocking to help us sleep.

From the date of my first visit to the rue de Vaugirard to the point at which Dominique and her brother were finally persuaded to accept my figures and sell the collection was thirteen long months. I confess that I found the waiting very trying. I sensed that attempts to put any kind of pressure on Dominique would be counter-productive.

At least three people, for each of whom I had a high regard and whose veracity I would normally have accepted unquestioningly, buttonholed me by letter at an early stage of my negotiations. One was Dick Ellmann, biographer of James Joyce, who wrote to me: 'Dear Anthony, As you may know, it was I who recommended you to Dominique Tiry to deal with her mother's papers. The papers include some unpublished letters from James Joyce and in the circumstances I have no hesitation in asking you if you would supply me with photostats of these letters when the archive is safely in your hands.'

Carlton Lake, Curator Emeritus of the French collection at the University of Texas, said in his missive 'Dear Anthony, I was glad to be able to recommend your firm to Dominique Tiry to handle the disposal of the papers that her mother, Marianne Rodker inherited. As you know the archive includes unpublished letters from James Joyce to Madame Savitzky and I think you will agree that it would be proper that you should give me first refusal of those letters.' The third appeal was on similar lines.

Thus it was that one morning in November, 1985, Dominique and I met in the rue de Vaugirard. All the material from the country farmhouse, together with the books and letters from the Paris apartment had been taken to the shop of a friendly Paris bookseller for shipping back to England for cataloguing. When the agreed amounts of banknotes and bank drafts had changed hands, and when Dominique and I were sitting down to drink a glass of wine together to set the final seal on the deal, I was emboldened to say to her 'Dominique, I don't want to name names at this stage but no fewer than three people have told me that it is thanks to them that I have had the chance of handling this material and that I am therefore under some obligation to them. I am prepared to do the right thing by them but I should like to know to whom I am really indebted for the recommendation.' Dominique threw back her head and laughed. 'Anthony,' she said, 'Your benefactor is my mother. She told me that of the various dealers she had met, and done business with in her lifetime, you were the one I could trust when my brother and I finally came to dispose of the remaining things.' She then punctured any bubble of self-satisfaction that might have been rising in my breast by adding, 'She said you were more honest than most!'.

'You are always welcome in a bookshop' ran the slogan of a publicity campaign organised by Britain's new book trade. By and large it is true, even allowing for the fact that some members of the public seem to think that the sign over the door reads 'Public Library,' 'Information Booth' or even 'Guide, Philosopher and Friend'. Certainly bookshops receive requests for some very weird things. The oddest I can remember was when a man came into our Vigo Street shop and asked for a packet of 'those little paper frills you put round the end of lamb cutlets'.

CHAPTER THIRTY-FOUR

THE OPTIMUM
GREGYNOG COLLECTION

AND MY FIRST ROLLS ROYCE

One of the exciting things about my job is that I never know what is going to be around the next corner. Even after nearly fifty years it is a peculiar day which does not bring me a book which I have never seen before. In my first months in my father's business this was especially true and new experiences and new impressions crowded in on me. It was then that I first came across the work of the great Welsh private press called Gregynog. First I had to learn to pronounce its name. The trick is to treat the letter 'y' as though it were a 'u' and thus effectively to say 'Greg-gun-nog'.

Wales owed the Gregynog Press, as it owed so much else, to the generous benefaction of the Davies family, whose fortune had been founded in the nineteenth century by David Davies, industrialist, builder of railways and coal mining magnate. His granddaughters the Misses Gwendoline and Margaret ('Daisy') Davies, established Gregynog Hall as a Welsh arts centre. The role of the Gregynog Press was 'to unlock the treasure house of Welsh literature, romance and legend, and to make it accessible to the English-speaking public'. The literature was to be presented 'in as perfect a form as we possibly can as regards the English translation and artistic treatment.'

No private press ever began life with greater financial support, not even Count Kessler's justly celebrated Cranach Press in Weimar. Nor were the books of any private press less influenced in design by the taste of its proprietors: although insistent on the highest standards (being willing to finance the scrapping of work that was less than perfect and a return to the proverbial drawing board), Gwendoline and Daisy Davies took little or no interest in the running of the Press and seldom visited it. They left the management in the hands of Dr Thomas Jones, Deputy Secretary to the Cabinet, and chairman of the Gregynog board, and a sequence of controllers of the press: R. A. Maynard, William McCance (husband of Agnes Miller Parker), Loyd Haberly, and James Wardrop. These controllers, together with successive artists in residence (H. W. Bray and Blair Hughes-Stanton) and master binders (first John Mason and then George Fisher, who was recruited in 1925 and was responsible for the binding of almost all the Press's books, as well as the three produced at Gregynog for private circulation), these were the people who influenced the contents of the Gregynog list and the appearance of the books.

Illustration was a key feature of Gregynog Press books. Thirty-three of the forty-two publications were illustrated, the artists including those named above (Agnes Miller Parker, H. W. Bray and Blair Hughes-Stanton, the last being responsible for those two spectacular folios *The Lamentations of Jeremiah* and *The Revelation of Saint John the Divine*), as well as John Farleigh, Gertrude Hermes, David Jones, and Reynolds Stone. The Gregynog edition of Robert Bridges' *Eros and Psyche*, with initial letters cut by Graily Hewitt, made the first use of designs drawn by Burne-Jones long before, but only now cut on wood (by the Press's American controller, Loyd Haberly, and by John Beedham).

It was at George Fisher's instigation that, in addition to the regular bindings, which themselves attracted much praise, the Press issued a few copies of each book, generally between fifteen and twenty-five, specially bound in the richest levant or oasis morocco. The earlier special bindings tended to be relatively simple, relying on the beauty of the colour and the quality of the leather to make their effect: later bindings include eight remarkably *avant garde* abstract designs by Hughes-Stanton. All have long been treasured.

Accordingly, when I was approached in 1992 about 'a collection of Gregynog Press books in special bindings' by someone giving his surname as 'Davies', my heart missed a beat. I soon found that it was as I had hoped: Mr Davies was a member of the Gregynog family and was contemplating selling what had been Daisy Davies's set of the forty-two publications, all in the special bindings and all virtually mint. What made this set specially attractive was the inclusion of two great rarities. One was one of only four copies of Bernard Shaw's *Shaw Gives Himself Away* out of the twenty-five in special bindings to be 'enriched' with additional morocco onlays. The other was one of just three copies (at this time Miss Dorothy Harrop, Gregynog's authoritative bibliographer, knew of the existence of only two) of one of Gregynog's rare forays into printing on vellum, *Llyfr y pregeth-wr (The Book of Ecclesiastes)*, with two wood-engravings by David Jones. Its blue levant binding was decorated with patterns of gilt rules and with lozenge-shaped onlays of coloured morocco, each outlined in gilt. It shone and sparkled like a jewel cave. This was a collection I simply had to handle.

Mr Davies told me quite frankly that he had already sought opinions and advice from two auction houses and two or three booksellers. As we talked I believe he sensed the strength of my feeling for these books. In any event we eventually reached an agreement under which I would take the collection on consignment. The day came when they were all delivered to me. As soon as I had unpacked them I telephoned Bill Fletcher who, although he was now in his eighties, still came in regularly to his bookshop in Cecil Court. Bill was something of an authority on fine bindings and I knew that he had a special interest in those from the Gregynog Press. I was sure he would enjoy seeing this set and also thought that I might learn something from his comments.

'Bill' I said 'I have just unpacked a complete set of Gregynog Press special bindings and I thought you might like to come round and look at them some time.' 'Thank you', he said, 'I'd love to see them; I'll come round as soon as I can manage it'.

I expected to see him in two or three days but in fact within ten minutes he was at my door. His eagerness confirmed what I thought of the desirability and rarity of such a set as this. Bill pored over the books lovingly, admiring this and criticising that. 'What do you want for them?' he asked after half an hour or so. I told him that I planned to price the set at £85,000. He pouted a little, thought for a moment and then said that it was more than he could pay but he 'supposed' I might well get that price.

In the months that followed I tried to do just that, but without success. I approached appropriate libraries on both sides of the Atlantic, and private collectors as well. Complete sets of Gregynog special bindings were indeed rare but institutions which took Gregynog Press books seriously tended to have a few special bindings already and none of them seemed both willing and able to fund the purchase of my set. My next step was going to be the preparation of a de luxe catalogue of the collection, with each binding reproduced in full colour. This would be a costly undertaking, but it would probably ensure the selling of the collection, and as a by-product would make an attractive and highly desirable work of reference.

At this juncture I went over to Amsterdam for a meeting of the Committee of the International League of Antiquarian Booksellers. I knew Amsterdam and its booksellers quite well but on this visit I had made a mental note to visit a newcomer to the scene, Dr Steven Bakker, who ran his business under the name of Der Zilverdistel, called after what was arguably the finest of Holland's private presses. I had done a little business with Steven Bakker by post and I telephoned him now to ask if I might call on him. (At that time he ran his business from an elegant apartment on the top floor of a tall, narrow house in an old quarter of the city: he did not have an open bookshop.) Steven received me kindly, introduced me to his staff and gave me the run of his shelves. His premises were beautifully fitted out and his shelves were laden with fine books. While Steven, his secretary and his cataloguer all beavered away, classical music filled the air. I worked around the room, selecting a few books for purchase. Steven and I chatted a little as the sight of a particular book moved me to comment or as a question happened to occur to him. What books from the Doves Press did I have in stock, he wondered? Did he have any clandestine printing from the Nazi occupation, I asked in my turn?

A few minutes and a cup of tea later Steven enquired 'What Gregynog Press books do you have in stock at the moment?' I chuckled. 'Well, to start with I have a complete set of the special bindings,' I boasted.

'How much to you want for them?' he asked.

'Eighty-five thousand pounds' I said.

'When do you go back to London?'

'On Monday' I replied.

'I'll be there first thing on Tuesday morning' he promised, and sure enough he was.

He wanted the books badly: that I could see. But he proved a tough negotiator, pressing for every penny in discount, and every day in credit terms. Eventually we shook hands on a figure and a date. Later I learned that he had the good fortune to resell the collection almost at once to a private customer whose prompt settlement enabled Steven to pay me before the promised date. We agreed to have a celebratory luncheon next time he was in London.

'I hope you did well out of it, Anthony', Steven said.

'Well I'm not complaining', I replied, 'But by the time you had had your discount, my profit was not enormous. Let's just say I shan't be buying my first Rolls Royce on the strength of it.'

Steven laughed.

When the time for our lunch came, Steven, his tall spare bespectacled figure topped by fair hair, introduced the attractive young lawyer who was his partner in life, if not in business, and, together with my wife, we set off for a table at *Le Palais du Jardin* just across the street from us in Long Acre. As we opened a preprandial bottle of champagne and began to toast the Davies family, the Gregynog Press, its various controllers, and above all George Fisher, Steven slipped across the table a gift-wrapped package. I opened it with eager fingers and what should emerge from the wrapping but a perfect scale model, not six inches long, of a Rolls Royce Silver Shadow and that is how I acquired my first and so far my only Rolls Royce.

CHANGING PLACES

In the seventy-eight years of the firm's history Bertram Rota Ltd has changed its premises rather often : once every ten years on average, as the list below shows. Most of the moves have been onwards and upwards, either metaphorically (as to better things) or literally (as to larger premises or, most recently, upstairs). Seldom have we gone very far, but the labour of moving the stock (something we have always done ourselves, not caring to entrust rare books to even the most careful of professional removal men) is just too great for me ever to contemplate moving again.

The shortest distance involved was when we went from Bodley House in Vigo Street to Nos. 4, 5 & 6 Savile Row, just 28 yards away. This was the easiest move to plan, for we were moving to a much larger space, all of it on the ground floor, and we had new shelving installed at our destination before a single volume was carried across the road. Working to a detailed brief we would take an armful of books off a shelf in Vigo Street, carry it 28 yards and set it down in its predestined place in Savile Row. I know the distance was 28 yards because I measured it, so why did it seem like half a mile by the middle of the afternoon?

This was the removal in the course of which we actually sold a book. We had just passed the halfway point in moving the alphabetically arranged stock of modern first editions, when a lady came through the open door and, oblivious of the work in progress all around her, asked if we had a copy of George Orwell's Shooting an Elephant. *'Madam' I said to her, 'a fine copy in the dust-wrapper has just gone out of the door. If you hurry you will catch it as it is put on a shelf across the street.' Which she did.*

Over the years our addresses have been : 109 Charing Cross Road, WC2, 1923-1927; 76A Davies Street, W1, 1927-1934; 14 Old Burlington Street, W1, 1934-1937; Bodley House, Vigo Street, W1, 1937-1965; 4, 5 & 6 Savile Row, W1, 1965-1977. In 1977 we moved to 31 Long Acre, WC2. In 1987 we sold the freehold of that building but retained the use of the first floor. From that date until 1994 we were at 9–11 Langley Court WC2, since when we have traded solely from our suite of rooms at 31 Long Acre.

Interior of the shop, Long Acre

CHAPTER THIRTY-FIVE

THE ONES THAT GOT AWAY

People who write their memoirs have a tendency to dwell on successes rather than failures, on triumphs rather than disasters. Let us be charitable and assume that the Freudian censor accounts for this by erasing the less happy outcomes from the writers' memory banks. In my own case not all my searches turned up desirable books and papers and not all negotiations resulted in a purchase or a sale. The two biggest fish to escape my net were Evelyn Waugh's library and archive, and, later, the Vladimir Nabokov archive. I wanted each of these collections desperately and failing to get them really hurt. Over the years I have looked back time and again and reviewed what happened and I still cannot see what I could have done differently that might have affected the outcome.

Evelyn Waugh's manuscripts and correspondence files and his considerable library, with its very special copies of the books he had written (some in small editions on tinted paper and in morocco or half morocco bindings), presentation copies of books by his friends and contemporaries, and his collection of Victorian books with chromolithographs and *papier mâché* bindings, were offered to selected institutional libraries by the Estate. Librarians were invited to submit bids by sealed tender. Will Ready, the iconoclastic head of libraries at McMaster University in Hamilton, Ontario, asked me to represent him, examine the material, make a 'fair market value' appraisal, and report to him on the usefulness or otherwise of the material to scholars. This was a commission I was glad to undertake and during one of winter's colder cold snaps I took the train down to Taunton. I spent the first day in snug offices, the first that of Waugh's solicitor and the second in Waugh's bank, where certain of the manuscripts were being kept in safe custody. Both rooms were really too warm, and had it not been for the excitement generated by handling such wonderful material, I do not doubt that I should have nodded off over my work.

The next morning Mrs Laura Waugh, Evelyn's widow, collected me from my hotel and took me to Waugh's home at Combe Florey. A notice on the gate, a witty variation on the old cliché, read 'No Admittance on Business'. The day was icy and the temperature in the house caused my breath to vaporize as I spoke. Mrs Waugh and her niece, who was staying with her to help with the books and papers, plied me with hot drinks and with brimming schooners of sherry, and these ministrations prevented the blood from actually freezing in my veins, but draughts howling through the window where two pieces of glass had been butted together as a cheap replacement when a larger piece broke, made this, like the Battle of Waterloo, 'a damned close-run thing'. I put the best face on it that I could and was proud of having kept my image burnished by comparison with the previous bidder, Lew David Feldman, of the House of El Dieff (note the pun) who had lodged in the house. Mrs Waugh's niece told me that 'Mr Feldman actually came to my aunt's lunch table in his overcoat!' The ladies clearly still felt outrage a couple of weeks later.

Lew blotted his copybook further, though it didn't affect the final outcome. On the dining room sideboard stood a portrait bust of Waugh himself. As a joke Waugh crowned it with his Royal Marine field service peaked cap, a joke which it was in order for Waugh, a Captain in the Marines (the 'Halbardiers' in the *Sword of Honour* trilogy) to play on himself as it were, but not for others to copy. Lew Feldman lifted the cap from the bust and tried it on his own head for size. Laura Waugh and her niece were horrified, but at the end of the day the bid from Feldman, who on this occasion was acting for the University of Texas, was more than others were willing and able to come up with for the manuscripts, and so the niceties of etiquette went by the board. I found it ironic that Lew should later telephone me to ask what figure he ought to put forward for the chromolithographs and the *papier mâché* bindings, two fields that were completely blind spots for him.

Actually Lew's wearing a Royal Marine cap was not too awful a thing, for he had been a top sergeant in the United States Marine Corps during World War II. He had come a long way since then, walking with a gold-knobbed cane, having his finger nails polished and travelling first class. He was useful to Dr Ransom in his role as one of the acquisitions agents for the Humanities Research Center at the University of Texas because of his seemingly limitless credit at the Chemical Bank in New York. Certainly he used to call Dr Ransom's secretary to enquire about her boss's travel plans. He would then call the airlines and book the adjacent seat: that was certainly a sound way of getting a quiet and uninterrupted audience with Harry. Before we leave the Waugh Library (its bookcases and Waugh's desk are now installed in Austin) it is worth remarking that over the door of the downstairs loo Waugh had caused to be engraved the words 'Abandon hope all ye who enter here'.

The Waugh material came onto the market during Warren Roberts's time as Director of the HRC. The Nabokov archive came up during the reign of Dr Decherd Turner, who was advised on the subject by Carlton Lake, Curator Emeritus of the French collections at HRC and a man intimately familiar with the field. Hearing that Nabokov's widow and his son, Dmitri, opera singer and racing car driver, were thinking of selling, Carlton persuaded Decherd to send me out to Switzerland to make an appraisal of the books and manuscripts that were on offer and to advise my principals about their scholarly worth and their market value. We were talking of a capital sum in six figures sterling, and I was a little hurt that Carlton thought it necessary to warn me to keep my expenses claim low: perhaps he had heard the story of George Lawson and the observatory? Be that as it may, I arrived at Montreux and made my way to the Grand Hotel where Mme Nabokov maintained the suite she had shared with her husband. She welcome me graciously, introduced me to Brian Butler, the antipodean scholar then working on his life of Nabokov and who was helping her sort the papers. Butler led me to the hotel's attics where much of the material was stored.

All the rare early books, those written and first published in Russian, were there. So were the original drafts of excessively clever crossword puzzles. Then too there were notes on the mating habits of obscure species of butterflies. All this was in addition to straight-forward manuscripts of books published in English, lecture notes for courses given at Cornell, translations of Pushkin and so on. I recommended a figure which I was sure it would command on the open market but I do not know how far Texas actually went towards it. I was subsequently told that Dmitri, through his agents, had suggested a complicated arrangement involving high valuations, and reciprocal 'gifts' in kind from the family. Dr Turner, an ordained Minister of Religion, would have nothing to do with it. In stepped a New York dealer who represented the Berg Collection of the New York Public Library. He was able to square the circle and keep both buyer and seller happy and I suppose he is to be congratulated on that. I take some small consolation from the fact that I did at least get to leaf through the archive before it entered the public world of that very private library.

In the early nineteen-seventies I was fortunate enough to have as my secretary-cum-personal assistant Virginia Murray, wife of John Murray VI who is now the head of the august publishing house whose name he bears. Virginia was being groomed to become Murray's archivist, looking after important Byron manuscripts and much else besides, and it was thought useful for her to get some bookshop experience, especially in cataloguing archival material. Virginia stayed with me for two happy years and when she left to take up her duties at Murray's we remained in touch. This is presumably why Murray's turned to my firm when they sought help over the matter of the file copies of Murray publications virtually from their company's inception to the point (around 1933) where the titles were still in copyright. This very considerable quantity of books, including many titles published over the imprint of their predecessor, Smith, Elder & Co. posed quite a storage problem. Murray's seldom if ever referred to the older books themselves and, if the right buyer could be found, they were prepared to sell.

We leaped at the chance of handling the sale for them (our dealings were with Hallam Murray, Virginia's brother-in-law, who was leaving the firm to devote himself to good causes) and had the books removed to our warehouse for cataloguing, appraisal and eventual display. The cataloguing was a gargantuan task and the appraisal hardly less so, but eventually we came up with a list and a price. Then all we had to do was find a buyer. There were conditions of sale. The collection was to be sold en bloc and the buyer was to undertake to keep it together. Although there were many exciting and valuable books in this collection of file copies, all of them virtually mint, there were also quite a few out-of-date medical books and other such things which had no immediate attraction to would-be buyers.

Even so it was not too long before we found the ideal purchaser, the University of North Carolina at Chapel Hill. I particularly liked the way that they raised the purchase price, which was not inconsiderable. Elsewhere I speak of a war between the English Department and the

Library on a certain campus. At Chapel Hill it was very different. The prime movers in the purchase were the English Department and they called in old IOUs and pledged their future funds in interdepartmental deals. The Manuscript Division of the Library was reminded of help it had received from English funds. The Library School was shown what good teaching aids the Murray file copies would make. The Art Department had it pointed out to them that some of the nineteenth century illustrated books could be of use to them too. The chairman of the committee controlling the President's Fund for Excellence was persuaded to go on side, as were one or two other trustees of small but useful sums of money. Nobody who was asked turned a deaf ear. Through this spirit of co-operation the funding was raised and the books went to Chapel Hill where they are richly appreciated as they tell the story of British book production in the nineteenth and early twentieth centuries. If only there were similar co-operation on every campus.

CHAPTER THIRTY-SIX

LOOKING BACK

This is a book of memoirs, not a definitive biography. It is therefore selective. There are aspects of subjects that I have barely touched on and others that I have not mentioned at all, chiefly for fear of straining the reader's patience too far. There are many tales I have not told. I have barely touched on my involvement in politics for example and have said relatively little about working for the Antiquarian Booksellers Association and the International League of Antiquarian Booksellers. I joined the ABA committee in 1959 (when Harry Pratley was President) and as a Past-President still have the right to attend committee meetings. Every now and then I turn up and surprise the present incumbents. Though I no longer have a vote the rules don't stop me speaking and I usually interject a remark or two. Today in both the ABA and the ILAB it is harder to find people willing and able to take on the large amounts of voluntary work that are involved. In an age of increasing professionalism, with government and bureaucracy ever extending their grip the workload of the trade associations has certainly increased – and that at a time when for the book trade 'Life is real! Life is Earnest!', as Longfellow has it. This is a shame. I for my part always found much pleasure in committee work and both at home and abroad it has brought me great friendships.

Working for the League had a particular savour. Its remit was to promote the cause of rare books and the highest ethical standards in dealing with them, among the thirty nations or more whose antiquarian book trade associations have banded together for the common good. The League's business is conducted by a seven-man committee under the chairmanship of the President. I served as Treasurer for three years during the presidency of the Danish bookseller Hans Bagger, one of the finest and most selfless men I have ever had the privilege to meet. I succeeded him in the chair in 1988 and served till 1991. My committee consisted of a Dutchman (Anton Gerits), a German (Konrad Meuschel), a Frenchman (Louis Loeb-Laroque), an American (Lou Weinstein), a Japanese (Mitsou Nitta of the Yushodo Company), and an Italian (Vittorio Soave). We met for a protracted session every six months. We managed without interpreters and the resulting latter-day Tower of Babel was really rather fun. We worked hard and we played hard, meeting in different locations such as Stuttgart, Paris, Amsterdam, London, Tokyo and Turin – either where one of us had his rare book business, or where there was an important Book Fair being held. Any disagreements of the day were washed away at night by good wine at dinner. Often the local booksellers acted as our hosts. I remember with particular pleasure a lunch that Vittorio Soave gave on the terrace of his rowing club on the River Po at Turin. I remember too the dedication and loyalty to the League and to myself shown by my admirable vice-president, Anton Gerits. Needing once to get the committee's reaction between meetings to a question that had arisen, I sent faxes to the various points of the compass. I hope Anton will forgive me if I paraphrase his reply:

'I have returned from holiday to find your fax. My desk is piled high with papers demanding my attention, but I answer you first.

On the question you put my opinion is (there followed a brief but cogent argument). If you should reach a different conclusion, Mr President, then your opinion is my opinion also.'

If working with these people was rewarding for the fun we had and the fellowship we shared, so too was helping collectors, some great and some quite modest, to build their collections. Equally so was working with librarians who were building great libraries. I remember the tales I used to hear from a retired dealer in jade who collected first editions by Somerset Maugham, whom he had once met on a boat on the Yangtse. A man who deserves a whole chapter to himself is the late Grenville Cook, who also collected Maugham. A local government officer, and a bachelor, he delighted in building author collections, usually with the intention of using them as the basis for a book or at least an article, but as soon as they were as complete as he could make them he would sell them to us en bloc and begin all over again, usually with a different author, though I know that he built and disposed of no fewer than three Maugham collections. When Anthony Hobson sold some of his modern first editions in a spectacularly successful sale at Sotheby's a year or two back I was proud to find my firm's help generously acknowledged. Certainly I had enjoyed handling his auction bids for modern books when he himself was on the rostrum.

How fortunate I was to get to know that legendary librarian Lawrence Clark Powell, whose enthusiasm for rare books made him such a successful missionary and proselytiser for the cause. Equally enthusiastic is Michael Meredith (a former Head of English, and now Librarian, at Eton) who actually encourages boys to study and use the rich material gathered into safe keeping there. Working with Michael on the building of the modern collection was its own reward.

I enjoyed first appraising and then negotiating the sale of Cyril Connolly's library, which he referred to as 'the Clapham Junction of literature'. I think back to the days when he would come into the Vigo Street shop on a Monday or Tuesday and suddenly launch into what appeared to be an unscripted monologue. The subject might be Proust, it might be Joyce or someone less famous, but we came to know that, lightly edited, the words Cyril uttered would form his column in the next issue of 'The Sunday Times.'

Of course there are catalogues for which I have a particular fondness. I think of No 180 devoted to books from the Libraries of the Rossetti family, of No 244 listing only books by members of the Powys family and their circle, and of No 286a offering only dedication copies of the books that it listed.

Is there anything in the blood or in the genes which can predispose a person towards such a calling as bookselling? I often ask myself this. My paternal grandfather, christened Carlo but brought up in this country as Charles Rota, was a corrector of the press or proofreader on one of the big financial newspapers. My father has told me how, when in retirement, Carlo would pick up the morning newspaper, open it to a double-page spread and even before he began to read it, would point his finger at a misprint which was, let us say, halfway down the third column of the second page. My father seemed to inherit this good eye for typographical errors. Something of this trait appeared to pass to me and I found it useful when in my first job I had to begin each morning by reading through the eleven national newspapers that England then boasted and mark for my boss, the director of publicity at 20th Century Fox, first in red crayon, all stories about 20th Century Fox and its films, and any stars under contract to us. Then in blue crayon I had to mark all other stories which touched on the cinema in any way at all. Since I wasn't given very long to perform this task, an ability to spot, not mistakes, but key words such as 'film', 'director', and 'star' that leapt at me from the page was very helpful. Both my sons, Julian, who works with me in the business, and Gavin, who works in television, also inherited this useful characteristic.

As I said at the beginning of this book, my parents' marriage broke down about the time that war broke out. My father joined the Royal Air Force and my mother took a job. This meant that as an only child I was thrown very much on my own resources. At the end of the school day and during the entire school holidays I become one of the public library's most avid readers, devouring the works of such writers as Herbert Strang (tales of smuggling and of shipwrecks) and Percy F. Westerman (stories of sea-scouts). Then I discovered Arthur Ransome, who was clever enough to make the exploits of his characters entirely within the compass of his readers so that they could imagine themselves actually living through the experiences of the Swallows and the Amazons. (Many years later I published in *The Book Collector* an essay on his work in the 'Uncollected Authors' series.)

But apart from the public library and the books that I bought for myself I had the run of the books my father had left behind in the big glass-fronted bookcase that dominated the living room in our home in Palmers Green. I think it was these volumes which first kindled my interest in books as physical objects, apart from the text.

They were not especially valuable (my father was not trying to form a collection in competition with his customers) but they were all interesting, were of diverse shapes and sizes and were good examples of their various kinds. From them I began to learn what page size was appropriate for what kind of text. I remember the thick royal octavo of O. Henry's *Collected Stories* and the duodecimo and 16mo of selections from Keats, Byron and Shelley. There were books bound in decorated parchment. There was a volume from the Roycroft Press bound in suede (a concept that I thought bizarre and in poor taste then as I do to this day). There were two quarto volumes in half-morocco being H. G. Wells's *The Outline of History*, bound up from the original fortnightly parts. There were privately printed books. There were books issued under pseudonyms. There were advance proof copies in drab brown wrappers. There were presentation copies, some inscribed to my father, others to the great and the good. I came to an appreciation of this diversity long before I knew the correct terms to use to describe them.

All these factors played their part in helping me to make my way as an antiquarian bookseller, a calling which has brought me the best of friends, a host of rich memories and the constant challenge of never knowing what the next day will bring.

BERTRAM ROTA

1903–1966

The following appreciation by the late Simon Nowell-Smith first appeared in The Book Collector, *Volume 16, No. 1, Spring 1967 and is here reprinted by kind permission of the Editor and of Simon Nowell-Smith's Executors.*

A young face, with eyes quick to smile, beneath a distinguished, white head-of-hair. You knew he was past 60: there had been a birthday party. But you never thought of him as of any particular age, or, if you did, you expected him to look just the same when his 70th birthday should come round. Last November he had a heart attack, his second. After a quick recovery he was all set to return to work, in spite of the tactful restraint of a devoted wife. Suddenly on 3 December he suffered a brain haemorrhage and died.

Cyril Bertram Rota was born on 22 June 1903. His mother's father was Bertram Dobell, rediscoverer of Traherne, friend and editor of James ('B.V.') Thomson, scholar, publisher and bookseller. His father, Carlo Rota, half Italian, was a printer's reader, father of his chapel, first at the *Morning Post* and later with Couchman's, the Stock Exchange printers. From one side of the family he derived (besides a preferred Christian name) his devotion to literature and sympathy with men of letters; from the other side, so scrupulous an attention to the printed word that in later life a misprint in one of his catalogues would give him a sleepless night. In 1918, the elder Dobell being dead, Bertram's uncles Percy and Arthur persuaded his mother to remove him from Hornsey County School – he was 14 – to help restore their bookshop to normal after the first world war. Perhaps because Percy was too busy to cast the spell of his own Restoration-to-Romantic interests over him, or because his inclinations lay elsewhere, he concentrated his youthful energies on the

Bodley House, drawn by Jock Hinchliffe, 1947

twentieth century, so that when after five years he set up on his own, the debt that he owed was mainly to his uncle Arthur, who indeed provided some of his first stock. He was 19; his capital was £100, his shop a single first-floor back above Marks's then premises at 108 Charing Cross Road. From there, in September 1923, was issued *A Catalogue of Modern Books, mainly first editions. No. 1. C. Bertram Rota* ... In 1927 Bertram took over the Davies Street shop which Percy Muir vacated when he joined Dulau's; in 1934 he moved to Old Burlington Street, and in 1937 to the pretty Regency house in Vigo Street (formally opened by Hugh Walpole) with which he will always be associated in the memory of his friends – Bodley House, one-time John Lane's and Elkin Mathews's Bodley Head. The grandeur of 4-6 Savile Row dates from 1965.

The 147 catalogues issued by Bertram Rota ('Limited' since 1942) would provide a microcosm of book-price history in the modern field over more than 40 years, but for two reservations. On the one hand, items like T. S. Eliot's *The Waste Land* (Hogarth Press 1923, 4s 6d; Rota, 7s 6d in 1924, £1 in 1937) would almost certainly after 1959 (£10) go to the customer heading a waiting list without benefit of catalogue. On the other hand, operating for many years with small capital and a small margin, Bertram was less affected by market fluctuations than some of his more ambitious rivals. Elkin Mathews, for example, hit by the 'slump', announced in 1931 a 'complete revaluation' of their stock: a 'fine, unfaded copy' of *The Old Wives' Tale* was marked down from £110 to £90 between one catalogue and another. (Bennett's own rebound copy was sold at auction for £20 at about the same time.) Bertram's catalogues in 1930-31 contained no *Old Wives' Tale*, and no Bennett items – indeed few books of any kind – priced as high as £10: nor for many years after. He built up his reputation, especially among young collectors, by selling at moderate prices clean copies of a wide range of modern books, many of them little known at the time. Success came gradually. It came, I believe, because he enjoyed reading; because if he liked a book he was confident – often rightly, and often, no doubt, wrongly – that it would one day come into its own;

and because he could respect, even when he did not share, the enthusiasms of his customers.

The occasional introductions to the catalogues recall some of the vicissitudes of the firm and its founder.

April 1940: 'As there are still books in Bodley House after half a year of war, here is another list of them . . . He who buys may be plucking a brand from the burning, a book from the bombs.'

Early 1941: 'I prophesied more truly than I knew. Bodley House was bombed in October. Half the stock was ruined.' (Much of the stock had been moved out to be bombed elsewhere.) Late 1941: 'This personal note is written from a Royal Air Force Station where I have the privilege of serving with the RAF Volunteer Reserve.' Flight-Lieutenant Rota's work on photographic interpretation and target intelligence culminated in the award of the King Haakon VII Liberty Cross: for Bertram Rota Limited the war meant an acute financial stringency from which it took years to recover.

Like most of us, Bertram had formed his taste in poetry by the time he was 25. He never lost his preference for the 'Georgian' – Eddie Marsh's 'proud ambiguous adjective'. But his puzzlement over the rejection of his favourites by his younger friends did not prevent him, either as conversationalist or bookseller, from moving with the times. Among prose writers he put T. E. Lawrence first: for him *Seven Pillars of Wisdom* was 'the one undoubted classic of our generation'. His thorough knowledge of D. H. Lawrence's work enabled him to build up George Lazarus's collection, unparalleled in private hands, of Lawrence's books and manuscripts. Among the 'archives' for which he found homes were those of H. G. Wells (now at the University of Illinois, except for Henry James's letters to Wells, which are in the Bodleian), and Eddie Marsh, correspondent of numberless Georgian and later poets (Berg Collection, NYPL; except the important Rupert Brooke papers which remain in this country). To the University of Texas, with which in recent years his connection was close, and NYPL and other libraries, he steered many of the multifarious papers of the literary agent, J. B. Pinker. Though *The Old Wives' Tale* in its marcescible binding eluded him in the thirties, he was in due time able to sell its manuscript to the voracious J. K. Lilly, of Indiana. Among writers who were his personal friends were Arthur Machen, Richard Llewellyn, A. E. Coppard, H. E. Bates and L. A. G. Strong, and he was a good friend in need to Dylan Thomas. Bodley House since the last war has been a congenial resort not only of collectors but of librarians, and not least of those American scholars with whom Bertram cemented friendships on business visits and lecture tours in the United States. This kind of recognition was none the less grateful for having come comparatively late.

There are 'ifs' in every man's biography. What would Bertram's career have been if he had not been taken away from school at 14? Perhaps not very different. His Dobell grandfather (who incidentally started life as a grocer's errand boy) and his uncle Percy were both scholar-booksellers: Percy's catalogue of Restoration literature and 18th-century verse are reference works of lasting value. Bertram used to say that he would have been a better scholar if he had had more schooling. Certainly he might have been less diffident about committing to paper the results of long study in a field where his experience and expertise were virtually unsurpassed. In fact he published little – checklists of Arthur Rackham and Constance Holme, articles and reviews in the *TLS, The Book Collector* and other journals. His reports on the larger collections which passed through his hands were far more learned than the mere business of selling demanded. But his most valuable contribution to bibliography lay in the assistance and advice he gave to others. (And his contribution to biography too, witnessed by his preparatory work on the papers that formed the basis of his friend Christopher Hassall's life of Marsh.) Cecil Woolf is not alone in claiming John Hayward and Bertram Rota as his 'twin bibliographical godfathers'. There can be few bibliographies of 20th-century authors in which Bertram's help is not acknowledged; in more than one instance – I shall name no names – the formal acknowledgment conceals the fact that without that help, time-consuming but unstinted, the bibliographer would have done better to remain ingloriously mute.

To be asked by Bertram to assist in worrying out some problem of his own, as happened to me on rare occasions, was both flattering and rewarding: by the end of the interview or correspondence he had always modestly imparted more truth and wit than he had received – or rejected.

APPENDIX II

TWELVE QUESTIONS TO ASK WHEN
VALUING MANUSCRIPTS AND ARCHIVES

By taking the time and trouble to attempt to answer the simple but extremely important questions set out below, a valuer builds a sure platform on which to base his appraisal figure. Those parties to whom his report is addressed can see at once thta there is a clear rationale behind his figures. I am proud of my firm's record in thi regard: in the firm's 78 years of trading no valuation we have made has ever been successfully challenged, be it by an insurer, the Inland Revenue in Great Britain, the Internal Revenue Service in the United States or any other relevant party.

1. What proportion of the author's work does the manuscript or collection of manuscripts represent? Too much can on occasion be like the celebrated surfeit of lampreys. When the price rises above a certain level, even if it represents good value, many potential buyers are ruled out because of budget limitations. It is then that those with long purses can pick up the greatest bargains.

2. Where are the rest of the manuscripts? Have they been lost or destroyed? Are they in institutional hands already? Might some come onto the market later, or is this the buyer's last chance?

3. What point has the author reached in his career? Is he likely to produce much more? An affirmative answer pulls both ways. Some buyers welcome the chance this implies to build a worthwhile collection, but others hesitate to commit themselves to what might become an expensive long-term project.

4. Is the author likely to rise in critical esteem? A promising poet may be seen by some as a latter-day Keats, but that does not yet make the manuscript of his first book of poems worth as much as that of *Endymion*.

5. Is this a typical or an atypical example of the author's work? Let us take the hypothetical case of William Golding. Are we deal-

ing with one of the relatively 'heavy' novels by which he has won
his reputation or is this, perhaps, the manuscript of his first – and
only – book of verse (*Poems*, by W. [sic] Golding, 1934). The typical
Golding novel will enjoy an obvious demand. The poems on the
other hand will have a rarity value. There are more buyers for
the former but how strongly does the unusual quality of the latter
weigh in the balance?

6. Is this a 'key' book of its time? (As *Ulysses* was: as *The Waste
Land* was.) Is it an 'intellectual landmark' in the manner of Keynes's
General Theory of Employment? Is it what Richard Landon, who
presides over the Fisher Library at the University of Toronto, aptly
calls a 'touchstone of civilisation'?

7. Is the 'manuscript' really a manuscript at all? i.e. is it written
in the author's hand (or even the hand of an amanuensis)? Or is
it what publishers, literary agents and all too many authors call
a 'manuscript' when it is in fact a typescript? If the latter, is the
author in the habit of composing on the typewriter, or are we
merely faced with a relatively clean secretarial transcription from a
discarded holograph draft?

8. What is the degree of correction? Is it very lightly corrected or
really heavily revised? (Both D. H. Lawrence and John Cowper
Powys would be promising candidates for the all-time record for
the greatest number of revisions to a single manuscript.) The answer
to this last question leads us to the next:

9. What does the piece tell us about the 'creative process'? In
other words, what does it tell us about the writer's method of
work? We have already considered the extent to which an author
revises. What does the manuscript or series of manuscripts show us
about the progression of his ideas? The novelist and short story
writer William Sansom used to begin with random thoughts jotted
on the back of cigarette packets. If one had the patience to arrange
the packets in the right order one could follow the germination of
a novel through manuscript and typescript to corrected proof.
Ronald Firbank also used to write down seemingly random names,
words and phrases, snatches of dialogue and descriptions of places

that occurred to him as he moved through life. (Happily, in notebooks – now in the Berg Collection – rather than cigarette packets).
Later they would be woven into the thread of his works of fiction.

10. Has the piece been published? If so does the manuscript contain material not in the published version?

11. Is the author 'taught'? The appearance of a name on a university syllabus has a more dramatic effect on prices and values in this
particular market than any incursion into the best-seller lists.

12. Do photocopies or microfilms exist? This last is important
if one remembers that libraries buy modern manuscripts not as
museum pieces but as the raw material for research. If that material
is not unique but is equally available through an indeterminate
number of photocopies, its value is less. Indeed several celebrated
institutions will not then buy at all.[1]

[1] At this point perhaps I should stress that in all my remarks about valuing MSS I am
referring only to the physical possession of a MS, to ownership of the paper and ink,
for in my experience it is rare for copyright to pass in sales of this kind. This is as
true of published MSS as it is of unpublished MSS – and equally as true of sales of
correspondence files : it is normal in these transactions for copyright to stay where it
was before.

AN EASIER WAY

For those not prepared to study the material they are appraising,
and to decide on the correct answers to my twelve questions, there
is of course an easier way. There always is. In this instance it is to let
someone else do the work and simply make use of their figures. I
still get angry when I recall occasions when my work was misappro-
priated in this way. The man who annoyed me most in this regard
was Frank Swinnerton (1884-1982), the novelist and man of letters. I
was introduced to him by George Sims when Swinnerton wanted
to sell his library, his correspondence files and his surviving manuscripts. Sims knew that I rather specialised in deals of this kind and
that I had the ear of the research libraries which were the major
players in this field.

He and I went down to see this 'grand old man' at his home in Old Tokefield in Surrey. Swinnerton was already well into his eighties. He received us kindly and we spent a pleasant day with him, listing and valuing, albeit feeling under some pressure from the clock. When we had completed our work George Sims and I added up our respective lists and arrived at a grand total. Let us say that it was £80,000. I put that figure to Mr Swinnerton who asked if he might have 'time to think it over'. That seemed fair enough, so I readily agreed, taking the opportunity to request that he did not reveal my offer to any other party. I was given satisfactory assurances about this and caught the next train back to London.

A week went by, and then three more days. I wrote to Old Tokefield to ask how the 'thinking' was going. I received the reply that Frank Swinnerton had concluded a sale to the University of Arkansas for 'a higher figure' than I had proposed. That was disappointing enough, but my chagrin was greater when I heard from my friend Ted Harris, head of the London branch of the international booksellers Stechert Hafner Inc., that he was handling the shipping of the Swinnerton material and that he was surprised I had let the deal get away from me for 'so small a margin.' 'What did you value it at Ted,' I asked. 'I didn't value it at all,' Ted replied. 'F. S. just told the library what you had offered and asked £5,000 more!'

On another occasion a friendly competitor whose firm specialised in first editions of the last hundred years, much as we did, admitted, almost boasted, that instead of viewing for himself the books coming up for sale at a particular auction, he would let me do the hard work and then simply reckon that he was safe in bidding one more time after I stopped. When I heard this I answered with the nearest noise to a noncommittal grunt that I could manage. That afternoon at Hodgson's saleroom my rival bought some very expensive books indeed. In all I believe he purchased some ten or a dozen lots before the penny dropped.

INDEX